P9-CKV-574

The Acting-Out Child:

COPING WITH CLASSROOM DISRUPTION

Hill M. Walker

University of Oregon

ALLYN AND BACON, INC.

Boston, London, Sydney

Library of Congress Cataloging in Publication Data

Walker, Hill M
The acting-out child.

Bibliography: p.
Includes index.
1. Classroom management. 2. Problem children—Education. 3. Acting out (Psychology) I. Title.
LB3013.W327 371.1'02 79-1054
ISBN 0-205-06576-7 (hardbound)
ISBN 0-205-06569-4 (paperbound)

Printed in the United States of America

Dedication

This book is dedicated to

MATILDA CLARK WALKER

a fine classroom teacher

Contents

Preface

The purpose of this book is to present a set of procedures for effectively managing the behavior of children who act out in a classroom setting. The material, if mastered, will give teachers in regular, special, and resource classrooms the necessary skills to effectively manage the behavior of acting out children as well as that of less disruptive children. The book will also be of value to school administrators and professionals who serve teachers in consultive roles, including counselors, school psychologists, and social workers. Tasks and exercises are provided at the end of Chapter 3 to test the reader's grasp of the material and to give practice in applying the information presented to hypothetical classroom situations.

Teachers at every level are well aware of the management problems presented by the child who consistently "acts out" against classroom rules, procedures, and accepted methods of instruction. Since the beginning of formal education, the disruptive behavior of such children has been a persistent challenge to effective teaching. Unless this behavior is controlled and managed effectively, it can disrupt the learning and achievement for an entire classroom and especially for the acting-out child.

For reasons that are not well understood, some children adjust to the school experience, with its new and unique demands, in very satisfactory ways, while other children experience difficulties with these same demands from the first day of school. There are a number of theories that attempt to explain the origins of disruptive classroom behavior. For example, some professionals suggest that the adequacy of a child's school adjustment is largely a result of the kinds of preschool experiences the child has had that are similar to those encountered in the regular school setting. This explanation seems to have some validity, but it doesn't explain the school adjustment patterns of all children.

Others suggest that the educational level of the child's parents and their general attitude toward learning and achievement have a profound effect upon how a child perceives and reacts to the school experience. This theory may be partially true, but it is not clear how it specifically operates to account for a child's school adjustment.

A third explanation holds that an acting-out child has not mastered the key "survival skills" needed for successful school adjustment upon entering first grade. "Survival skills" are the minimum behavioral requirements necessary for the child to effectively consume instruction. These include paying attention, listening to instructions, following directions, and complying with teacher demands (Cobb, 1972). It is suggested that failure to master these skills early in the educational process can handicap a child's school adjustment in both academic and social areas and may lead eventually to the development of severe behavior problems. While this explanation seems highly plausible, it has not been established as yet that acting-out children identified in later school grades are deficient in survival skills upon entering first grade.

Until careful longitudinal studies are carried out on the specific processes involved in successful and unsuccessful school adjustment, the various theories accounting for the origins of acting-out behavior will remain only theories. Although we cannot, at present, determine precisely how and why some children develop disruptive behavior patterns, we do possess the technological means to effectively reduce acting-out behavior. In the last ten to fifteen years, an effective behavior management technology has been developed for remediating both *behavioral deficits* such as social withdrawal, and *behavioral excesses* such as acting-out behavior. This technology is based upon principles of social learning that determine how human behavior is acquired, maintained, and eliminated.

This body of knowledge consists of a series of proven techniques for changing human behavior that have been validated in literally hundreds of studies reported in the professional literature. These techniques have been applied with a great deal of success in such varied settings as regular classrooms, special classrooms, homes, playgrounds, clinics, and institutions. They have developed to the point where it is feasible for teachers to apply them in the regular classroom in order to improve the conditions of learning for all children. They are especially applicable to remediation of the learning and behavioral problems of the acting-out child.

It is intended that the material in this volume will give the classroom teacher the skills necessary to successfully apply these techniques to the acting-out child and to manage the general classroom environment more effectively. Increasing pressures are being placed upon the management skills of classroom teachers with the current emphases upon individualizing instruction, mainstreaming handicapped children, and accommodating a greater range and diversity of behavior patterns in the regular classroom. It is hoped that this book will be responsive to the needs of classroom teachers in designing an optimal learning environment; one that will facilitate development of both academic and social competencies in acting-out children.

REFERENCE

Cobb, J. A. The relationship of discrete classroom behavior to fourth grade academic achievement. *Journal of Educational Psychology*, 1972, 63, 74–80.

ACKNOWLEDGMENTS

The author's family, Jan and Seth, were very supportive, encouraging, and tolerant during the period in which this manuscript was produced. Their understanding is sincerely appreciated.

CHAPTER
I

The Acting-Out Child in the Classroom Setting

(The scene in Mrs. Moore's second-grade classroom is typical of those found in thousands of classrooms each day. Following a teacher-led discussion of that day's reading assignment, Mrs. Moore instructs her class to complete a series of reading worksheets during the remaining twenty minutes of the reading period. The children begin organizing themselves to work on the assignment; all, that is, except Tracy, who leaves his seat and begins moving in the direction of the pencil sharpener.)

Mrs. Moore: Tracy, what are you doing?

Tracy: I'm going to the pencil sharpener.

Mrs. Moore: You know what the class rule is. You're supposed to sharpen all the pencils you need before class starts—not after. Besides, you're supposed to raise your hand before getting out of your seat.

Tracy: I only have two pencils. I broke the tips off both of them working on my math assignment.

Mrs. Moore: All right! Hurry up and sharpen them and get to work.

(Tracy continues moving toward the pencil sharpener. Mrs. Moore turns to answer a question about the assignment from another student. Tracy engages several peers in conversation about nonacademic matters. Mrs. Moore notices and begins to get visibly angry.)

Mrs. Moore: Tracy, I told you to sharpen your pencil and get to work! Now I mean it. You'd better do what I tell you.

Tracy: Okay, okay. I'm going.

(Tracy has the attention of nearly the entire class and seems to be enjoying it. He also seems to enjoy Mrs. Moore's obvious irritation with his behavior. He approaches the pencil sharpener and slowly begins to sharpen his pencils, making a production of it and continuing to exchange glances and gestures with the peers to whom he was talking. Mrs. Moore observes this and does a slow burn.)

Mrs. Moore: Tracy, I'm telling you for the last time to sharpen your pencils and get to work. You're getting behind in your work and you're keeping others from doing theirs.

Tracy: I'll be through in just a minute. I'm going as fast as I can.

Mrs. Moore: I'm going to stand right here beside you until you finish and escort you back to your seat.

(Mrs. Moore takes Tracy by the arm and leads him to his seat. She waits beside him while he takes out his assignment and begins to work.)

Unfortunately, the exchanges between Tracy and Mrs. Moore are too often typical of the interactions between acting-out children and their teachers. Whatever the reasons, the acting-out child has not learned to pay attention, listen to instructions, follow directions, and comply with teacher requests promptly. To make matters worse, the acting-out child often engages in social behaviors (hitting, yelling, screaming, throwing tantrums) that have a disruptive effect on the classroom and are extremely unpleasant for classmates and teacher.

Children like Tracy are very difficult for teachers to manage. They tend to dominate the teacher's valuable time; time that could be spent in instructing other children. Teachers are pulled into endless confrontations with such children in vain attempts to control their behavior.

The confrontation between Tracy and Mrs. Moore illustrates some important points about the behavior of acting-out children and their relationships with teachers and peers. For example, it is the acting-out child who is usually in control of the behavioral episodes occurring with the teacher. It is the acting-out child, and not the teacher, who normally decides when the confrontation will end. Second, the acting-out child's deviant behavioral repertoire is strongly developed and is very resistant to change. As a rule, the further along acting-out children have progressed in school the more resistant is their behavior pattern to change due to the massive amounts of teacher and peer attention they have received for disruptive behavior throughout their school careers. Third, the amount of emotional intensity and the level of direct control exerted by the teacher in confrontations with the acting-out child are usually related to how long the child decides to prolong the confrontation. In some cases, the teacher must resort to ever higher levels of emotional intensity and direct control in order to get the acting-out child to terminate the inappropriate behavior. In such cases, the emotional and psychological costs of managing acting-out children can be extremely high.

BEHAVIORAL CHARACTERISTICS OF THE ACTING-OUT CHILD

Characteristically, the acting-out child in the classroom setting is one who defies teacher-imposed rules, structures, and/or procedures. She/he is a consistent rule breaker and spends a great deal of time in nonacademic pursuits. Because the acting-out child spends so much time on nonacademic matters, she/he is often deficient in key academic skills and is below grade level in achievement (Walker & Buckley, 1974).

Frequently, the acting-out child's disruptive behavior pattern develops early in the school career (Zax, Cowen, Izzo, & Trost, 1964). She/he becomes identified as a difficult-to-manage child and develops a reputation that can follow him/her from teacher to teacher, from year to year, and from school to school. Sometimes this reputation becomes a self-fulfilling prophecy; that is, teachers and peers expect the child to misbehave, so it happens.

The acting-out child, with accompanying academic disabilities, finds academic performance a generally unrewarding activity. Because of deficient skills and an often negative attitude toward learning, the acting-out child generally finds it difficult to obtain teacher praise for academic efforts. The low probability of success or praise being associated with academic performance decreases the frequency of appropriate academic responding in a downward spiraling process; e.g., the less praise, the less academic work attempted, and the less work attempted, the less praise. In addition, the aversive nature of the acting-out child's behavior further reduces the chances of his/her receiving positive attention and approval from the teacher and classmates.

It should be mentioned that not all acting-out children are deficient in academic skills; some achieve at or above grade level expectations in spite of the relatively large amounts of time they spend in nonacademic pursuits. In such cases, the acting-out child's disruptive social behavior is probably not a direct function of his/her academic skill level; whereas, for acting-out children with severe academic deficits, there probably is a relationship between their disruptive behavior and deficient academic skills. To date, however, the exact nature of this relationship has not been precisely described.

The acting-out child's noncompliance with teacher instructions and commands and consistent failure to abide by established classroom rules are two of the qualities classroom teachers find most irritating. However, acting-out children engage in a number of other inappropriate behaviors that are highly disruptive of classroom atmosphere and optimal instructional conditions. These include running around the room, hitting, yelling, disturbing others, complaining, arguing, having temper tantrums, and provoking others. The high intensity of such behaviors makes them very difficult to tolerate. Usually, these behaviors precipitate either controlling or avoidance responses from the child's teacher and/or peers. The end result of this spiraling process is often a confrontation, which proves to be even more disruptive of classroom atmosphere.

The acting-out child's relationships with peers are frequently characterized by angry, hostile social exchanges of a verbal or physical nature. If the acting-out child is sufficiently powerful, he/she may be able to intimidate peers and force them to submit, which often causes them to avoid direct social or personal contact whenever possible. If such is not the case, the acting-out child's relationship with them may be simply antagonistic and characterized by mutual hostility.

Table 1.1 contains a list of classroom and nonclassroom behaviors that are descriptive of the way in which acting-out children characteristically behave in school (Hops, Beickel, & Walker, 1976).

It should be noted that acting-out children are different from their normal peers not so much in the quality of their behavior but in its quantity. For example, most children at one time or another fail to comply with teacher commands, hit or shove a peer, disrupt the classroom, talk out, and so forth. However, normal children are clearly differentiated from acting-out children in terms of the frequency with

TABLE 1.1. *Characteristic Behaviors Displayed by Acting-Out Children in School*

1. Out of seat	11. Does not comply with adult commands or directions
2. Yells out	12. Argues (talks back)
3. Runs around room	13. Ignores other teachers
4. Disturbs peers	14. Distorts the truth
5. Hits or fights	15. Has temper tantrums
6. Ignores teacher	16. Excluded from activities by peers
7. Complains	17. Doesn't follow directions
8. Fights excessively	18. Doesn't complete assignments
9. Steals	
10. Destroys property	

which they engage in such classroom behavior(s). Consequently, in managing acting-out children in the classroom, the key task is to reduce the level of inappropriate behavior to manageable proportions, rather than to attempt to produce a change in the acting-out child's personality.

The acting-out child's inappropriate behavior is not limited to the classroom. Teachers often complain most vigorously about the behavior of acting-out children in such nonclassroom areas of the school as the playground, hallways, and lunchroom. The behavior of normal as well as deviant children is usually more disruptive and at a much higher frequency in these areas of the school due to such factors as reduced supervision, less structure, and less clearly defined standards governing appropriate and inappropriate behavior.

The behavior of acting-out children is frequently out of control in these areas and is usually more difficult to manage than in the classroom. Due to the acting-out child's traditional lack of self-control and to the reduced behavioral constraints operating in these areas, there is a high probability that she/he will engage in disruptive and rule breaking behavior. Further, the quality of her/his behavior may also differ in that it is more likely to involve physical aggression and hostile verbal exchanges with peers due to the nature of the activities children engage in within these areas (active games, running, shouting, jumping, yelling, etc.).

Some children are deviant in the classroom but not in other school settings, while other children are deviant in nonclassroom settings but not in the classroom. Both Patterson (1974) and Johnson, Bolstad, and Lobitz (1976) have found that children who are identified as deviant at home are likely to be deviant at school, and vice versa. As a rule, the more deviant the child, the more likely he/she is to engage in inappropriate behavior across all school settings. Acting-out children characteristically "act out" in both classroom and nonclassroom areas of the school.

THE DEVELOPMENT OF DEVIANT, DISRUPTIVE BEHAVIOR IN ACTING-OUT CHILDREN

The origin of deviant patterns of behavior in children in general and in acting-out children in particular is a subject of continuing debate and controversy. There is little agreement on this issue and numerous theories exist as to why some children develop normally while others become deviant. The complexity of this problem is overwhelming and the specific reasons as to why some children become deviant and others do not are not clearly understood at present.

In spite of our inability to identify the specific causes of deviant, disruptive behavior in children, disruptive behavior in the school setting is an increasing concern of educators and parents. Children's school behavior seems to be becoming more difficult to manage. Increasing school resources are being devoted to managing the behavior of problem children. Teachers' unions are beginning to negotiate for special services for difficult to manage children in order to make their behavior more controllable and less aversive within the classroom setting. Further, school systems are having to invest thousands of dollars each year in order to maintain the security of grounds, buildings, and teaching staffs. In some large urban school districts, police are required to patrol school grounds in order to insure the physical safety of children and teachers. All of these developments suggest that the concerns of parents and educators are well founded and that school behavior problems seem to be approaching new levels of severity.

What accounts for the dramatic rise in children's disruptiveness and deviance levels within the school setting? There appear to be no easy answers. For example, the changed social conditions that exist in the larger society are no doubt reflected in the school behavior of children. Such changes include (1) increases in the crime rate, (2) a breakdown in the authority of institutions, and (3) a general disruption and weakening of the family as the primary unit of socialization in society. There is no doubt that these social conditions are contributing to increased levels of child deviance and disruption in school. However, the manner in which they operate to *specifically* account for such increases is relatively obscure at present.

A popular viewpoint in accounting for deviant child behavior, particularly in school settings, is to blame the school in general and classroom teachers specifically. There is no doubt that children *can* learn deviant patterns of behavior in school and that schools sometimes inadvertently build in and strengthen deviant, disruptive child behavior. Some have suggested that inappropriate child behavior is a direct function of ineffective teaching and the teacher's lack of skill in managing child behavior. According to this view, deviant child behavior can be accounted for by simply examining the instructional and management behavior of the teacher.

It is difficult to accept unconditionally such a view of why children display deviant behavior in schools. For example, it is obvious that some children display highly deviant, disruptive patterns of behavior from the very first day of school. Such children could not have learned these behavior patterns in school, and the teacher cannot be held accountable for the child's disruptive behavior. It is apparent that such children have learned deviant patterns of behavior outside the school setting and continue to engage in them upon entering school. Unfortunately, studies have shown that schools can maintain and actually strengthen such deviant behavior patterns even though they were learned and acquired outside the school setting (Bostow & Bailey, 1969; Thomas, Becker & Armstrong, 1968; Walker & Buckley, 1973).

It is apparent that a child's behavior pattern at school is the result of a complex interaction of: (1) the behavior pattern the child has been taught at home, including attitudes toward school, (2) the experiences the child has had with different teachers in the school setting, and (3) the relationship between the child and his/her current teacher(s). Trying to determine in what proportion the child's behavior pattern is attributable to each of these learning sources is an impossible and unnecessary task. Deviant child behavior can be changed very effectively without knowing the original causes for its acquisition and development. The major purpose of this book is to present a set of strategies for achieving this goal.

SCHOOL RESPONSES TO CHILD DEVIANCE

Intense pressures have developed both within and outside schools for the application of more effective methods of dealing with child deviance in the school setting. How have schools responded to such pressure?

The first response has usually been to try and fix blame for the child's inappropriate behavior pattern. School personnel have tended to blame parents for their children's disruptive behavior in school. In the past, schools have frequently referred parents to mental health clinics because of their child's behavior problems in school. The clear implication is that the parents are to blame and that it is the parent's responsibility to insure that the child's behavior problems are reduced to acceptable limits at school.

As would be expected, parents are not always receptive to this view of their child's behavior problems. Instead, they often blame the school for its inability to control their child's school behavior. The criticism is frequently voiced by parents that schools are not adequately teaching their children and assisting them in developing socially and emotionally.

The task of fixing blame and defining responsibility for a child's behavior problems at school is a fruitless one. Parents are usually not convinced of the school's point of view and vice versa. Johnson (1975), for example, reported that in a study of referrals to mental health clinics, the highest frequency of cancellations of family therapy were by families who were referred by school systems because of their child's behavior problems at school. Clearly, these types of interactions between parents and schools over child deviance at school have not resulted in adaptive, positive responses to the behavior problems of children in school settings.

Another popular response to child deviance at school has been drug therapy. Provided that it is effective, drug therapy for a given child can have a number of obvious advantages for the teachers and parents who must manage the child's behavior. For example, the rate or frequency of the child's behavior is greatly reduced, it tends to become less disruptive, and presumably the child becomes more receptive to instruction and other forms of therapy. Given that drug therapy makes a child's behavior more compliant and less disruptive, it is not surprising that children experiencing behavior problems at school are often referred to physicians for possible placement on drug therapy programs. In fact, some school districts have placed intense pressures upon parents to allow their children to participate in drug programs in order to make their behavior more compliant at school.

In recent years, there has been increasing public concern over the possible undesirable side effects of drug therapy programs (Bendix, 1973; Connors, 1973; Ladd, 1970; Novack, 1971; Walker, 1974). These include (1) the risk of drug dependency in later years, (2) suppression of growth, and (3) increased heart rate or blood pressure (Cohen, Douglas, & Morganstern, 1971; Knights & Hinston, 1969; Rapoport, Quinn, Bradbard, Riddle, & Brooks, 1974; Safer & Allen, 1973). This issue is by no means resolved, and critics have charged that the news media has greatly exaggerated the magnitude of potential problems with the use of drugs for children (Comly, 1971).

Two of the more common stimulant medications used with acting-out and/or hyperactive children are (1) dextroamphetamine and (2) methyphenidate. There is little doubt that such drugs can have a powerful impact upon child behavior (Comly, 1971; Conrad, Dworkin, Shai, & Tobiessen, 1971; Denhoff, Davids, & Hawkins, 1971). However, even when the correct dosage is found, drug therapy of this type is effective with only one-half to two-thirds of cases (Fish, 1971; *Journal of Learning Disabilities*, 1971).

The goal of drug therapy with children is generally not to "cure" a given child's behavior problems and/or disorders. Drug therapy does not produce enduring changes in child behavior nor does it have an impact upon a child's personality. Studies have shown that a child's behavior quickly reverts to pre-drug levels of intensity and frequency when the drug program is terminated (Ayllon, Layman, & Kandel, 1975). Essentially, drug therapy suppresses the more undesirable features of child behavior but does not teach the child strategies for controlling her/his behavior.

It has been argued that drug therapy does not "cure" behavior disorders but *may* make the child more accessible to educational and counseling efforts. It is suggested that stimulant drugs do not provide a chemical straitjacket nor do they act as a sedative. They are designed to increase the child's abilities to focus on meaningful stimuli and to organize her/his body movements more purposefully (*Journal of Learning Disabilities*, 1971). The extent to which this occurs is not entirely clear at present. Further, the extent to which drug therapy facilitates academic performance and/or achievement is also not clear in spite of the claims by drug therapy proponents to the effect that stimulants make children more receptive to instruction.

Ayllon, Layman, and Kandel (1975) conducted a study in which they evaluated a drug treatment for three hyperactive children versus a behavior intervention program implemented for the same children.

Specifically, they were interested in the effects the two treatments would have upon the children's academic performance and hyperactivity.

Three children, two boys and a girl, served as subjects in the study. All three had been clinically diagnosed as hyperactive and all were receiving drugs to control their hyperactivity. The girl was eight years old and the boys were nine and ten years old, respectively.

The children's hyperactivity was evaluated across two academic periods, math and reading. A simple check-point system with backup rewards was used to reinforce the children's academic performance in math and reading. The children were awarded checks by the teacher on a simple index card. One check was recorded for each correct academic response. The checks could be exchanged for a large array of backup reinforcers later in the day. The backup rewards ranged in price from one check to seventy-five checks and included such items and activities as candy, school supplies, free time, lunch in the teacher's room, and picnics in the park.

Each child's daily level of hyperactivity and academic achievement, on and off medication, were observed and recorded before the behavioral program was introduced. The results were nearly identical for all three children.

When the medication for hyperactivity was discontinued, there was a gross increase in the level of hyperactivity for all three children in both subject areas (reading and math). The hyperactivity level increased from about 20 percent to approximately 80 percent. There was only a slight correlated increase in math and reading performance. However, introduction of a behavioral program for academic performance in reading and math, during no medication, controlled the children's hyperactivity at a level comparable to that when they were on drugs (about 20 percent). At the same time, math and reading performance for the three children increased from about 12 percent correct during baseline to a level of over 85 percent correct during intervention.

The results showed that each child performed optimally in both behavioral and academic areas without medication. In contrast to the usual expectation, the drug therapy program did not appear to make the children more responsive to academic instruction, judging from the comparative effects in academic performance produced by the two treatments. The behavior management program provided a highly effective alternative to medication for controlling hyperactivity while simultaneously allowing the children to achieve well academically.

It is apparent that drug therapy is a relatively easy to administer, low in cost, and often effective treatment procedure for children. Its major disadvantages are that (1) it teaches children nothing about methods or techniques for managing their own behavior and (2) it does not produce enduring changes in child behavior, that is, the child's behavior is changed only so long as the drug program is in effect. The possible undesirable physical side effects of stimulant drugs are another consideration in their use. It would seem that whenever feasible, non-drug alternatives should be pursued vigorously in the treatment of child behavior problems, especially at school. Some additional promising work in the area of developing behavioral treatment alternatives to the drug treatment of hyperactive/behavior-problem children has recently been reported by O'Leary, Pelham, Rosenbaum, and Price (1976).

A third response of school systems to the problem of disruptive, inappropriate child behavior in the classroom has been to remove them from mainstream educational settings. The behavior of acting-out children often places intense pressures upon the management and instructional skills of classroom teachers. Such children are extremely difficult to manage and teach effectively. Consequently, the treatment of choice for them traditionally has been placement in settings external to the regular classroom, e.g., in resource rooms, special classrooms, or institutional settings. The principal effect of such placement decisions has been to relieve the teacher and normal peers of the burdens imposed by the acting-out child's disruptive behavior. However, removal from the regular classroom simultaneously deprives the child of the opportunity to develop a behavioral repertoire that would insure entry into and maintenance within the educational mainstream. Further, research has shown that treatment gains achieved in a special class setting tend not to be maintained after reintegration into the regular class setting (Walker & Buckley, 1974).

It is entirely understandable why regular classroom teachers would be motivated to have acting-out children assigned to special settings, especially since teachers have been encouraged by special services personnel to refer behavior-problem children for possible placement in such settings. However, the mainstreaming movement and the advent of Public Law 94–142 have created equally powerful pressures for handicapped children, including behavior-problem children, to be brought into contact with effective treatment services and to be educated in the *least* restrictive educational setting possible. The regular classroom setting is viewed by the courts and Congress as the least restrictive of available educational placements.

The implications of these developments for regular classroom teachers are direct and far reaching. For example, placement of larger numbers of such children in regular classrooms will severely test the management and instructional skills of regular classroom teachers. Extensive consultative services from special educators will accompany assignment of such children to regular classrooms in most cases; however, teachers, in the final analysis, will be responsible for educating these children effectively. In order to do so, many regular classroom teachers will need to acquire some relatively complex skills in the areas of behavior management and instructional programming.

Counseling and psychotherapy have also been used frequently as vehicles for coping with the disruptive classroom behavior of acting-out children. The focus of this treatment approach is generally upon getting the acting-out child to identify and understand the reasons for her/his disruptive and rule breaking behavior. Usually, acting-out children are quite aware of the appropriateness or inappropriateness of their behavior and are sensitive, in many cases, to the effects it has upon others. Unfortunately, there is no evidence to indicate that an acting-out child's awareness of the probable causes of his/her disruptive behavior has any effect upon his/her actual classroom behavior. Providing the acting-out child with feedback about the extent to which she/he is following classroom rules also appears to have little effect in reducing his/her disruptive behavior. In fact, studies have consistently shown that classroom rules alone have little effect in changing the behavior of any children (Greenwood, Hops, Delquadri, & Guild, 1974). This would be especially true of acting-out children.

Ullman and Krasner (1965) make the point that a person's verbal behavior concerning one's problems in a counselor's or psychotherapist's office bears little relationship to how one behaves in natural settings. In the author's opinion, this is a correct view of human behavior. Study after study reported in the professional literature shows that behavior tends to change only in those settings where *formal* intervention procedures are actually implemented and not in those settings or situations where such procedures are not implemented (Kazdin & Bootzin, 1972; O'Leary & Drabman, 1971). Thus, counseling or psychotherapy designed to have an impact upon a child's classroom behavior has been a weak treatment procedure. Its relative impact upon an acting-out child's behavior would be even weaker.

Developing intervention procedures for changing the acting-out child's behavior in the regular classroom setting has been one of the least frequently selected treatment alternatives. The reasons for this development are not clear at present. Possible reasons might include the following: (1) It may be that the teacher's tolerance for the child's inappropriate behavior and her/his relative inability to cope with it causes the teacher to reject the child and become less than receptive to in-class procedures for changing the child's behavior. (2) Teachers may be perceived as either too busy or not sufficiently skilled to implement such procedures effectively in the classroom. (3) Given that the child can be referred to a resource or special classroom, wherein the child is taken off the teacher's hands for a period of time, teachers may be relatively unmotivated to develop and implement in-class treatment procedures designed to change the inappropriate behavior. (4) It may be that the necessary behavior technology and/or sufficiently skilled teacher consultants (psychologists, counselors, resource teachers, etc.) have not been available to make this alternative a reality. Whatever the reasons, it is apparent, given the mainstreaming emphasis and the advent of Public Law 94–142, that this alternative will be pursued increasingly by school personnel in the future.

One advantage of this approach is that the child's behavior is treated within the setting(s) where it is a problem. However, only recently have sufficiently powerful techniques been developed for changing disruptive behavior within the regular classroom setting (Becker, Engelmann, & Thomas, 1976; Walker & Buckley, 1974). It is anticipated that this approach will be used to a much greater extent in the future due to the increasing pressures for mainstreaming handicapped children of various types and due to its potential for reducing deviant behavior in the setting(s) where it is actually problematic—the regular classroom.

The more successful classroom intervention strategies have been based upon behavioral procedures. Systematic behavior management programs have been used increasingly to cope with disruptive child behavior in schools primarily because of their comparative effectiveness in reducing child behavior problems. If implemented correctly, these procedures can be highly effective in controlling disruptive behavior and in teaching children new patterns of constructive, prosocial behavior.

Ironically, the actual success of behavior modification procedures has helped to make them increasingly controversial. The power of behavior modification procedures has raised fears that they represent a too powerful form of control over human behavior. It has even been suggested that behavioral procedures can be used to change children's basic values in a deleterious fashion. There is no evidence that either of these criticisms is true.

However, there are a number of issues associated with the use of behavioral procedures that are of concern to social agents charged with their implementation. These include (1) the bribery issue associated with the use of rewards, (2) the issue of fairness as it relates to equitable treatment of individuals (it appears unfair to reward one child in a class and not others), (3) the issue of denying privileges to individuals in schools and institutional settings in order to motivate them to behave differently, and (4) the issue of generalization and maintenance of changed behavior (treatment effects associated with behavioral procedures tend to not maintain once treatment procedures are withdrawn or to generalize to nontreatment settings.) These issues need to be confronted and dealt with directly by the proponents of behavioral procedures. Portions of Chapter 4 of this volume address each of these issues.

It is apparent that few school systems have dealt systematically with the problems presented by disruptive, acting-out children in either a constructive or effective manner. Excluding children from the educational mainstream and suppressing their behavior through the use of drugs do not appear to be fair or just responses to child deviance. Behavioral procedures seem to represent a constructive alternative to such methods of dealing with the behavior of acting-out children. To date, however, we have not been entirely successful in adapting these procedures for use by teachers in a maximally cost effective manner. Hopefully, the material in this book will constitute some progress in this area.

TEACHER ATTEMPTS TO COPE WITH THE ACTING-OUT CHILD

Teachers have tried a variety of techniques for controlling and/or managing the behavior of acting-out children. Unfortunately, most of the practical techniques used by teachers to respond to acting-out children are only of limited effectiveness and some, such as reprimands, can actually strengthen the behavior they are designed to suppress or terminate.

No two teachers respond to acting-out children in exactly the same way. However, there is considerable similarity among teachers in their general attempts to manage the acting-out child's behavior. Most often, the teacher responds in a way that is designed to get the acting-out child to stop her/his disruptive or noncompliant behavior and to behave more appropriately. In these situations, peers usually provide support for the child's inappropriate behavior. The teacher's attention in these situations and the support provided by peers strengthen the acting-out child's behavior and make it more likely that she/he will act out again in the future to obtain attention and approval. It is indeed ironic that the teacher's direct efforts to get the acting-out child to stop misbehaving are very often instrumental in maintaining the inappropriate behavior.

Teachers are usually quick to respond to the acting-out child's inappropriate behavior because of its disruptive and aversive properties. As noted, their management efforts are directed at getting him/her to terminate the inappropriate behavior as soon as possible. The success of teachers in this task has been highly variable.

The acting-out child learns, for reasons that are not clearly understood, that it is easier to get attention from her/his peers and the teacher by engaging in disruptive, noncompliant behavior than by following classroom rules, completing assignments, and developing positive social relationships with peers. The acting-out child learns a set of behaviors and adopts a strategy that forces his/her teachers and peers to respond to her/his initiations, often in a negative way. Even though the attention received from peers and the teacher is usually negative, critical, and disapproving, it is attention just the same and serves to maintain the behavior. In fact, many acting-out children seem to thrive on the hostile confrontations they have with their teachers. Their ability to irritate the teacher and keep him/her upset is rewarding for them and is often subtly approved of by their peers.

Some teachers attempt to ignore the acting-out child's inappropriate behavior in the hope that if it doesn't receive attention, it won't continue. This would be a sound strategy if the behavior were maintained only by teacher attention; however, peers often provide massive support for the acting-out child's misbehavior. Further, teachers usually find the acting-out child's disruptive behavior very difficult to ignore for any length of time since such children have learned to escalate their demands of the teacher in the face of a limited teacher response.

Teachers are more likely to respond in an active fashion in dealing with the acting-out child. This frequently involves the use of negative reprimands, disapproval, and criticism(s). The effectiveness of these techniques in controlling the acting-out child's inappropriate behavior is highly variable. Sometimes they will produce a temporary reduction in the inappropriate behavior; at other times, they seem to have no discernible effect. Unfortunately, the attention the acting-out child receives in this process is probably instrumental in maintaining her/his inappropriate behavior over the long term. In addition, the teacher's obvious irritation with his/her behavior, her/his ability to get the teacher upset, and his/her control of the situation can all combine to strengthen the acting-out child's inappropriate behavior and make it very difficult to change.

Studies of the classroom interactions between teachers and disruptive children have shown that (1) such interactions are more likely to be negative than positive, (2) the teacher is much more likely to critically reprimand inappropriate behavior than to approve of appropriate behavior in these interactions, and (3) disruptive children tend to monopolize the teacher's time (Walker & Buckley, 1973, 1974). While these findings do not apply to all teachers, they are descriptive of the interactions that occur between many teachers and disruptive children in their classes.

Walker, Hops, and Fiegenbaum (1976), for example, carried out a study illustrating the points made above. Five teachers from five different elementary schools each referred an acting-out child to a demonstration classroom for treatment due to disruptive classroom behavior. The interactions between these teachers and the referred children were observed and recorded over a two-week period in the regular classroom prior to assignment to the demonstration class. Results showed that the five teachers praised and approved of the acting-out children's appropriate behavior an average of .6 times per hour (about once every two hours), or approximately 2.4 times within a normal school day. However, in contrast, the same teachers showed active disapproval of the children's inappropriate behavior an average of 9.1 times per hour or approximately 36 times per day.

Further, as a group, the five children consumed an average of 14 percent of the teacher's time per child. With an average teacher/child ratio of 1 to 24, each child could expect to receive approximately 4 percent of the teacher's available time. Thus, the acting-out children consumed considerably more of the teacher's time than did their peers, and the majority of this time was spent in negative interactions with the teacher. It is ironic that this huge investment of teacher time was largely ineffectual in reducing the children's inappropriate behavior.

Walker and Buckley (1973) carried out a study in which they examined the way in which a regular elementary teacher responded to deviant and nondeviant children enrolled in her fifth-grade classroom. The results were quite revealing.

A combination of teacher ratings and observation data was used to select the three most deviant and the three least deviant children in her classroom. The interactions between these six children and the teacher were then systematically recorded over a two-week period.

There were 144 separate interactions between the teacher and the six children during the two-week observation period. Seventy of the 144 interactions were a result of the child initiating to the teacher, and 74 were a result of the teacher initiating to one of the six children. Of the 74 interactions resulting from the teacher initiating to the children, 57 or 77 percent involved the three deviant children, and 17 or 23 percent involved the three nondeviant children. For the deviant children, 51 of the 57 interactions (89 percent) were a result of the teacher attending to their inappropriate behavior. In contrast, 14 of the 17 interactions (82 percent) with the nondeviant children were a result of the teacher attending to their appropriate behavior.

These results showed that the teacher responded in a clearly different fashion to deviant and nondeviant children enrolled in her classroom. In her interactions with the three deviant children, there were nine times as many interactions involving her attention to their inappropriate behavior as there were interactions in which she attended to their appropriate behavior. For the three nondeviant children, the ratio was 5 to 1 in favor of interactions in which she attended to their appropriate behavior.

As in the Walker, Hops, and Fiegenbaum study, the deviant children in this study consumed a large amount of the teacher's time. The three deviant children in this study were involved in approximately 3.3 times as many interactions with the teacher as were the three nondeviant children within the same time period.

The dynamics of these interactions were also quite different for the deviant and nondeviant children. For example, when the teacher directed her attention to the inappropriate behavior of the nondeviant children, they would usually stop the behavior in question on the first or second consequation attempt. However, the deviant children sometimes would not terminate their inappropriate behavior until the fourth, fifth, or even sixth attempt by the teacher to get them to do so. At other times, they would terminate the inappropriate behavior on the first or second attempt. Thus, it seemed that the teacher's consequating behavior was partially under the control of a schedule of compliance furnished by the deviant children. This was clearly not the case for the nondeviant children, who consistently complied with the teacher's instructions to terminate the inappropriate behavior on either the first or second attempt.

These studies illustrate how frustrating it is for teachers to deal with acting-out children. It often appears that the harder a teacher tries to control an acting-out child's behavior, the less effective she/he is. This process can be physically draining and emotionally exhausting. In situations such as this, the acting-out child's behavior is a constant reminder that the classroom atmosphere is not what the teacher would like it to be.

In nonclassroom settings (playground, hallways, lunchroom), the most commonly used techniques for controlling disruptive behavior include warnings, reprimands, threats, removal from on-going activities, and systematic exclusion. These techniques have variable effects upon children's behavior. Normal children are more likely to respond to warnings and reprimands while acting-out children often require either temporary removal from the area or systematic exclusion in order for their behavior to be controlled. Even though removal and exclusion are effective in terminating an acting-out child's inappropriate behavior and in teaching her/him to control the grosser forms of his/her behavior, they do not teach prosocial skills that would lead to the development of positive behavior patterns in these settings.

To change this situation, very powerful treatment procedures have to be applied to the acting-out child's behavior. The application of these procedures (to be discussed in Chapters 4 and 5) requires a fairly substantial investment of teacher time initially; however, as the child's behavior changes from inappropriate to appropriate, the teacher will be required to devote less and less time to management of her/his behavior. Further, the time that is invested will be much more effective in producing the desired results and is more likely to be positive instead of negative. If these procedures are implemented properly and consistently, the teacher should not be required to invest any more time with the acting-out child over the long term than with other children.

THE SITUATIONAL SPECIFICITY OF THE BEHAVIOR OF ACTING-OUT CHILDREN

Much of personality theory rests upon the assumption that human behavior is characterized by relatively stable traits (Allport, 1966; 1974). Trait labels are frequently used in the description of human behavior. For example, it is common for individuals to describe the behavior of others using such labels as sensitive, conscientious, aggressive, hostile, loving, independent, capricious, dependent, warm, and so forth. The list of labels goes on and on.

Such labels *do* communicate information about human behavior. However, they are based upon the assumption that the behavioral dimensions being described are stable and relatively unchanging over time. That is, if we describe someone as conscientious, dependent, or sensitive, it is assumed that he/she displays manifestations of these behavioral dimensions consistently over time and across settings.

Mischel (1969) argues persuasively that while cognitive and intellectual dimensions of human functioning show evidence of such consistency, personality and interpersonal behavior do not. Mischel (1968), in a comprehensive review of the available research evidence on this issue, concludes that the evidence is overwhelming as to the situational specificity of human behavior. That is, human behavior tends to be a function of the specific situation(s) in which it occurs. Another way of saying this is that behavior is highly reactive and sensitive to the conditions that exist in the situation in which it occurs.

In practical terms, this means that not everyone is aggressive, warm, dependent, or conscientious *all* the time. It is much more likely that people are, as a rule, aggressive, warm, dependent, or conscientious only some of the time or in some situations. Individuals may be aggressive in some situations and not in others or dependent in some and not in others. An individual who is generally regarded as "aggressive" may simply engage in aggressive behavior at a higher frequency and in more situations than normal. However, it is extremely unlikely that any individual is aggressive *all* the time and across *all* situations.

The implications of this view of human behavior bear directly upon strategies for explaining and changing it. For example, if one's behavior is markedly different in two different situations, a major portion of this difference *may* be accounted for by whatever differences exist in the conditions within those situations. By way of illustration, some children are deviant at school and not at home, while others are deviant at home and not at school. Studies by Johnson, Bolstad, and Lobitz (1976) and Patterson (1974) show that approximately half of the children who are deviant in either the home or school setting are also deviant in the other setting. When a child is deviant in one setting and not in another, it is obvious that at least part of the explanation of this difference can be attributed to differing conditions in the two settings of which the child's behavior is a function.

Mischel (1969) argues that cross-situational consistency of human behavior should only be expected if the conditions within situations are similar. To the extent that they are different, one can expect cross-situational differences in behavior or lack of behavioral consistency.

Given that human behavior is highly sensitive to differing conditions that exist across situations, it is probably also true that behavior is equally sensitive to changing conditions *within* situations. Evidence seems to be accumulating that children in general and acting-out, disruptive children in particular, are highly sensitive to differing conditions across situations and to changing conditions within them (Johnson, Bolstad, & Lobitz, 1976; Kazdin, 1973; Kazdin & Bootzin, 1972; Meichenbaum, Bowers, & Ross, 1968; O'Leary & Drabman, 1971).

Kazdin (1973) conducted a study which illustrates the relative sensitivity of deviant and nondeviant children to conditions within the regular classroom setting. A group of deviant and nondeviant children was selected for the study in a series of first-, third-, and fourth-grade regular classes. Five deviant and five nondeviant children were selected from each of six classrooms. Some of the children were told that they would be rewarded (with tokens exchangeable for backup rewards) for behaving appropriately. Others were rewarded for appropriate behavior but not given any instructions. Children in another group were told they would be rewarded for their appropriate behavior but were actually rewarded on a *random* (chance) basis. Still another group was rewarded randomly but given no instructions regarding what they were being rewarded for.

The results of the study showed that both deviant and nondeviant children responded when they were rewarded for appropriate behavior regardless of whether the teacher told them what they were being rewarded for. As would be expected, when the children were given *no* instructions and rewarded on a strictly chance basis, neither deviant nor nondeviant children responded. However, when the children were *told* they would be rewarded for their appropriate behavior and were actually rewarded on a random (chance) basis, the nondeviant children improved; however, the deviant children's behavior showed no change whatever.

This is an important finding since it illustrates how deviant and nondeviant children respond differently to treatment procedures designed to improve their behavior. For example, nondeviant children can be given a general set through instructions that they will be rewarded for their appropriate behavior, and even though this does not occur, they still respond positively. This is probably a result of the tendency of nondeviant children to generally follow instructions given them by adults and to accept their credibility uncritically.

However, deviant children in general, and acting-out children in particular, are very sensitive to the relationship between the instructions and/or directions given them by adults and the consequences that back them up. They are also equally sensitive to whether consequences delivered by adults are applied consistently. Thus, in the Kazdin study, it is not surprising that the deviant children weren't deceived by teacher instructions to the effect that they would be rewarded for their appropriate behavior when in fact they were not.

This finding can also be used to illustrate another characteristic of acting-out children; that is, their ability to "read" contingencies within a given situation and to respond appropriately. Contingencies refer to the relationships that exist between the stated rules or behavioral expectations in a situation, e.g., classroom, home, playground, and the consequences that back them up. Thus, an acting-out child's behavior may be quite different in two situations or settings where the contingencies differ radically. If, for example, the relationship between rules and backup consequences is not clear or the rules are not consistently backed up by consequences, the acting-out child may follow the rules only infrequently. If, however, rules are clearly stated and always consequated promptly, the acting-out child, as well as normal children, are much more likely to behave appropriately.

Numerous studies have shown that child behavior which has been changed through the application of behavioral procedures tends to be specific to the setting(s) in which such procedures are implemented (O'Leary & Drabman, 1971; O'Leary & O'Leary, 1976; Walker & Buckley, 1974). This is no doubt in part due to the ability of children in general, and particularly deviant children, to discriminate the presence and absence of behavioral treatment procedures across different settings.

The implications of these findings for the management of deviant, disruptive child behavior seem obvious. The behavior of such children is likely to be responsive to systematic intervention procedures; however, one should expect behavior to change only in those settings where the intervention procedures have been implemented. Further, once such procedures have been terminated, child behavior is likely to revert to pre-intervention levels unless maintenance procedures are implemented to support the changed behavior over the long term. Thus, if one wishes a child's behavior to be changed throughout the entire school day, then intervention procedures must be implemented throughout the total day and not just a part of it. Chapter 7 of this volume deals with the issue of generalization and maintenance of classroom treatment effects and describes techniques for facilitating its occurrence.

IDENTIFYING THE ACTING-OUT CHILD

Because of the high frequency and aversive nature of their behavior, acting-out children are easily identified by their teachers and peers. Teachers are usually quite sensitive to acting-out children since they spend so much time in trying to control their disruptive behavior. Further, evidence exists that classroom teachers can reliably identify their worst behaved, best behaved, and average behaved pupils (Bolstad, 1974).

A number of rating scales, behavior checklists, and observation instruments have been constructed to assist teachers and other school personnel in identifying children with behavior problems, including the acting-out child (Maes, 1966; Ross, Lacey, & Parton, 1965; Walker, 1970). These instruments are generally norm referenced in that norms (average scores) are developed by administering the scales to large numbers of children at different grade levels. Any child's score can then be compared against her/his normative group to determine whether he/she is average, above average, or below average. Thus, if a given child receives an exceptionally high score (compared to members of her/his normative group) on a checklist of problem behaviors, he/she may qualify for special treatment services.

One advantage of checklists and rating scales of this type is that the teacher, or the one rating, is required to make a series of judgments about whether or not a child possesses a problem behavior and in some cases how often it occurs. The rating process requires the teacher to carefully evaluate the child's behavior and to pinpoint specific problem behaviors. These pinpointed problem behaviors can be extremely valuable in planning a treatment program for the child.

Less frequently, behavioral observation data are used as a supplement in the identification of behavior problem children. Normative data also exist for observation instruments (Walker & Hops, 1976). For example, numerous studies of classroom behavior using systematic observation procedures indicate that the normal range for appropriate behavior in most classrooms is 70 to 80 percent; that is, the children observed were engaged in appropriate behavior for 70 to 80 percent of the time they were observed (Patterson, Cobb, & Ray, 1972).

Over a four year period, 71 acting-out children with relatively severe behavior problems were referred for treatment in a demonstration classroom maintained by the author. Observation data were recorded on each of these children in their regular classrooms prior to referral. As a group, they averaged 40 to 50 percent appropriate behavior during these observations, with a range of approximately 25 to 75 percent. Thus, as a group, these children were considerably below their peers in their levels of appropriate classroom behavior.

In some cases, a combination of teacher ratings and observation data is used to identify acting-out children (Hops, Beickel, & Walker, 1976; Walker & Buckley, 1974). However, such formal procedures as rating scales, checklists, and observation data are not required for a teacher to initially identify acting-out children in the classroom. These instruments do give some structure to the selection process and they can provide a validity check on the teacher's informal observations of the behavior of children in her/his class. For these reasons, they have value in the evaluation of child behavior and in the process of determining whether a given child qualifies for available services.

The Buros Mental Measurements Yearbook, available in any university library, contains a number of checklists, rating scales, and inventories that can be used to identify problem children and describe their classroom behavior. Two popular scales often used for this purpose are the Devereux Scales (1966) and the Walker Problem Behavior Identification Checklist (1970).

SUMMARY

The purpose of this chapter has been to describe the acting-out child and her/his behavioral characteristics. Also described were traditional school and teacher responses to the behavior problems presented by acting-out children.

An attempt was made to provide a perspective on human behavior in general and on deviant child behavior in particular. How one views child behavior can have a powerful impact upon one's general responsiveness to methods for explaining and changing it.

This book presents a highly effective technology for managing the behavior of acting-out children. Teacher expectations concerning this technology are an important component in determining how effectively they will implement it in managing the behavior of acting-out children.

REFERENCES

Allport, G. Personalistic psychology: A trait approach to personality. In W. S. Sahakian (Ed.), *Psychology of personality: Readings in theory*, Chicago: Rand McNally, 1974.

Allport, G. Traits revisited. *American Psychologist*, 1966, *21* (1), 1–9.

Ayllon, T., Layman, D., & Kandel, H. J. A behavioral-educational alternative to drug control of hyperactive children. *Journal of Applied Behavior Analysis*, 1975, *2*, 137–146.

Becker, W. C., Engelmann, S., & Thomas, D. *Teaching 1: Classroom management*. Chicago: Science Research Associates, 1976.

Bendix, S. Drug modification of behavior: A form of chemical violence against children? *Journal of Clinical Child Psychology*, 1973, *2* (3), 17–19.

Boldstad, O. *The relationship between teacher's assessment of students and student's actual behavior in the classroom*. Doctoral Dissertation, University of Oregon, 1974.

Bostow, D. E. & Bailey, J. B. Modification of severe disruptive and aggressive behavior using brief timeout and reinforcement procedures. *Journal of Applied Behavior Analysis*, 1969, *2*, 31–37.

Cohen, D., Douglas, V., & Morganstern, G. The effect of methylphenidate on attentive behavior and autonomic activity in hyperactive children. *Psychopharmacologia*, 1971, *22*, 282.

Comly, H. Cerebral stimulants for children with learning disorders? *Journal of Learning Disabilities*, 1971, *4* (9), 20–26.

Connors, C. K. What parents need to know about stimulant drugs and special education. *Journal of Learning Disabilities*, 1973, *6* (6), 349–351.

Conrad, W. C., Dworkin, E. S., Shai, A., & Tobiessen, J. E. Effects of amphetamine therapy and prescriptive tutoring on the behavior and achievement of lower class hyperactive children. *Journal of Learning Disabilities*, 1972, *4* (9), 509–517.

Denhoff, E., Davids, A., & Hawkins, A. B. Effects of dextroamphetamine on hyperkinetic children: A controlled double blind study. *Journal of Learning Disabilities*, 1971, *4* (9).

Fish, B. The "one child, one drug" myth of stimulants in hyperkinesis. *Archives of General Psychiatry*, 1971, *25*, 193–203.

Freedman, D. X., panel chairman, Panel of fifteen participants, Report of the conference on the use of stimulant drugs in the treatment of behaviorally disturbed young school children. *Journal of Learning Disabilities*, 1971, *4* (9).

Greenwood, C. R., Hops, H., Delquadri, J., & Guild, J. Group contingencies for group consequences in classroom management: A further analysis. *Journal of Applied Behavior Analysis*, 1974, 7, 413–425.

Hops, H., Beickel, S., & Walker, H. M. *CLASS (Contingencies for Learning Academic and Social Skills): Manual for consultants.* Eugene, Ore.: Center at Oregon for Research in the Behavioral Education of the Handicapped, University of Oregon, 1974.

Johnson, S. M., Boldstad, D. D., & Lobitz, G. K. Generalization and contrast phenomena in behavior modification with children. In E. J. Mash, L. A. Hamerlynck, & L. C. Handy (Eds.), *Behavior modification and families.* New York: Brunner/Mazell, 1976.

Johnson, S. M. *Personal Communication*, 1975.

Kazdin, A. E. & Bootzin, R. R. The token economy: An evaluative review. *Journal of Applied Behavior Analysis*, 1972, *5*, 343–372.

Knights, R. & Hinston, G. The effects of methylphenidate (Ritalin) on motor skills and behavior of children with learning problems. *Journal of Nervous Mental Disorders*, 1969, *148*, 643.

Ladd, E. T. Pills for classroom peace? *Saturday Review*, November 1970, 66–83.

Maes, W. R. The identification of emotionally disturbed children. *Exceptional Children*, 1966, *32*, 607–613.

Meichenbaum, D. H., Bowers, K. S., & Ross, R. R. Modification of classroom behavior of institutionalized female adolescent offenders. *Behavior Research and Therapy*, 1968, *6*, 343–353.

Mischel, W. Continuity and change in personality. *American Psychologist*, 1969, *24* (11), 1012–1018.

Mischel, W. *Personality and assessment.* New York: John Wiley, 1968.

Novack, H. S. An educator's view of medication and classroom behavior. *Journal of Learning Disabilities*, 1971, *4* (9).

O'Leary, K. D. & Drabman, R. Token reinforcement programs in the classroom: A preview. *Psychological Bulletin*, 1971, *75*, 379–398.

O'Leary, K. D., Pelham, W. E., Rosenbaum, M. A., & Price, G. H. Behavioral treatment of hyperkinetic children: An experimental evaluation of its usefulness. *Clinical Pediatrics*, 1976, *15* (6), 510–515.

O'Leary, K. D. & O'Leary, S. G. Behavior modification in the school. In H. Leitenberg (Ed.), *Handbook of behavior modification and therapy*, Englewood Cliffs, New Jersey: Prentice-Hall, Inc., 1976.

Patterson, G. R. Intervention for boys with conduct problems: Multiple settings, treatment, and criteria. *Journal of Consulting and Clinical Psychology*, 1974, *42*, 471–481.

Patterson, G. R., Cobb, J. A., & Ray, R. S. Direct intervention in the classroom: A set of procedures for the aggressive child. In F. W. Clark, D. R. Evans, & L. A. Hamerlynck (Eds.), *Implementing behavioral programs for schools and clinics*. Proceedings of the 3rd Banff International Conference on Behavior Modification, Research Press Co., 1972.

Rapoport, J. L., Quinn, P. O., Bradbard, G., Riddle, D., & Brooks, E. Imipramine and methylphenidate treatments of hyperactive boys. *Arch. Gen. Psychiatry*, 1974, *30*, 789.

Ross, A. O., Lacey, H., & Parton, D. The development of a behavior checklist for boys. *Child Development*, 1965, *36*, 1013–1027.

Safer, D. J., & Allen, R. P. Factors influencing the suppressant effects of two stimulant drugs on the growth of hyperactive children. *Pediatrics*, 1973, *51*, 660.

Spivack, G. & Swift, M. S. The Devereux elementary school behavior rating scales: A study of the nature and organization of achievement related disturbed classroom behavior. *Journal of Special Education*, 1966, *1*, 71–90.

Thomas, D. R., Becker, W. C., & Armstrong, M. Production and elimination of disruptive classroom behavior by systematically varying teacher's behavior. *Journal of Applied Behavior Analysis*, 1968, *1*, 35–45.

Ullman, L. P. & Krasner, L. *Case studies in behavior modification*. New York: Holt, Rinehart & Winston, 1965.

Walker, H. M., Hops, H., & Fiegenbaum, E. Deviant classroom behavior as a function of combinations of social and token reinforcement and cost contingency. *Behavior Therapy*, 1976, 7, 76–88.

Walker, S. Drugging the American child: We're too cavalier about hyperactivity. *Psychology Today*, 1974, *8* (7), 43–48.

Walker, H. M. & Buckley, N. K. *Token reinforcement techniques: Classroom applications for the hard to teach child*. Eugene, Ore.: E-B Press, Inc., 1974.

Walker, H. M. & Buckley, N. K. Teacher attention to appropriate and inappropriate classroom behavior: An individual case study. *Focus on Exceptional Children*, 1973, *5*, 5–11.

Walker, H. M. & Hops, H. Use of normative peer data as a standard for evaluating classroom treatment effects. *Journal of Applied Behavior Analysis*, 1976, *9*, 159–168.

Walker, H. M. *The Walker problem behavior identification checklist*. Los Angeles, Calif.: Western Psychological Services, 1970.

Zax, M., Cowen, E. L., Izzo, L. D., & Trost, M. A. Identifying emotional disturbance in the school setting. *American Journal of Orthopsychiatry*, 1964, *34*, 447–454.

CHAPTER 2

Rules Governing Classroom Behavior

This chapter presents a series of key rules that govern the behavior of acting-out children and their peers. The social learning foundations for each rule are described and practical examples are given to illustrate how the rule operates. Classroom applications of each rule are also discussed.

A knowledge of these rules and how they operate in the classroom setting will give the teacher a greater understanding of why children behave as they do. An understanding of causal factors governing deviant as well as nondeviant behavior can be of invaluable assistance to a classroom teacher in improving her/his behavior management skills. Chapter 4 discusses how to use specific classroom management techniques that are based upon these rules.

HUMAN BEHAVIOR IS LEARNED THROUGH A SERIES OF INTERACTIONS WITH ONE'S ENVIRONMENT

Social Learning Foundations

John Locke, the English poet, regarded the newborn child as a "Tabula Rasa" or as a blank tablet to be written upon. The child's unique life experiences determined what was written upon this tablet. The person the child eventually developed into and his/her personality characteristics were the sum total of these life experiences.

Locke's view of human development saw the child as highly malleable and as being greatly influenced by her/his life experiences. If John Locke were alive today, he would probably subscribe strongly to the nurture side of the "nature-nurture" controversy in explaining the development of intelligence and personality. He felt that environmental influences played a powerful role in determining how children develop and learn and that all knowledge was acquired empirically —through experience.

Children are born with almost limitless capacities for learning. In the early stages of development, what the child learns is to a large extent acquired through contact with environments such as the home or school. Environmental influences upon the child's development are transmitted primarily through interactions the child has with key social agents in these settings including parents, siblings, teachers, and peers. The quality of these interactions and the kinds of feedback children receive regarding their behavior are instrumental in shaping what is learned.

Specific behavior patterns as well as values and attitudes are taught through this process. This gradual training process is known as *socialization* and is the primary vehicle through which children absorb their culture and acquire the skills they need to cope effectively in society.

In this training process, children become highly sensitive to the feedback they receive regarding their behavior. If a particular response produces a positive result from the environment, it is likely to be strengthened and become a part of the child's behavioral repertoire. If the behavior is punished or consistently ignored, it will not be strengthened and will eventually cease. In the course of development, the child "tries out" literally hundreds of such behavioral responses in home and school environments. Whether or not they are acquired depends upon the effect they have upon the environment. If the effect is positive, they will probably be acquired; if it is negative, they probably will not be acquired.

It is clear that learning is, to a large extent, an interactive process. Much of a child's learning is social in nature and involves social exchanges with key social agents in the environment. However, the child also learns and acquires skills through interactions of a nonsocial nature.

For example, children learn to discriminate relevant features of the physical environment through contact with materials that teach size, shape, color, and so forth. After basic reading skills are developed, much learning of a nonsocial nature occurs through interaction with a wide variety of educational materials.

Adults (usually parents and teachers) are responsible for guiding this interactive process along lines that insure healthy and normal development. Parents and sometimes teachers are not always aware of the remarkable extent to which they can influence the developmental learning processes of children.

Classroom Applications

Since no two home environments are exactly the same, children's learning histories differ and the behavioral repertoires they bring to school reflect these differences. When they begin school, children are expected to behave in certain carefully prescribed ways in order to participate in the learning process. That is, they must learn to listen to teacher instructions, follow directions, sit quietly for relatively long periods, attend to tasks, raise their hand before asking questions, cooperate with other children, and respond when called upon. That is, they must learn to be socially responsive to adults and classmates.

Due to their unique learning histories, some children experience great difficulty in adjusting to these behavioral demands. If these difficulties are not resolved, the result can be a seriously impaired school adjustment and the development of conflict between the child and teacher.

The kinds of interactions a child has with her/his teachers and classmates can have a dramatic impact upon the learning process and subsequently upon academic achievement. Some children enter school with well developed social skills, are responsive to instructions or commands from adults, and are motivated to learn. Such children are easy to teach in that they generally learn quickly, require only limited amounts of teacher time, and interact constructively with the teacher and their peers. Their interactions with teachers are generally also positive and of a cooperative nature.

Acting-out children, on the other hand, are another story. Their interactions with the teacher and peers are very often negative and characterized by mutual hostility (Walker & Buckley, 1973). The disruptive effects of these interactions upon the learning and achievement of the acting-out child and, in many cases, that of his/her classmates are well documented (Hops, Beickel, & Walker, 1976). It is nearly impossible for efficient instruction to occur under such conditions since teachers naturally require a certain level of appropriate behavior before dispensing instruction. Further, the emotional reactions of adults to child behavior(s) that they find highly irritating or aversive are slow to subside and can condition the teacher's instructional and management behavior toward the child long after the specific behavior(s) in question has terminated.

As mentioned earlier, because of the aversive nature of her/his behavior, the acting-out child systematically trains classmates and peers to either (a) avoid social interactions with him/her or (b) to respond to his/her social initiations in a negative or hostile fashion. Consequently, the acting-out child loses valuable opportunities to learn prosocial patterns of behavior from peers through mutually positive and reciprocal social exchanges with them.

In the classroom setting, it seems apparent that positive interactions can facilitate learning processes in general and specifically those occurring between the teacher and pupils, and among pupils. If such interactions are aversive and characterized by mutual hostility, little in the way of *constructive* learning may occur.

DEVIANT AS WELL AS NONDEVIANT BEHAVIOR IS LEARNED

Social Learning Foundations

Probably no parent or teacher would deliberately teach a child to act out, be disruptive, or engage in deviant behavior. Yet it is ironic that many parents and teachers systematically teach children to be aggressive, noncompliant, and generally irritating.

This happens because the same principles that govern the learning and acquisition of appropriate behavior also control the acquisition of inappropriate behavior. Whether a child learns appropriate or inappropriate behavior depends largely upon the consequences that are supplied to these two types of behavior.

The manner in which children are systematically taught to misbehave can be illustrated in a number of ways. For example, most parents and teachers communicate a general expectancy to children that they should behave appropriately, follow rules, obey instructions, and so forth. However, children very often receive no (or only limited) adult attention for doing so. The number of positive consequences (spontaneous compliments, social praise, privileges) that are received for behaving appropriately are even fewer. In such situations, if a child wants attention and feedback, she/he learns that it is more likely to be received for such things as *not* following rules, *not* obeying instructions, and *not* paying attention to the task at hand. Even though it is negative, this kind of attention is far superior to none at all.

It would be desirable and certainly much more convenient for adults if children would learn to behave appropriately in the absence of positive attention and support for doing so. It is true that some children seem to receive only very small amounts of positive attention and feedback for their appropriate behavior and still manage to develop very constructive behavior patterns at home and school. However, such children are probably relatively rare.

Praising and providing positive feedback to children (and each other) do not seem to be "natural" activities for most adults. We are much more likely to ignore long periods of constructive, prosocial child behavior and to respond only to those child behaviors that we find irritating, disruptive, or inappropriate. Consequently, one can see how the adage "the squeaky wheel gets the oil" applies directly to the development of deviant behavior in children.

Whining is an example of a behavior that is systematically, although inadvertently, taught to children by parents and sometimes teachers. If a child has difficulty obtaining parental or teacher attention, he/she sometimes learns that whining will produce an immediate response to her/his demand(s). Adults find whining extremely irritating and generally respond quickly so as to terminate it. This behavior pattern then becomes established and mutually supported since the child is rewarded by adult attention and acquiescence to his/her demand(s), whereas adults are rewarded by termination of the whining (Patterson & Reid, 1970). Consequently, many children learn that whining is an instrumental response that produces an immediate reaction from adults.

Children are also taught to misbehave through a general lack of consistency by adults in their efforts at shaping and controlling the child's behavior. Sometimes a child receives negative feedback and unpleasant consequences for engaging in a particular behavior. At other times, the child receives no consequences or feedback at all when engaging in the behavior. Consequently, the child is taught that sometimes he/she "gets caught" for engaging in a certain deviant behavior and at other times, no negative or unpleasant consequences are forthcoming. Thus, the child learns that occasionally and, in some cases, frequently, it is possible to engage in deviant behavior and suffer no unpleasant consequences for it. If the child finds the deviant behavior rewarding, this can be a very serious problem.

Adults are inconsistent in their efforts at managing child behavior for different reasons. For example, sometimes adults have not completely made up their minds about whether a particular behavior is appropriate or inappropriate. Children are usually quick to sense such ambivalence and respond accordingly. At other times, adults may be too tired to consequate the child's behavior consistently, or it may be inconvenient to do so. Sometimes adults also have difficulty remembering how they have responded to a particular behavior in the past. Whatever the reason(s) for lack of consistency in the management of child behavior, the resulting effects are uniformly the same and very often undesirable.

Children can also learn to misbehave because of differing behavioral standards held by social agents charged with managing their behavior. For example, one parent may be very strict and highly consistent in requiring a child to follow established rules, whereas the other parent may be much less strict and inconsistent in this respect. Thus, the child would learn that one parent maintains consistent behavioral standards while the other does not. The child's behavior in the presence of the two parents is likely to be markedly different with appropriate behavior displayed in the presence of the strict parent and inappropriate behavior displayed in the presence of the less strict and less consistent parent. This kind of child rearing experience can teach a child to discriminate among social agents in terms of the type of behavior that will be tolerated and to respond accordingly.

Doubtless, the situations outlined above are not the only ways in which children are inadvertently taught to not follow rules and to misbehave. However, they do illustrate how easy it is for children to learn patterns of misbehavior.

Classroom Applications

Children are systematically taught patterns of misbehavior by teachers in the same way they are taught by parents. In some respects, the problem is more acute with teachers than with parents. For example, teachers are charged with the effective management and instruction of twenty to thirty children at any one time. Great demands are placed upon the teacher's time in this process with little attention available for individual children. Consequently, most teachers develop a set of classroom rules governing appropriate social and academic behavior and then communicate an expectancy that all children should follow them. Because of the obvious time constraints, children who follow the rules, do their work, and don't create problems for the teacher are generally ignored, while those who act out and are disruptive of classroom atmosphere receive a great deal of teacher attention even though it is usually negative and directed toward the child's inappropriate behavior.

Lack of teacher consistency in the management of child behavior is also a very serious problem in the school setting. Because of the sheer numbers involved, teachers find it extremely difficult to be consistent in the consequences they supply to children's appropriate and inappropriate classroom behavior.

The problem of differing behavioral standards held by social agents who manage the child's behavior is a relatively greater problem at school than at home. An elementary pupil can have up to seven or eight different teachers in an ordinary school day, all of whom may have different standards in relation to the child's overall behavior. Children in general, and acting-out children in particular, become very discriminating when it is apparent that their teachers hold different behavioral standards and enforce those standards differentially. Instead of learning a consistent, prosocial behavior pattern that is maintained across settings, some children learn to try and "get away" with whatever the situation will bear as a result of their learning experiences. The unfortunate result may be the acquisition of a consistent pattern of misbehavior that can permanently handicap a child's school adjustment.

OBSERVATIONAL LEARNING EXPLAINS THE ACQUISITION OF MUCH HUMAN BEHAVIOR

Social Learning Foundations

In the course of their development, children acquire a great deal of information through the simple process of observation. The capacities of children for observation and their sensitivity to what they observe are sometimes truly amazing. Through observation, children develop an understanding of how the environment works as well as an awareness of relationships existing among situations and between individuals within the environment.

Observation is one vehicle through which children acquire new behavioral responses. For example, a young child will observe another sibling or parent performing a certain behavior and may attempt to reproduce it. This process is called *modeling* and is an attempt by the child to behaviorally reproduce what she/he has observed through imitation.

Usually a child's first attempts at imitating a new behavior are unskilled and poorly developed. With practice, however, the child's skill level increases and the behavior in question comes to approximate more closely that of the model. This acquisition process is facilitated if the child receives positive feedback or consequences for attempting to imitate the behavior. If ignored or punished, the child may cease all such attempts, thus reducing the chances that the behavior will be acquired (Bandura, 1969).

Parents are well aware of the power of observation and modeling as methods through which children are educated and socialized. A number of behavioral responses and attitudes are transmitted from parents to children through this process. Unfortunately, the child is just as likely to imitate undesirable attitudes and behavior patterns as desirable ones. When parents give their children advice to the effect, "Do what I say, not what I do!" children are much more likely to imitate their parents' actual behavior than to follow their instructions to the contrary.

Children are more likely to observe and imitate the behavior of individuals whom they see as having power and high social status. Consequently, children are more likely to be influenced by their parents (at least in their younger years) than any other social agents with whom they have contact. Thus, parents' actual behavior as observed by the child and their expressed attitudes can have a profound effect upon the child's development.

Research has shown that children respond positively to symbolic models (in film) and will acquire new behavioral responses through this process (Bandura, 1969; O'Connor, 1969). Children acquire a great deal of information through viewing television and often imitate the behavior of television models. In recent years, substantial controversy has developed around the issue of whether children are influenced adversely by televised violence. There seems to be no clear cut answer to this question at present; however, a large number of parents and educators remain concerned about this issue.

Research has also shown that children learn by simply observing the behavior of others, by taking note of the consequences of their behavior (Kazdin, 1973). This is called *vicarious* learning. If a child observes a model receiving a positive consequence for engaging in a certain behavior, that behavior is more likely to be modeled. If the model is observed being punished for engaging in a particular behavior, that behavior is not likely to be modeled by the observing child.

Modeling and vicarious learning operate at all levels of society. These two processes explain the acquisition of much human behavior. In recent years, there has been an increasing awareness of how teaching methods based upon these processes can be used to develop complex skills and behavior patterns.

Classroom Applications

In the school setting, a child learns from the teacher and from other children through observational processes. Teachers make use of modeling techniques to teach certain academic and social skills. Teachers will often use verbal instructions to explain a skill to be learned, model the skill for the children, and then provide positive feedback and encouragement as the children attempt to master it (Becker, Engelmann, & Thomas, 1976). If used correctly, this is a highly effective teaching strategy.

Children imitate each other's behavior in the classroom and acquire behavior patterns from each other. High status, popular children are more likely to be modeled than low status children. Children who are perceived as having power and influence are also likely to be modeled by their peers (Bandura, 1969). Acting-out children frequently model deviant behavior patterns for their peers and thus contribute to a higher rate of deviant behavior in the classroom than may otherwise be the case.

Vicarious learning processes operate constantly in every classroom. The teacher's interactions with children are constantly being observed and evaluated by peers. The teacher's consistency in managing children's behavior and the consequences applied to both prosocial and inappropriate behavior are carefully noted. The classroom behavior of children is thus powerfully affected by what they have learned through these observational processes.

Children in general, and acting-out children in particular, become very sensitive to the contingencies that exist in different settings through observational learning processes. Where contingencies differ markedly across settings, children's behavior is likely to reflect those differences and vary accordingly.

Children can learn to imitate prosocial, appropriate behavior, especially if positive consequences are provided for doing so. Some teachers will occasionally single out a child who is following classroom rules and praise him/her publicly in order to provide a model for the class. Some teachers will also use modeling procedures to consequate deviant behavior; that is, if a child is acting-out or misbehaving, the teacher will select a child nearby and praise him/her aloud for following the rules. Thus, the correct behavior is modeled for the misbehaving child and it is learned that teacher attention will be received for appropriate rather than inappropriate behavior. Both of these techniques have proven effective in changing classroom behavior.

Traditionally, modeling and vicarious learning processes have been used primarily to explain how behavior is acquired. Increasingly, however, productive applications of these processes are being developed for the purpose of changing behavior from inappropriate to appropriate and for teaching complex academic and social skills (Kazdin, 1973; O'Connor, 1969; 1972). Their demonstrated effectiveness will no doubt lead to the development of additional applications in the future.

A BEHAVIOR FOLLOWED CLOSELY IN TIME BY A REWARDING CONSEQUENCE WILL TEND TO OCCUR MORE OFTEN IN THE FUTURE

Social Learning Foundations

This principle is referred to as reinforcement. It means that if a consequence, which the child finds rewarding, immediately follows a particular behavior, the child is more likely to engage in that behavior in the future in order to produce the reward. This principle is fundamental to the way all children learn (Skinner, 1953).

From birth onward, children learn to respond in ways that produce rewarding consequences from the environment. For example, an infant quickly learns that crying is usually followed by maternal attention accompanied by efforts to identify the source of the crying. The mother's efforts to change the condition(s) (pain, hunger, trauma, fear, etc.) causing the crying gradually teaches the child that crying is an instrumental response, which will usually prompt attention from adults, expressions of concern, and changes designed to eliminate the reason for the crying. Such consequences are highly rewarding to most children and increase the chances that crying will occur again in the future under similar circumstances.

There is almost a limitless number of consequences that can be considered rewarding. However, what is rewarding for one child may not necessarily be rewarding for another. Some events that are commonly assumed to be rewarding for most children are hugs, smiles, kisses, expressions of approval, attention, compliments, free time, sympathy, money, toys, games, candy, and food in general. If a child is willing to work hard to earn a given reward, that may be a good indication of whether it is rewarding for her/him.

Activities can be rewarding or nonrewarding. People sample a very large number of activities over the course of their lives. Some of these activities are found to be rewarding and others are not. As a general rule, people tend to avoid those activities they find unrewarding and to spend time in those activities they enjoy and do find rewarding.

How such preferences develop is a complex and not well understood process. Their formation is probably influenced by a host of genetic, biological, psychological, and environmental factors.

The reasons why someone finds an activity or event rewarding are not really important in explaining human behavior. The important point to remember is that people usually behave in ways designed to maximize their chances of obtaining, receiving, or engaging in consequences they find rewarding.

Classroom Applications

The principle of reinforcement explains much of the classroom behavior of the acting-out child and her/his peers. Perhaps the most powerful rewarding consequence available to all the children in most classrooms is teacher attention. At any given time, twenty to thirty children are simultaneously competing for the teacher's attention. Some are more successful than others in this process. For example, children with deficient academic skills require larger amounts of the teacher's time and attention than do their more academically skilled classmates. Other children are highly dependent upon the teacher for encouragement, feedback, and reassurance in the completion of tasks and thereby consume large amounts of teacher attention. However, the acting-out child far and away consumes the largest amounts of the teacher's time and attention. As noted in Chapter 1, huge amounts of the teacher's time are devoted to the task of simply managing the acting-out child's classroom behavior. Acting-out children learn to dominate the teacher's time and are very skilled in coercing attention from the teacher, even when the teacher does not have the energy, time, or willingness to give it.

It is apparent that acting-out children have learned to "act out" to obtain teacher attention and that the attention they receive in this process, though often negative and designed to suppress their behavior, is at least partially instrumental in strengthening it and making it more likely that it will occur again in the future.

Normal children on the other hand learn to engage in appropriate behavior for long periods of time and receive only minimal amounts of the teacher's attention and time. As mentioned earlier, there are a number of theories, none of them validated, to explain why some children learn this behavior pattern and others do not.

Even though it is not known why some children learn this behavior pattern and other do not, it is clear that teacher attention is a highly rewarding consequence for both acting-out children and their normal peers. Because of its potency, teacher attention can be a valuable tool in changing the acting-out child's behavior from inappropriate to appropriate. Through a gradual process, the acting-out child can be taught that his/her appropriate behavior is more likely to produce teacher attention than is inappropriate behavior. This is no easy task and at least initially it may be necessary to supplement this teaching process with more powerful treatment procedures in order to change a long established behavior pattern. However, because of its rewarding qualities and its availability, teacher attention can be one of the most effective tools at the teacher's disposal for changing the acting-out child's behavior.

A PREVIOUSLY REWARDED BEHAVIOR THAT IS NO LONGER REWARDED WILL EVENTUALLY EXTINGUISH

Social Learning Foundations

The process of withholding rewards from a previously rewarded behavior is referred to as placing the behavior on extinction. If rewards are consistently withheld from the behavior for a sufficient period of time, it will decrease in frequency and may cease altogether. When the behavior no longer occurs, extinction is said to have occurred.

Laboratory studies have shown extinction to be an effective technique for reducing a variety of behavioral responses. In controlled settings, such as a laboratory, it is a fairly simple task to insure that a response is no longer rewarded, thus maximizing the effectiveness of extinction. However, in real world settings such as the home and classroom, it's much more difficult to control all the sources of reward for a particular behavior, especially if attention from others is the primary rewarding consequence.

Careful studies of the extinction process have shown that there are characteristic patterns of responding during extinction (Ferster & Skinner, 1957). When the behavior is first placed on extinction, there is usually an increase in its frequency, magnitude, or intensity followed by a gradual and sometimes irregular decline prior to eventual cessation. The initial increase in the behavior results from attempts to produce the reward that is no longer forthcoming. Eventually, it is learned that the behavior will not be rewarded and it ceases to occur.

If the pressures that are applied to produce the reward are occasionally successful in the early stages of extinction, then extinction procedures will be unsuccessful in reducing the behavior. In fact, this could result in the behavior in question being maintained at higher levels of intensity, magnitude, or frequency for a period of time. Consequently, if extinction is applied incorrectly, it may produce the opposite effect from that intended.

Classroom Applications

If applied to the right behaviors and used correctly, extinction can be a practical behavior management tool for the classroom teacher. Extinction can be used to reduce certain "attention getting" behaviors that may be minimally disruptive to the classroom setting. Extinction, in the form of ignoring, can be applied successfully to such "teacher irritant" child behaviors as dawdling, pencil tapping, asking irrelevant and unnecessary questions, and minor rule breaking. If the child engages in these behaviors primarily to irritate the teacher and to get attention, then systematically ignoring them may be quite effective in reducing their rates of occurrence.

It is impossible to determine in advance how long it will take for a given behavior to extinguish for a particular child. If a decision to use extinction is made, the teacher should be prepared to stick with it until it has proven successful. The teacher should also be reasonably confident that all sources of reward for the behavior to be extinguished can be controlled effectively and that it is feasible to consistently ignore the behavior. If not, the teacher's use of extinction will be an exercise in futility.

There are certain classroom behaviors for which extinction is not appropriate. For example, high magnitude behaviors such as tantrums, fighting, and teacher defiance are not, as would be expected, appreciably affected by extinction procedures applied in the classroom setting. These behaviors usually occur at a relatively low frequency, but at extremely high levels of intensity. They are highly disruptive of classroom atmosphere, usually cannot be tolerated, and require the application of much more powerful procedures than simple ignoring by the teacher and/or peers. Other classroom behaviors such as talking out, out of seat, not completing assignments, noncompliance, and off-task also generally require procedures other than simple extinction. As a general rule, extinction should be applied only to those inappropriate behaviors that are minimally disruptive to classroom atmosphere and that are maintained primarily by teacher attention.

A BEHAVIOR FOLLOWED CLOSELY IN TIME BY A PUNISHING CONSEQUENCE WILL TEND TO OCCUR LESS OFTEN IN THE FUTURE, PARTICULARLY IN THE PRESENCE OF THE PUNISHING AGENT

Social Learning Foundations

Punishment refers to the application of an aversive consequence to a behavior. If the aversive consequence suppresses the behavior to which it is applied, it can be classified as a punishing consequence. Laboratory studies have shown that punishment procedures, if powerful enough, can produce almost a complete suppression in responding (Azrin & Holz, 1966).

The use of punishment in controlling human behavior has been a highly controversial issue in our society. Arguments over punishment have ranged from whether to use spanking to encourage children to behave, to whether capital punishment reduces the incidence of violent crimes. Professionals and nonprofessionals alike seem to be divided over the issue of punishment.

A number of moral and ethical arguments have been developed against the use of punishment. Further, it has been suggested that punishment only teaches a child to suppress behavior in the presence of the punishing agent and not at other times.

If used in isolation as a behavior change technique, punishment is likely to be ineffective, especially if the behavior being punished continues to be reinforced by other social agents in the same setting or by social agents in different settings. If all sources of reinforcement for the punished behavior are controlled, and an incompatible appropriate behavior is reinforced while punishment is applied to the inappropriate behavior, then punishment as a behavior change technique is likely to be much more effective. In managing child behavior, it is sometimes difficult to achieve this goal.

Even though punishment can be effective in changing behavior under certain conditions, a number of difficult questions remain unresolved as to the generality of its effects and whether side effects are associated with its use. Continuing research on the use of punishment in applied settings such as the classroom should provide information on these questions.

Classroom Applications

The role of punishment in the classroom has also generated a great deal of controversy and discussion in recent years. A number of schools in this country use corporal punishment (spanking, paddling) as one means of controlling child behavior. Statutes allowing corporal punishment have been a part of the legal code for a long time. The legal foundation for the use of corporal punishment in the schools was only recently reaffirmed by the United States Supreme Court.

Given what is known about the management and control of classroom behavior, it does not appear that the use of corporal punishment can be justified by school personnel as a method for controlling child behavior. Further, corporal punishment in the forms of spanking and paddling are easily abused and can result in inadvertent injury to the child. Long term, traumatic emotional effects can also result from corporal punishment.

Techniques such as timeout, loss of privileges, and temporary suspension are equally as effective as corporal punishment in controlling child behavior. Further, the risks associated with corporal punishment are usually not associated with the use of these techniques.

One of the most heavily used punishing consequences employed by teachers to control child behavior is the reprimand. The unfortunate thing is, reprimands only control the behavior of some children and not others. One study found that the teacher's use of sit down commands actually *increased* rather than decreased the number of times children were out of their seats (Madsen, Becker, Thomas, Koser, & Plager, 1968). Occasionally, reprimands will produce a short term reduction in an inappropriate behavior but the teacher attention received in this process may actually strengthen the behavior over the long term. As a general rule, reprimands should be avoided as a technique for controlling classroom behavior.

There is no substitute for good teaching methods, explicit classroom rules, and a positive behavior management system to reduce the necessity for using punishment procedures in the classroom. Some very deviant children may require the use of mild punishment procedures for a period of time for their behavior to be controlled effectively. However, such procedures should be used only in conjunction with a positive reinforcement system. Two forms of mild punishment that have been used effectively in classroom settings include *timeout* and *cost contingency*. These two techniques will be defined and their classroom applications discussed in Chapter 4.

BEHAVIOR IS CONTROLLED BY ANTECEDENT EVENTS (CONDITIONS THAT PRECEDE IT) AND BY CONSEQUENT EVENTS (CONDITIONS THAT FOLLOW IT)

Social Learning Foundations

Human behavior is controlled by events and conditions that precede it as well as by events and conditions that follow it. Controlling events/conditions that precede behavior are called *antecedents*, while those that follow behavior are called *consequences*. (See diagram below.)

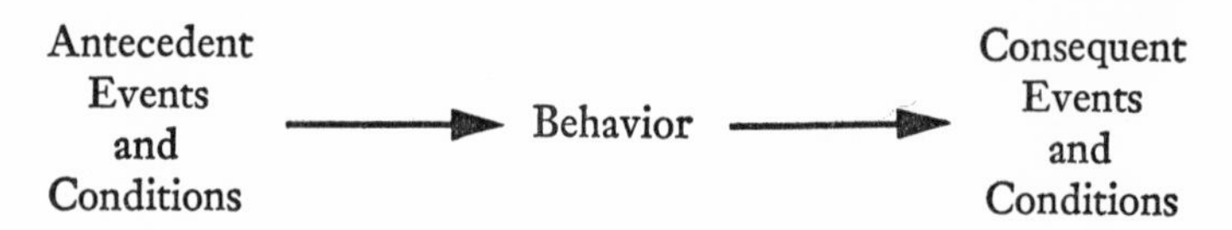

Antecedent events and conditions either set the stage for behavior to occur or actually prompt its occurrence. Consequences follow the behavior and determine whether it is strengthened or weakened.

The controlling relationship between antecedents and subsequent behavior is illustrated in the following examples. A teacher's classroom rules governing appropriate behavior are vaguely defined; consequently, child behavior is unpredictable and often out of control. Two children frequently argue over who gets to play with a favorite toy; the presence of the toy leads to squabbling, bickering, and sometimes fighting. A preschool child falls down and skins his arm at nursery school, but expresses only mild discomfort; however, when his mother picks him up about thirty minutes later, he bursts into tears and gives a long account of how badly he hurt himself on the playground. A mother and father usually have violent arguments around dinner time; their children become upset and begin to show visible signs of anxiety as dinner approaches.

The consequences to child behavior that have been supplied by adults in the above examples have no doubt contributed to the controlling relationship that exists between the antecedent stimuli and child behavior. This process is known as the stimulus control of behavior (Patterson, 1974). For example, if classroom rules are not clearly specified and child behavior is frequently disruptive and out of control, the teacher may spend more time in attempting to manage the class than in instructing the children. The teacher attention dispensed in this process may strengthen the children's inappropriate behavior and make it more likely that such behavior will occur in the future. In the case of the two children arguing over a favorite toy, squabbling, bickering, and fighting will often require parental intervention and the attention received makes it more likely that an argument will occur again in the near future. The preschool child who cries over a minor injury received thirty minutes before has learned that he can obtain sympathy, expressions of concern, and maternal attention by crying and complaining of aches, pains, and injury. When children are emotionally upset and anxious over their parents' arguing, their behavior may become aberrant or unusual, thus prompting the attention and concern of one or both parents following the argument. The result may be to actually strengthen the children's aberrant or unusual behavior.

Antecedents and consequences are equally powerful in the control they exert over behavior. However, we are often much more concerned with the consequences supplied to behavior than we are with the situations that actually prompt its occurrence. If we were more sensitive to such situations and conditions, it would be possible to *prevent* the occurrence of inappropriate or undesirable behavior in many instances.

Classroom Applications

The classroom teacher is the most powerful influence in any classroom. One reason for this is that the teacher has such direct control of the antecedents and consequences that precede and follow child behavior.

Teachers engage in four classes of behavior in relation to antecedents and consequences. That is, teachers arrange situations and conditions in the classroom that lead to both appropriate and inappropriate child behavior. Similarly, teachers supply positive consequences to appropriate child behavior and negative consequences to inappropriate child behavior.

Unfortunately, many teachers arrange classroom conditions, albeit inadvertently, that lead to inappropriate child behavior without recognizing that their own behavior is indirectly responsible for the undesirable behavior of the children. For example, a situation common to all classrooms concerns getting the attention of the class before giving instructions for an assignment or activity. To facilitate the ability of all pupils to perform the assignment or activity correctly, it is necessary that each pupil have a clear understanding of the accompanying instructions. It is important that the teacher have the attention of the *entire* class before giving instructions. In actual practice, however, many teachers give instructions with only a portion of the class attending to them. This can lead to yelling, shouting, and general teacher frustration. Further, the teacher may find him/herself repeating instructions over and over to those students who were not attending.

As mentioned earlier, teachers spend a great deal of time supplying negative consequences to children's inappropriate behavior. In many cases, teachers have to respond this way in order to cope with deviant child behavior that has been prompted by inappropriate antecedent conditions.

It would be desirable and more productive of child achievement if teachers could spend a greater portion of their time supplying consequences to appropriate child classroom behavior. However, in order to do this, it would be necessary to simultaneously rearrange antecedent conditions so that situations leading to inappropriate behavior would be reduced to the maximum extent possible.

BEHAVIOR CAN BE CHANGED BY EITHER ALTERING CONTROLLING ANTECEDENT EVENTS AND CONDITIONS AND/OR BY MANIPULATING CONSEQUENCES

Social Learning Foundations

The great majority of studies concerned with changing child behavior have focused upon manipulating consequences that follow behavior. Relatively few studies have systematically investigated methods for altering and controlling antecedent conditions so as to permanently change behavior. As a general rule, in the process of changing behavior, one should examine antecedent variables *first* as a means of possibly changing the behavior in question before resorting to the manipulation of consequences.

If it is discovered that inappropriate child behavior is a function of a certain antecedent condition or event, then the teacher may be able to simply rearrange the antecedent(s) and change the behavior. There are several advantages to this approach. For example, if altering an antecedent does change a behavior(s), the behavior change is likely to be *permanent* as long as the changed antecedent conditions remain in effect. Further, once the change has been made, the teacher no longer has to worry about it; that is, the personal response cost to the teacher required to change the child's behavior can be extremely low when antecedents are used.

If there are no antecedent conditions that can be changed, then one should consider manipulating consequences in order to change behavior. There are several types of consequences that can be manipulated. For example, rewarding consequences (teacher praise, awarding privileges, free time, etc.) can be used to motivate a child and to increase performance. Similarly, extinction procedures (ignoring) and mild punishment (timeout, loss of privileges) can be used to decrease inappropriate behavior. Rewarding and punishing consequences can also be applied simultaneously to increase appropriate behavior at the same time that inappropriate behavior is decreased.

In order for consequences to be effective in changing behavior, they must be applied consistently. It is sometimes difficult for adults to apply such consequences over a long period of time. Therefore, if one has a choice of rearranging antecedents or of manipulating consequences in order to change behavior, antecedents should be the preferred method unless special circumstances make it inadvisable.

Classroom Applications

If a child is not learning and achieving in school, it is up to the school system to determine why and to arrange conditions that will facilitate learning. There are a number of antecedents that could be examined in the task of finding the cause of the child's inability to learn.

For example, one should determine whether the academic performance expectations for the child are consistent with her/his intellectual potential. Examinations should be given to check for sensory deficits that could account for the learning failure, e.g., hearing and/or visual problems. The possibility of a central nervous system insult or neurological problems should also be considered as an explanatory variable, as well as the child's general health status. Finally, instructional formats and assignment levels should be evaluated carefully in terms of their appropriateness for the child. A number of different instructional formats, sequences, and programs could be tried out to see if they have an effect on reducing the learning deficit.

If all of these antecedent variables prove to be unrelated to the child's inability to learn, then the effect of consequences following the behavior could be investigated. It could be, for example, that the child is not receiving the necessary feedback regarding his/her performance and the child's attempts at learning are being placed on extinction. The problem could be a motivational one. Thus, teacher praise in combination with a formal reinforcement system may be required to motivate the child to achieve.

In some cases, it may be necessary to manipulate both antecedents and consequences in order to effectively remediate a behavioral or learning problem. Simultaneous manipulation of antecedents and consequences is probably the most powerful and effective method available for changing behavior. An example of the manipulation of both antecedents and consequences would be in the case where a teacher carefully defines classroom rules and then allows children to accumulate minutes of free time for following them.

A COMBINATION OF REINFORCEMENT FOR APPROPRIATE BEHAVIOR AND MILD PUNISHMENT FOR INAPPROPRIATE BEHAVIOR WILL PRODUCE MORE RAPID AND SUBSTANTIAL CHANGES IN BEHAVIOR THAN EITHER ONE ALONE

Social Learning Foundations

Many intervention programs use either reinforcement alone or punishment alone in order to change and/or control child behavior (Hall, Lund, & Jackson, 1968; Tyler & Brown, 1967). It is relatively unusual for reinforcement and punishment procedures to be used in combination (Walker, Hops, & Fiegenbaum, 1976). This is somewhat ironic since a combination of rewarding and punishing techniques, applied simultaneously, appears to be much more powerful than either one applied in isolation (Patterson & Gullion, 1968).

If a child is normal or only minimally disruptive, a reinforcement system alone can be used successfully to change her/his behavior. When used correctly, this process is called *differential positive reinforcement.* It means that the rewarding consequence is awarded differentially; that is, if the child is behaving appropriately and following the rules, she/he is reinforced, while reinforcement is withheld when the child is not behaving appropriately or following rules. This procedure gradually teaches the child to discriminate between appropriate and inappropriate behavior and motivates him/her to behave appropriately. A number of studies have manipulated positive teacher attention to increase the study behavior and appropriate classroom behavior of minimally disruptive children (Becker, Madsen, Arnold, & Thomas, 1967; Hall, Lund, & Jackson, 1968). However, it should be noted that the more deviant the child the less likely it is that teacher praise or attention by itself will be effective in controlling and/or changing the inappropriate behavior.

Punishment procedures have been traditionally applied, in isolation, in order to control more disruptive forms of child behavior (hitting, yelling, parent or teacher defiance, inappropriate language, fighting, tantrums, and so forth). The most popular punishment technique used to control such behavior is timeout (Patterson & White, 1969). Almost all parents, at one time or another, have sent children to their rooms for misbehaving. This is called timeout since the child must spend a portion of *time out* from ongoing activities. If the activities from which the child is excluded are rewarding to him/her, then timeout can be a very effective technique, especially in the home setting. Another popular form of punishment is loss of privileges for misbehaving. Going to bed without supper and loss of TV time are examples of this form of punishment. As mentioned earlier, punishment is most effective if used in conjunction with a positive reinforcement system (Patterson & Gullion, 1968). However, the types of punishment described above have proven effective in controlling child behavior when applied in isolation (Patterson & White, 1969), since they involve either removal from a reinforcing situation or loss of privileges that the child finds rewarding.

One clear finding seems to be emerging from research on the use of positive reinforcement and punishment techniques in applied settings. That is, rewarding and punishing techniques applied in combination generally produce an immediate and dramatic change in behavior that usually exceeds that which would be produced by either one in isolation. Further, the more deviant and disruptive a child's behavior, the more likely it is that reinforcement and punishment will be required to effectively change the child's overall behavior (Bostow & Bailey, 1969; Walker, Hops, & Fiegenbaum, 1976; Walker, Mattson, & Buckley, 1971).

Classroom Application

The most frequently used combinations of rewarding and punishing techniques in classroom settings are positive social or token reinforcement applied in conjunction with either timeout or cost contingency (loss of earned points for engaging in deviant behavior). In applications of this type, a number of rules for appropriate behavior are identified for the child and she/he is told that teacher praise and points will be earned for following them. Conversely, inappropriate and disruptive classroom behaviors are also identified and the child is informed that earned points will be subtracted for engaging in them. If timeout is being used, the specific behaviors resulting in timeout are labeled for the child.

Walker, Hops, and Fiegenbaum (1976) investigated the effectiveness of different combinations of teacher praise, token reinforcement (points), and cost contingency (loss of earned points) in changing the classroom behavior of acting-out children within an experimental classroom. Teacher praise alone had a minimal effect in increasing the appropriate behavior for four of the five children in the study. One child's behavior was completely unaffected by teacher praise. When a token system (points earned for appropriate behavior and exchanged for backup rewards) was added to teacher praise, there was a moderate increase in the appropriate behavior of all five children (from approximately 47 percent to 79 percent). When cost contingency (subtraction of earned points for inappropriate behavior) was added to teacher praise and token reinforcement, the appropriate behavior level of all five children showed an immediate increase. With cost contingency in effect, the children's appropriate behavior averaged 95 percent. This study demonstrated that a combination of teacher praise, tokens and cost was more effective than either teacher praise alone or teacher praise and tokens in combination.

In a later study, Walker, Hops, Greenwood, Todd, and Garrett (1977) evaluated effects of the same three treatment variables upon the interactive behavior of socially aggressive children. Six children with extremely high rates of negative social interaction with their classmates served as subjects in the study and were referred to an experimental classroom for treatment. To begin with, the authors evaluated effects of teacher praise alone upon the children's positive social interactions with each other. When the teacher praised the children for interacting positively with each other, there was a decrease in their rate of positive interactions. On the first day of teacher praise, the children's percent of total positive interactions dropped from approximately 80 percent to 40 percent. When a token system was later added to teacher praise, there was an initial increase in the children's positive interactive behavior. However, over a five-day period, the children's interactive behavior gradually returned to pretreatment levels. Only when cost contingency was added to teacher praise and tokens was the children's negative interactive behavior controlled effectively. The children were told that they could earn three points for each positive interaction with peer(s); however, if they engaged in any negative social behavior within an interaction, they would lose six of the points they had already earned. With cost in effect, the children's negative interactions were reduced to near zero levels. Their percent of interactions that were positive averaged 95 percent and above during this period.

These two studies clearly demonstrate that a combination of rewarding and punishing techniques can be extremely effective in changing the behavior of moderately to severely deviant children. In the author's opinion, the children in the second study were substantially more deviant than those in the first. It is interesting that while teacher praise was minimally effective with the acting-out children in the first study, it caused the socially aggressive children's appropriate interaction to actually decrease. This may be, in part, a result of the long history of hostile interactions that such children have had with adults; that is, they are so used to receiving negative reprimands and criticisms from adults that praise from adults is, at least initially, an aversive consequence for them. Other studies reported in the literature have also shown that some deviant children are unresponsive to adult praise (Thomas, Becker, & Armstrong, 1968).

It would have been impossible to effectively change the behavior of either group of children without a combination of rewarding and punishing consequences. It appears that the more deviant a child is, the more likely it is that such a combination will be necessary to effectively change his/her behavior.

REFERENCES

Azrin, N. H. & Holz, W. C. Punishment. In W. K. Honig (Ed.), *Operant behavior.* New York: Appleton-Century-Crofts, 1966, 380–447.

Bandura, A. *Principles of behavior modification.* New York: Holt, Rinehart and Winston, 1969.

Becker, W. C., Engelmann, S., & Thomas, D. *Teaching 1: Classroom management.* Chicago: Science Research Associates, 1976.

Becker, W. C., Madsen, C. H., Arnold, C. R., & Thomas, D. The contingent use of teacher attention and praise in reducing classroom behavior problems. *Journal of Special Education,* 1967, *1,* 287–307.

Bostow, D. E. & Bailey, J. B. Modification of severe disruptive and aggressive behavior using brief timeout and reinforcement procedures. *Journal of Applied Behavior Analysis,* 1969, 2, 31–37.

Ferster, C. B. & Skinner, B. F. *Schedules of reinforcement.* New York: Appleton-Century-Crofts, 1957.

Hall, R. Y., Lund, D., & Jackson, D. Effects of teacher attention on study behavior. *Journal of Applied Behavior Analysis,* 1968, *1,* 1–12.

Hops, H., Beickel, S., & Walker, H. M. *CLASS (Contingencies for Learning Academic and Social Skills): Manual for consultants.* Eugene, Ore.: Center at Oregon for Research in the Behavioral Education of the Handicapped, University of Oregon, 1976.

Johnson, S. M., Boldstad, O., & Lobitz, G. Generalization and contrast phenomena in behavior modification with children. In E. J. Mash, L. A.

Hamerlynck, and L. C. Handy (Eds.), *Behavior modification and families*. New York: Brunner/Mazell, 1976.
Kazdin, A. E. The effect of vicarious reinforcement on attentive behavior in the classroom. *Journal of Applied Behavior Analysis*, 1973, *6*, 71–78.
Madsen, C. H., Becker, W. C., Thomas, D., Koser, L., & Plager, E. An analysis of the reinforcing function of "sit down" commands. In R. K. Parker (Ed.), *Readings in Educational Psychology*. Boston: Allyn & Bacon, 1968.
Mischel, W. Continuity and change in personality. *American Psychologist*, 1969, *24* (11), 1012–1018.
Mischel, W. *Personality and assessment*. New York: John Wiley, 1968.
O'Connor, R. D. The relative efficacy of modelling, shaping, and the combined procedures for the modification of social withdrawal. *Journal of Abnormal Psychology*, 1972, *79*, 327–334.
O'Connor, R. D. Modification of social withdrawal through symbolic modelling. *Journal of Applied Behavior Analysis*, 1969, *2*, 15–22.
Patterson, G. R. A basis for identifying stimuli which control behaviors in natural settings. *Child Development*, 1974, *45*, 900–911.
Patterson, G. R. & Gullion, E. *Living with children*, Champaign, Ill.: Research Press Co., 1968.
Patterson, G. R. & White, G. P. It's a small world: The application of "timeout from positive reinforcement." *OPA (Oregon Psychological Association) Newsletter*, February, 1969.
Skinner, B. F. *Science and human behavior*. New York: The Macmillan Co., 1953.
Thomas, D., Becker, W. C., & Armstrong, M. Production and elimination of disruptive classroom behavior by systematically varying teacher's behavior. *Journal of Applied Behavior Analysis*, 1968, *1*, 35–45.
Tyler, V. O. & Brown, G. D. The use of swift, brief isolation as a group control device for institutionalized delinquents. *Behavior Research and Therapy*, 1967, *3*, 1–9.
Wahler, R. G. Setting generality: Some specific and general effects of child behavior therapy. *Journal of Applied Behavior Analysis*, 1969, *2*, 239–246.
Walker, H. M., Mattson, R. H., & Buckley, N. K. The functional analysis of behavior within an experimental class setting. In W. C. Becker (Ed.), *An empirical basis for change in education*. Chicago: Science Research Associates, 1971.
Walker, H. M. & Buckley, N. K. Teacher attention to appropriate and inappropriate classroom behavior: An individual case study. *Focus on Exceptional Children*, 1973, *5*, 5–11.
Walker, H. M., Hops, H., & Fiegenbaum, E. Deviant classroom behavior as a function of combinations of social and token reinforcement and cost contingency. *Behavior Therapy*, 1976, 7, 76–88.
Walker, H. M., Hops, H., & Johnson, S. M. Generalization and maintenance of classroom treatment effects. *Behavior Therapy*, 1975, *6*, 188–200.

Walker, H. M., Hops, H., Greenwood, C. R., Todd, N., & Garrett, B. *The comparative effects of teacher praise, token reinforcement, and response cost in reducing negative peer interactions.* CORBEH Report #25. Eugene, Ore.: Center at Oregon for Research in the Behavioral Education of the Handicapped, University of Oregon, 1977.

CHAPTER

3

Observing and Recording Child Behavior in the Classroom

The purpose of this chapter is to give the teacher the skills necessary for measuring the classroom behavior of acting-out children and to use the information in making decisions about their behavior. For the teacher's measurement of child behavior to be productive and useful, it must be defined carefully and specified in a very precise and concrete manner.

Also, in order to change the classroom behavior of the acting-out child, the teacher must be able to clearly specify those behaviors that are inappropriate and disruptive as well as those that are considered appropriate. These behaviors must be communicated to the acting-out child and, if necessary, demonstrated for her/him. We cannot expect the acting-out child's behavior to change if we are unable to clearly identify and describe classroom behaviors we consider inappropriate and appropriate.

The relationship between adults' informal estimates or judgment of behavior and the actual frequency of such behavior is notoriously low. However, when systematic observation and recording procedures are used as a basis for making such estimates, this relationship is greatly improved.

This is especially true of the teacher's judgment of children's classroom behavior. It is nearly impossible for the classroom teacher to develop accurate estimates of children's daily classroom behavior while relying only upon his/her informal judgment. To make accurate judgments about overt classroom behavior, it is essential that systematic observation and recording procedures be used to code precisely defined categories of child behavior. It is equally essential that such procedures be used in making decisions about the behavior of acting-out children, since classroom teachers are likely to greatly overestimate the frequency of classroom behaviors they find especially irritating or difficult to tolerate when relying upon their subjective judgment.

Teacher recorded data can serve three very useful purposes in the classroom. These are: (1) the identification of specific problem behaviors, (2) general monitoring of child behavior, and (3) evaluation of treatment procedures designed to change child behavior. The resulting information can be very useful in planning procedures to improve the social and academic adjustment of acting-out children.

This chapter presents information on three topics important to the precise measurement of classroom behavior. These are: (1) defining classroom behavior, (2) observing and recording classroom behavior, and (3) interpreting classroom behavior.

DEFINING CLASSROOM BEHAVIOR

Teachers frequently describe the classroom behavior of acting-out children by using such terms as aggressive, belligerent, lazy, unmotivated, hyperactive, and so forth. These terms are commonly referred to as trait labels; that is, they are labels used to describe characteristic patterns of human behavior.

On one level, these terms are descriptive of human behavior. They are commonly used by adults to describe the behavior of children and of other adults, and they do communicate a certain amount of information about behavior.

However, while most adults have a general idea of what is meant by such terms as aggressive, hyperactive, and belligerent, they do not communicate *precise* information about specific child behavior. For example, the behavioral manifestations of a term such as "frustrated" could range from biting one's nails, to cursing, to berating oneself, to having a temper tantrum. One could *infer* that an individual was frustrated if she/he were observed engaging in one or more of these overt behaviors. However, this inference would be subject to considerable error in many cases. In contrast, we could say with a great deal of confidence that an individual was in fact biting his/her nails, cursing, berating her/himself, or having a tantrum if the behavior were precisely defined and if he/she were actually observed engaged in the behavior. Thus, when relying upon trait labels to describe behavior, we must resort to inferential statements that may or may not be correct. In contrast, if we define behavior in overt, observable terms, we can describe it precisely without resorting to error-prone inferential statements.

In referring to child behavior for instructional or therapeutic purposes, it is generally better to rely upon descriptions of overt, observable behavior rather than upon trait labels. In order for a teacher to reliably change the behavior of an acting-out child, she/he must be able to specify the behavior to be changed. This specification process can be best illustrated through the concept of pinpointing behaviors. Pinpointing requires attention to the overt features of child behavior. Classroom behaviors that are capable of being pinpointed are characterized by being: (1) controllable, (2) repeatable, (3) containing movement, and (4) possessing a starting and ending point. Instances and noninstances of classroom behaviors that qualify as behavioral pinpoints are listed below.

Instances of Good Pinpoints	*Noninstances of Good Pinpoints*
1. Argues	1. Hyperactive
2. Steals	2. Lazy
3. Does not comply with directions	3. Belligerent
4. Out of seat	4. Angry
5. Talks out	5. Hostile
6. Has temper tantrums	6. Frustrated
7. Hits peers	7. Unmotivated
8. Looks away from assigned tasks	

All of the classroom behaviors in the left hand column above are observable and can be specified in terms of overt behavior. Each one meets the four criteria for a pinpointed behavior. The entries in the right hand column are trait labels, are not observable, and do not meet any of the criteria for a pinpointed behavior. Consequently, they are essentially nonfunctional in the processes of instructing children and/or changing their behavior.

If procedures are implemented to change one or more of the acting-out child's classroom behaviors, the target behaviors must be pinpointed in order to be changed. Pinpointing also makes it possible to evaluate precisely the extent to which behavior(s) has been changed as a result of treatment.

Teachers very often have a negative set concerning the acting-out child. It is extremely rare to find a child who spends all or even nearly all of his/her time engaged in deviant behavior. Yet teachers are often so angry or frustrated by specific behaviors the acting-out child engages in, that they tend to see all of her/his behavior as inappropriate. In actuality, most acting-out children spend considerable amounts of time engaged in appropriate behavior which is often ignored by the classroom teacher.

There may be a relatively small number of behaviors that are contributing to the teacher's overall impression of the acting-out child. If the inappropriate classroom behaviors of the acting-out child were pinpointed by the teacher and specific classroom rules identified which the child violates or does not follow, the teacher would have a much clearer perspective on the child's overall behavioral adjustment. A changed perspective, based upon such precise information, could lead eventually to a more positive teacher attitude toward the acting-out child and to a more optimistic view of her/his potential for change.

There are some general rules the teacher should follow in defining the classroom behavior of acting-out children. For example, the teacher should insure that the same rules and expectations that are applied to the acting-out child's behavior are also applied to the other members of the class. Sometimes, acting-out children generate so much hostility in teachers through their classroom behavior that the teacher's behavioral standards for the acting-out child inadvertently change and in some cases become unrealistic. Consequently, in evaluating the acting-out child's behavior, it is essential that this possibility be considered.

Second, the teacher should determine that the rules governing classroom behavior are reasonable, precisely defined, and clearly communicated to all the children in the classroom, including the acting-out child. Many teachers have a very clear idea of what the rules are in their classrooms but have not effectively communicated them to the children. Classroom rules should be defined in concrete, observable terms and, if necessary, role-played for the children. It is most helpful to write them on a wall poster and display them on a permanent basis in the classroom. If *all* the children understand and are aware of the classroom rules, then this can be ruled out as a possible cause of inappropriate behavior on the part of the acting-out child or his/her classmates.

Third, the teacher should identify those specific classroom behaviors of the acting-out child that are considered inappropriate. Each behavior should be pinpointed using the criteria described earlier. For purposes of observation and recording, the teacher should define each behavior in such a way that two adults could agree that the behavior did or did not occur when relying upon the definition to code the child's behavior. This requires defining the behavior in overt, observable terms. For example, if the behavior "hitting" were defined as *trying to hurt someone else*, adults would likely experience considerable disagreement in using this definition since it requires an inference to the effect that hitting is done with the purpose of inflicting pain or injury. Even though "hitting" is an observable, overt behavior, there would be many instances in which it would be extremely difficult to make this determination using the definition above. It would be better to define "hitting" as physical contact directed at another child using a closed fist. Whether or not the hitting was done in a friendly or hostile manner is a secondary decision to be made on the basis of additional information (if available) such as gestures, expressions, and physical attitude of the participants involved. Thus, it is possible to make a judgment about appropriate versus inappropriate hitting. However, the judgmental foundation for making this decision is much less sound than that required in hitting versus no hitting. (Task II at the end of this chapter presents a number of purposefully vague and purposefully clear definitions of overt classroom behavior and the reader is asked to discriminate between them.)

Finally, prosocial, appropriate behaviors should be defined in the same way that inappropriate behaviors are defined. Acting-out children may rarely engage in such behaviors, or if they do, at a relatively low rate. However, the appropriate behaviors should be communicated to the acting-out child as goals and observed and recorded when the teacher deems it appropriate to do so.

OBSERVING AND RECORDING CLASSROOM BEHAVIOR

Classroom behavior can be observed and recorded on either an individual basis or on an overall basis. For example, appropriate and inappropriate classroom behaviors can be pinpointed, observed, and recorded as they occur. However, it is usually not feasible to record more than two or three child behaviors at once. If an acting-out child hits, yells, and defies the teacher, it would be possible for the teacher to record all three behaviors simultaneously, depending upon the rate with which they occur. However, it would be much more feasible to record them one at a time.

In contrast, the teacher can observe and record all of the child's behavior at once. That is, the teacher can make an overall judgment about whether the child is following classroom rules and code her/his behavior as appropriate or inappropriate.

Both methods yield important information. Whether one or the other is preferred depends upon the child's behavior pattern, the teacher's objectives, the classroom situation, and the type of information being sought by the teacher.

When classroom behavior is observed and recorded on an individual basis, the recording procedure can involve either counting or timing. Counting yields a frequency measure while timing yields a time or proportion measure. For example, say a teacher wishes to record the social interactive behavior of a shy, withdrawn child. There are a number of recording options available to the teacher in this instance. The teacher could count the number of times the child initiates to other children, the number of times other children initiate to the child being observed, or simply the number of times the child has a social interaction with one or more classmates, regardless of who initiated it. It would be possible to count each of these behaviors separately (one at a time) or to count all three at once.

Instead of counting, the teacher could record the child's interactive behavior by timing it. For example, the teacher could use a stopwatch to record the length of each of the child's social interactions with peers. By noting the actual amount of time which the child's behavior was observed, it is possible to compute the percentage of time the child spent engaged in social interaction with peers. For example, if the teacher observed the child's behavior from 10:00 to 10:20 A.M. and found that she/he engaged in social interaction for a total of four minutes during that time, then the percentage of time in which social interaction occurred is 20 (4 minutes divided by 20 minutes equals 20 percent). It would also be possible to record the length of each social interaction, the length of each initiation, and the length of initiations by peers, if this information were of interest to the teacher.

When recording classroom behaviors on an individual basis, the most commonly used method is counting, since the frequency of the behavior is usually of interest. However, when recording certain behaviors, such as social interaction, it may be appropriate to record time in addition to frequency.

As mentioned, a stopwatch is generally used to time behavioral responses. Classroom behaviors can be counted by simply tallying their occurrence on a piece of paper. However, golf counters (worn on the wrist) have gained a great deal of popularity in many classrooms and school settings. Single and multiple channel counters that allow recording of one versus multiple behaviors, respectively, are relatively inexpensive and quite practical for classroom and playground use. Further, the process of recording behavior with a wrist counter is a relatively unobtrusive process.

If the starting and ending times are noted when a behavior (or behaviors) is observed and counted, then it is possible to compute the rate with which it occurs. Computing rate makes it possible to compare the frequency of occurrence of a behavior across observation periods of unequal lengths. For example, say a behavior such as "talks out" is observed and counted by the teacher for five consecutive days where the observation sessions were, respectively, 15 minutes, 10 minutes, 20 minutes, 30 minutes, and 5 minutes in length. The frequency with which "talk outs" occur in each of the sessions is, respectively, 3, 2, 4, 6, and 1. If we wish to compare the rate of occurrence for "talk outs" across the five observation sessions, we must first convert the data to a rate measure. This is done by dividing the amount of time observed into the frequency of the behavior during the observation session. For example, the rate for the first observation session is 3 (the frequency) divided by 15 (the length of the observation session) which equals .20 or a rate of one "talk out" for each 5 minutes of time observed. The rate for the second observation session is 2 divided by 10 or a rate of .20 also. In the example above, the rate is .20 for each of the five observation sessions. If rate is not computed, then the only way to compare behavior across observation sessions is to hold the length of the observation sessions constant.

When child behavior is recorded on an overall basis, the two most commonly used recording techniques are the interval method and the stopwatch method. The interval method requires that the child's behavior be coded as either appropriate or inappropriate (+ or —) during successive time intervals. Time intervals usually range from 2 or 3 seconds to as long as 20 seconds, with 10 seconds as perhaps the most commonly selected interval length. An observation form is used to record behavior with the interval method. Observation forms are easy to construct and use. Figure 3.1 shows an example of an observation form along with a sample use of the form in coding child behavior.

The grid below marks off 36 minutes of time, divided into 216, 10-second intervals. There are 24, 10-second intervals in each horizontal line equalling 4 minutes.

To use the form, the teacher or observer should fill in the information required at the top of the form. Next, the time at which the observation begins should be noted. After the observation is completed, the ending time should be recorded and the total time observed recorded.

The approximate amount of time which the child's behavior is to be observed should be decided upon in advance. With the interval method, a given child's behavior is usually observed for no more than 15 to 30 minutes at any one time. The interval method requires the full-time attention of the observing individual for the length of time observed. Consequently, the interval method may be impractical for many teachers to use if they do not have a teacher aide or the available time to conduct such observations.

In using the observation form in Figure 3.1, an entry has to be made in each 10-second interval. The observer makes an overall judgment of whether the child has followed the classroom rules for each 10-second interval and records either a "+" or a "—" for that interval. Only one "+" or "—" is recorded per interval. In order for a "+" to be recorded, the child's behavior must be appropriate for the *entire* 10-second interval. If the child's behavior is inappropriate for any portion of the interval then a "—" is recorded and the entire interval is counted as inappropriate.

If the teacher approves of the child's behavior during the interval by attending positively to it or by praising it, then a circle (○) is also recorded in the interval. If the teacher actively disapproves of the behavior by reprimanding or criticizing it, then a slash (/) is recorded in the interval.

Pupil James Stafford School Sunset
Teacher Mrs. Lynch Date 2-3-79
Classroom Activity Math (Individual Seat Work)
Time Start: 10 A.M. Time Stop: 10:01 A.M.
Total Time: 1 minute

Child Behavior	+ Appropriate
	− Inappropriate
Teacher Consequences	○ Praise
	/ Disapproval

Instructions: Code child's behavior as appropriate or inappropriate by recording a "+" or a "−" in each successive 10-second interval. Record teacher consequences in the same interval, if they occur, by using a circle (○) for praise and a slash (/) for disapproval.

Consecutive 10-Second Intervals

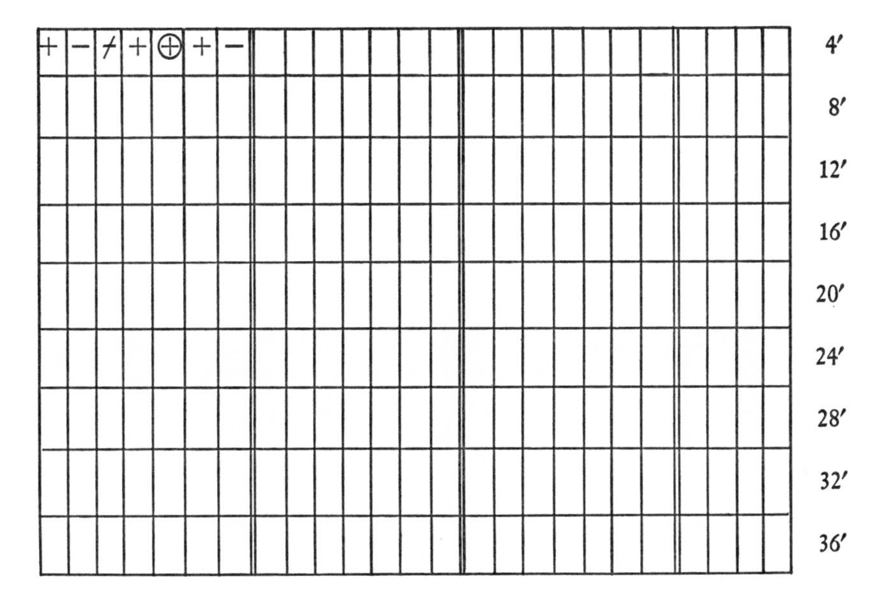

FIGURE 3.1

The interval method requires either a watch with a second hand or a stopwatch to designate 10-second intervals. With a little practice, a teacher can become very proficient at observing a child's behavior in 10-second segments and recording it on an observation form. The procedure to follow is to observe the child's behavior continuously for

10 seconds (or whatever the interval length is), quickly record the child and/or teacher's behavior, and then observe for another 10 seconds and repeat the recording procedure. This is continued until the observation session is terminated.

The first seven intervals of the sample observation form in Figure 3.1 are coded. In this instance, the child's behavior was appropriate in the first interval, inappropriate in the second and third, appropriate, for intervals four, five, and six, and inappropriate in interval seven. The teacher disapproved of the child's behavior in the third interval and approved of it in the fifth interval.

To compute the percentage or proportion of time in which the child's behavior was appropriate, simply count the number of 10-second intervals in which the child's behavior was appropriate, divide this figure by the total number of intervals observed, and multiply the result by 100. For example, in Figure 3.1, the child's behavior was appropriate 57 percent of the time in which it was observed. There were four intervals coded appropriate, divided by the seven intervals observed equals .57. When this figure is multiplied by 100, the result is 57 percent.

The stopwatch method is much easier to use than the interval method and yields essentially the same information. The teacher begins by noting the starting time for the observation session. During the observation session, the stopwatch is allowed to run and accumulate time as long as the child being observed is behaving appropriately and following the rules. Whenever the child's behavior is inappropriate, the stopwatch is turned off. At the end of the observation session, the child's percentage of appropriate behavior is found by dividing the length of the observation session into the amount of time on the stopwatch. For example, if a teacher observed a child's behavior from 1:05 P.M. to 1:30 P.M. and there was a total of 19 minutes on the stopwatch, the percent of time spent in appropriate behavior would be 76 percent (19 minutes divided by 25 minutes × 100 equals 76 percent).

Both the stopwatch method and the interval method require that the teacher have clearly defined classroom rules and that the child's behavior be observed continuously for a period of time. There appear to be a number of advantages for the classroom teacher in using the stopwatch method for recording child behavior on an overall basis. The only information not given by the stopwatch method is on teacher consequences which can be recorded with the interval method. The stopwatch method is unobtrusive and easy to use, requiring only a stopwatch to record behavior. Further, it is more accurate than the interval method since an entire 10-second interval is coded as inappropriate if the child's behavior is judged inappropriate for any portion of the interval. In contrast, with the stopwatch method, time accumulates only when the child's behavior is appropriate thereby producing a more accurate estimate of the child's appropriate behavior. With the stopwatch method, the teacher would be able to work observation and recording into ongoing classroom activities. This would be much more difficult with the interval method since this method requires an active response from the observer every ten seconds. Consequently, unless the teacher has a special reason for using the interval method, the stopwatch method should be the technique of choice for observing and recording child behavior.

An important consideration in measuring child behavior is how often to observe and record it. A general rule is that *representative* samples of her/his behavior should be obtained in order to make adequate judgments that are reliable and valid. Ideally, a child's behavior should be observed and recorded throughout the entire school day so that errors associated with sampling child behavior would be eliminated. As a rule, this is not feasible unless the behavior being recorded occurs at a very low rate. Behaviors such as stealing, fighting, and having tantrums meet this requirement. However, most classroom behaviors occur at a much higher rate and cannot be recorded throughout the school day. Thus, the teacher must try to obtain a representative sample of the child's behavior. This is done by recording the child's behavior for brief periods of time, one or more times each day. Usually a 15- to 30-minute recording period per day is sufficient for this purpose.

If the teacher has reason to believe that the rate with which the behavior occurs varies with the time of day, with instructional content (reading versus math), with classroom structure (group versus individual), or with setting (playground versus classroom), then efforts should be made to sample each of these conditions so a truly representative sample of the child's behavior will be obtained. If there is no reason to believe that the child's behavior varies with any of these factors, then observation and recording can occur at the same time each day. Sometimes it is difficult to make this determination. Consequently, as a matter of course, it is a good idea to sample a variety of times, settings, instructional activities, and classroom structures in the process of observing and recording child behavior in the classroom.

Another important consideration in observing and recording classroom behavior has to do with criteria for determining when behavior is appropriate or inappropriate. One solution to this problem is to ask whether the child's behavior is excessive or deficient in relation to that of his peers under identical classroom conditions (Walker & Hops, 1976). For example, if an acting-out child inappropriately talks out an average of once every thirty minutes of class time, the question can be asked, "Is this more, less, or the same as the rate exhibited by the child's peers?" Only by observing and recording the behavior of peers can this question be answered precisely. Similarly, if an acting-out child averages approximately 55 percent of the time spent following classroom rules, is she/he above, below, or the same as peers in this respect?

There are several ways to approach this task. For example, the whole class, excluding the target child, can be treated as one child. In this method, the entire class is observed simultaneously on the same dimension(s) as the target child. For example, if the acting-out child above averages 55 percent of his/her time spent following classroom rules, a stopwatch can be used to find out what proportion of time the rest of the class follows the rules. That is, all children in the class are observed simultaneously, excluding the acting-out child, and whenever the whole class is following the rules, the stopwatch runs and accumulates time. If one or more children are not following the rules, the watch is stopped. The percent of time in which the whole class follows the rules is then computed in the same way as it is for an individual child (time following the rules is divided by the time observed). The resulting percentage is a figure for the entire class and not for any individual child. However, it gives the teacher a basis for judging the acting-out child's behavior.

Another way to answer the question about the comparative level of appropriateness of the acting-out child's behavior is to select a representative peer or peers and observe their behavior in exactly the same way and under the same conditions as for the acting-out child. Thus, the teacher could select a child whom he/she considers representative of the class and record a series of observations on the child's behavior. If the child is representative of her/his peers, then data recorded on his/her behavior will form a sound basis for comparison with the acting-out child's behavior. The teacher can also select several peers rather than one and average their percentages together in order to form a basis for comparison. Several peers would be more representative of the class than one peer; however, in most cases, data recorded on a carefully selected representative peer would be sufficient for judging the appropriateness of the acting-out child's behavior.

The same procedure can be used for behaviors that are counted rather than timed. For example, if an acting-out child is continually out of seat, comparative rates of out of seat could be obtained for the class as a whole using either of the methods illustrated above. For example, if an acting-out child's out of seat rate is .14 or approximately once every seven and a half minutes, and the teacher recorded the out of seat frequency for the whole class, the average rate for an individual child would be computed by dividing the obtained frequency by the amount of time observed and then dividing again by the number of children in the class, excluding the acting-out child. If the teacher observed the entire class for a period of fifteen minutes and found that four children were out of seat during this time, 4 divided by 15 yields a rate of .266 for the whole class. However, to find the rate for a comparative individual child, it is necessary to divide .266 by the number of children in the class. In this intance, if there are twenty children in the class, .266 divided by 20 yields an average individual rate of .01 or one out of seat per child once every 100 minutes of class time. In this example, the acting-out child's out of seat rate was .14 or 14 times per 100 minutes. One would conclude that the acting-out child's rate was much higher than that of her/his peers.

The question could also have been answered by selecting one or more peers and observing their out of seat rate(s) in the same way as for the acting-out child. Where the rate of occurrence is relatively low for the entire class, the observed rates for selected peers is likely to be near zero or zero. Consequently, when recording behaviors of this type, it may be more useful to observe the entire class simultaneously in order to obtain a representative estimate for the entire class.

Normative data recorded on the behavior of an acting-out child's peers can serve two very useful purposes in evaluating the acting-out child's classroom behavior. It can be used as a basis for determining whether an acting-out child's behavior is in fact deviant and inappropriate when compared to that of peers under the same classroom conditions. If the child's behavior is judged to be inappropriate and problematic on this basis, and a treatment program is applied to decrease its frequency, normative peer data can be used to determine whether the acting-out child's behavior changes and, if so, does it change to within normal limits as judged by the behavior of peers?

INTERPRETING CLASSROOM BEHAVIOR

After the teacher has recorded the child's behavior, he/she is faced with the task of interpreting it. Interpretation of child behavior involves evaluating data representative of the child's performance and making decisions based upon such evaluation.

In order to properly inspect child performance data, it should be graphed so that trends and changes in the child's behavior can be detected. The most commonly used graph for recording behavior is the *frequency polygon.* As a general rule, the behavior being recorded is plotted along the vertical axis of the graph, while observation sessions are plotted along the horizontal axis. Figure 3.2 illustrates how a frequency polygon is used to graph out of seat behavior.

In Figure 3.2, twelve days of data on the child's out of seat behavior are graphed. Close inspection of the data reveals a good deal of information about the child's behavior. For example, during the twelve days in which the child's behavior was observed and recorded, the out of seat frequency ranged from approximately 4 (on days 4 and 11) to approximately 10 (on day 10). The frequency hovered around 4 or 5 for the first four days it was recorded. From days 5 to 10, there was a gradual accelerating (increasing) trend in the out of seat frequency. However, during the last three days (10, 11, and 12), the behavior showed a decreasing trend with the frequency on day 12 equalling that on day 1.

More than one behavior or more than one child's performance can be plotted on the same graph to facilitate comparative evaluations.

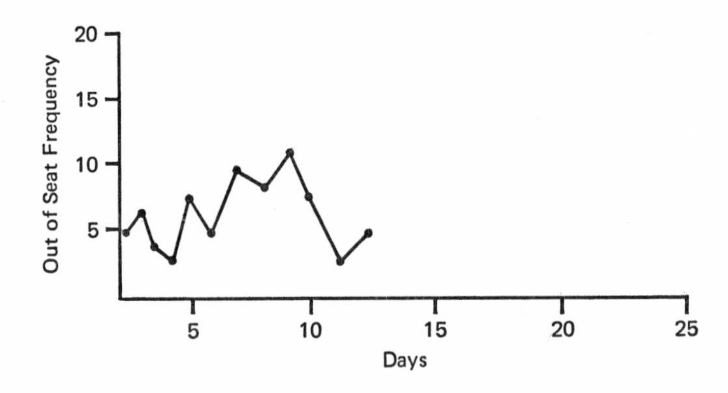

FIGURE 3.2

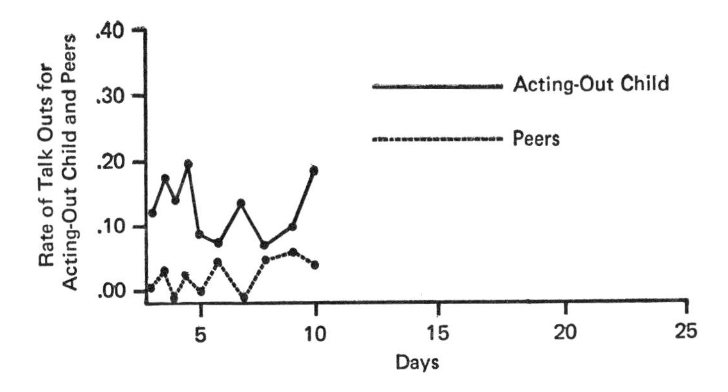

FIGURE 3.3

For example, if a teacher records the talk out rate for an acting-out child and her/his peers, and the teacher wishes to determine whether the acting-out child's rate is below, above, or the same as that of his/her classmates, these data would be graphed as shown in Figure 3.3.

The data in Figure 3.3 indicate that the acting-out child's talk out rate was consistently higher than that of peers. There was no overlap among the two rates during the 10-day recording period; that is, at no point was the acting-out child's rate as low as that of the average peer within the classroom. In this case, the teacher would conclude that the acting-out child's rate of talk outs was clearly excessive and higher than the average rate for her/his peers. Based on this information, the teacher would probably decide that an intervention program is required to reduce the acting-out child's talk out rate to within normal and acceptable limits.

Figure 3.4 shows how three inappropriate classroom behaviors can be plotted for the same child on the same graph. Say the three behaviors are "talk outs," "out of seat," and "hits." The teacher observes these three behaviors simultaneously for a 15-minute period each day. The data are plotted in Figure 3.4.

Figure 3.4 yields some interesting information about the frequency of talk outs, out of seat, and hits, respectively, as well as about the relationships among them. For example, the frequency of hits is clearly lower than that of talk outs and out of seat. Hits show a slight and gradual accelerating trend until day 10, and then does not occur for the last three days of the recording period. The daily frequency for talk outs and out of seat is approximately the same. If the daily

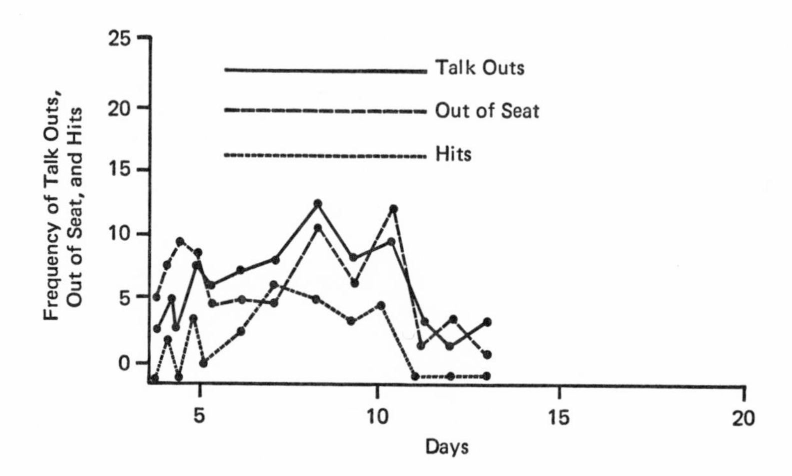

FIGURE 3.4

frequencies for these two behaviors were each averaged for the thirteen days of recording, the overall means (or averages) would be approximately the same—around 5 to 6 per day. Careful inspection of the daily frequencies for talk outs and out of seat indicates that they tend to *covary;* that is, when one is high, the other is high and when one is low, the other is low. These two behaviors are essentially tied together and may be triggered or enhanced by the same classroom conditions. It is a common occurrence, for example, for acting-out children to also talk out while they are out of seat. Either or both of these behaviors may be more likely to occur during individual seatwork periods than during teacher led discussions.

Further inspection of Figure 3.4 indicates that the frequency of all three behaviors is dramatically reduced on days 11, 12, and 13. This could be due to simple random variation or cycling in these behaviors, or it could be a result of systematic changes in classroom conditions that control their rates of occurrence. Continued simultaneous observation of these behaviors and careful noting of any associated changes in classroom conditions could provide clues as to the variables or events that control the rates of occurrence of these three behaviors.

Different behavioral measures, e.g., counts versus duration, can be recorded simultaneously and plotted on the same graph. For example, in observing and recording the social interactive behavior of a shy, withdrawn girl, the teacher may wish to count the number of interactions she has with peers and to time their duration in seconds as well. These two measures can be plotted so that the relationship between frequency and duration can be inspected on a daily basis. Figure 3.5 illustrates how this is done.

Figure 3.5 allows one to inspect the relationship or covariation between the frequency and duration of social interactions. The frequency of social interactions is plotted along the left, vertical axis, while their average duration is plotted along the right vertical axis.

The social interaction frequency data indicate that the child averaged approximately two interactions for that portion of the day in which her behavior was observed and recorded. During this same time period, her social interactions averaged approximately nine seconds each. Further inspection of the frequency and duration plots indicates that there was a tendency for the average length of social interactions to increase as the frequency of social interactions increased. In other words, they tended to covary.

Graphing data is also an extremely valuable tool for evaluating intervention programs designed to either accelerate appropriate behavior or to decelerate inappropriate behavior. When plotting data for this purpose, the graph is usually divided into phases. The number of phases used depends in part upon the purpose of the intervention program and upon the amount of energy, time, and resources the teacher is willing to invest in changing the child's behavior.

Most classroom intervention programs consist of two phases: a *baseline* phase and an *intervention* phase. The baseline phase consists

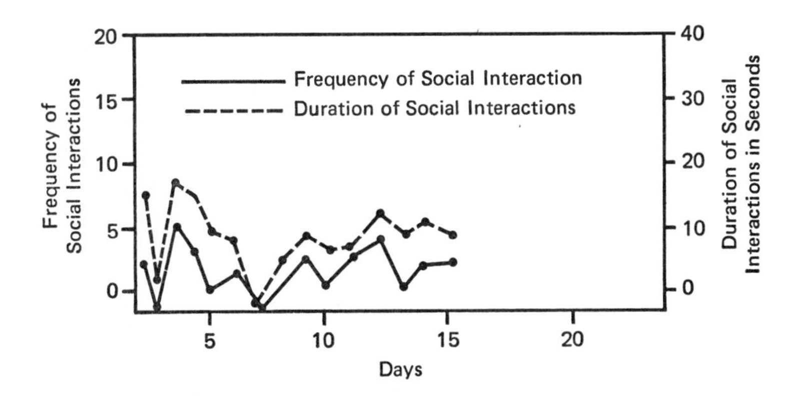

FIGURE 3.5

of data recorded on the child's behavior prior to the implementation of any treatment procedures. The intervention phase consists of data recorded on the child's behavior during implementation of the treatment program or procedures. Some classroom projects also add *posttreatment* and *followup* phases. The posttreatment phase contains data recorded after the treatment program is over (generally immediately after), and the followup phase contains data recorded well after the posttreatment phase. Long term followup is usually considered to be a year or more, while anything sooner than this is referred to as short term followup.

As a rule, an immediate change is expected in behavior after the treatment program is implemented and the intervention phase begins. By plotting and inspecting the data on a daily basis, it is possible to determine to what extent the treatment program is effective in changing the child's behavior. If the program is having no effect, then it can be changed or altered to increase its effectiveness. Only by recording data on the child's response to the treatment is the teacher in a position to evaluate precisely its effectiveness and to change it if necessary.

There are a number of criteria that can be used to judge the effectiveness of treatment. The most commonly used criteria are: (1) changes in the absolute level of the behavior, (2) changes in the trend of the behavior over time, e.g., accelerating or decelerating, and (3) changes in the variability of the behavior.

If, after being exposed to the treatment procedure, an inappropriate behavior shows a decrease in level or an appropriate behavior shows an increase in level, the treatment is usually judged to be a success. Sometimes, there is no change in the level of the behavior immediately following introduction of treatment. However, there may be a gradual accelerating trend in the data which suggests that the effects of treatment are not immediately apparent. Finally, there may be no change in either behavioral level or trend, but the variability (fluctuations) in the child's behavior may be reduced. In some situations, a treatment producing this effect would be judged a success, albeit a limited one.

Figure 3.6 below illustrates a change in the absolute level of a child's attending behavior from baseline to intervention. Inspection of this data clearly indicates the presence of a treatment effect. Further, this effect was evident as soon as the intervention program was introduced. During baseline, the child was observed engaged in attending behavior an average of 38 percent (dotted line) of the time. During

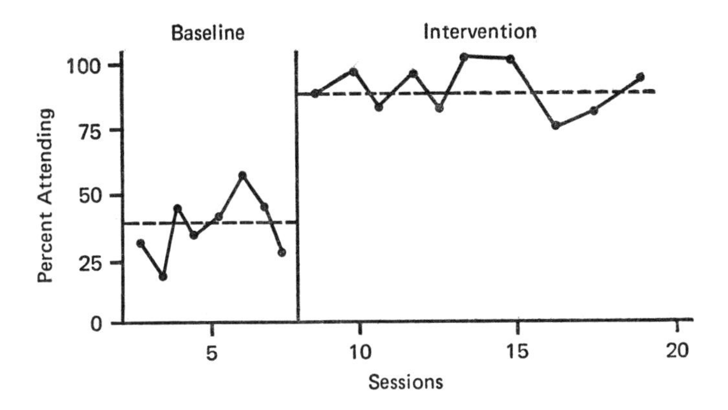

FIGURE 3.6

the intervention phase, this figure was approximately 83 percent. There was no overlap among the data points for the baseline and intervention phases. Based on these results, the teacher would conclude that (1) the child's behavior had changed, and (2) the intervention program was a success.

Figure 3.7 demonstrates a gradual accelerating trend in the proportion of time an acting-out child complies with teacher instructions. The data points for the first four sessions of the intervention phase do not show a treatment effect. However, the intervention program's effect is very apparent during the next six data points. Gradual ac-

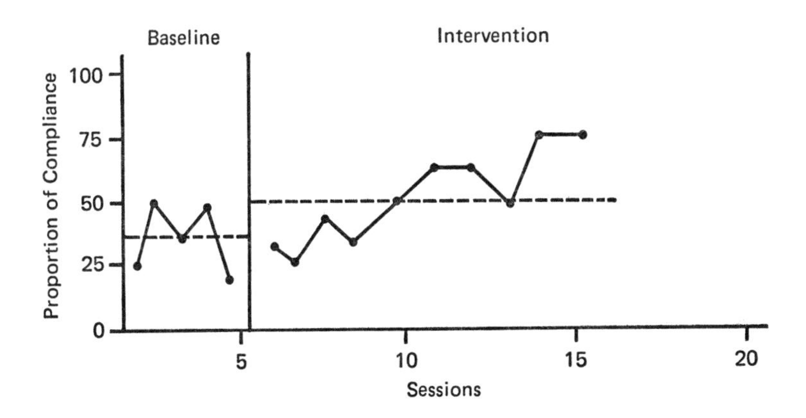

FIGURE 3.7

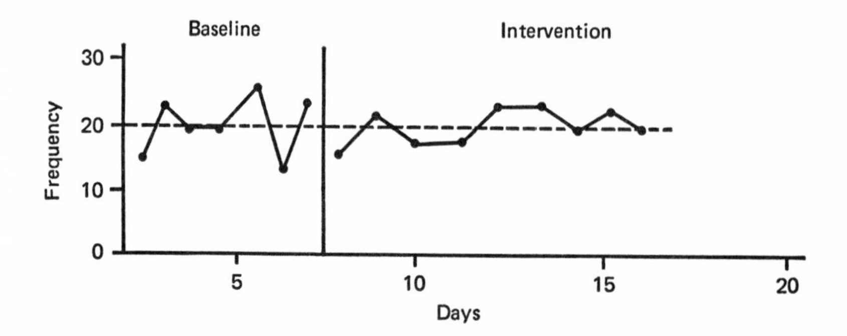

FIGURE 3.8

celerating trends of this type are a fairly common occurrence in the educational setting. Because of the accelerating trend in the data, the intervention program in Figure 3.7 would be judged a success in spite of the modest increase in the overall level of the behavior.

Figure 3.8 presents data for an intervention program designed to reduce an acting-out child's frequency of asking irrelevant and unnecessary questions. It is obvious from the data that the intervention program cannot be judged a success in terms of either an absolute change in behavioral level or in terms of an accelerating trend. However, there did appear to be a slight reduction in the daily variability of the behavior. It is often difficult to make a case for a successful treatment when results such as these are obtained. However, there are occasions where a reduction in variability can make the behavior easier to manage.

Figure 3.9 presents an acting-out child's rate of completing math

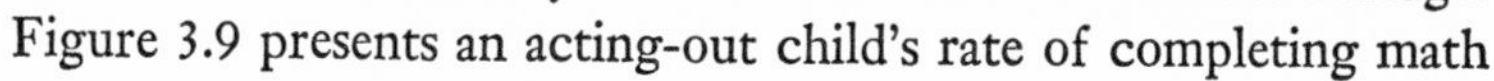

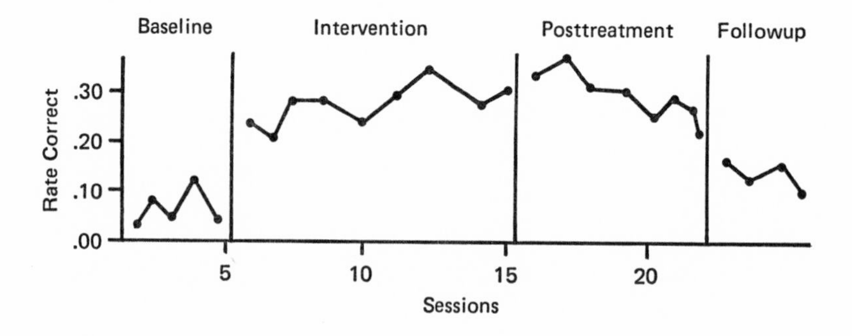

FIGURE 3.9

facts correctly across four phases: *baseline*, *intervention*, *posttreatment*, and *followup*. The data indicate a low rate of correct math facts completion during the baseline phase. With the introduction of treatment, there was a substantial increase in the child's correct rate, accompanied by a slight accelerating trend. After the intervention program was terminated (posttreatment), there was a gradual decelerating trend in the data. When the followup data were recorded sometime later, there was a significant decrease in its level to near baseline levels.

When intervention procedures are abruptly withdrawn, there is likely to be a decrease in the level of the behavior. There *are* cases where a behavior that is increased with a specific treatment program continues to maintain at a high level following withdrawal of the intervention procedures. However, such a result seems to be the exception rather than the rule (O'Leary & Drabman, 1971). There are a number of techniques that can be used to facilitate the persistence of treatment effects following termination of formal intervention procedures. Chapter 7 is devoted to this topic.

The importance of systematically observing and recording child behavior in the classroom cannot be overemphasized. The information produced can be invaluable in the process of instructing and managing the classroom behavior of children in general. This is especially true of acting-out children.

Many teachers observe and record classroom behavior because they have been told that it is an important component of good teaching. However, such data are not always used in reaching decisions about the child's behavior. This is unfortunate and represents a waste of energy, time, and resources. Unless such data are used in a meaningful way in decision making, it makes little sense to collect it.

TASK 1.

Discriminating Observable from Nonobservable Behavior

Instructions: Read the definitions for the classroom behaviors listed below and make a judgment as to whether each is observable or nonobservable. If observable, place an O on the line next to the behavior; if it is not observable, place an NO on the line. Answers are provided at the end of this exercise.

A behavior should be coded as observable if it is specified in overt terms: if two or more teachers could agree that the behavior occurred when using the definition, and if the definition of the behavior does not require additional explanation or elaboration. If the definition does not meet these requirements, it should be coded as nonobservable.

1. ____ (Argumentative): is stubborn and has to have the last word.
2. ____ (Talks out): talks out of turn and engages in verbal exchanges with peers about nonacademic matters when she/he is supposed to be working.
3. ____ (Steals): takes property of others without their awareness or permission and claims material as his/her own.
4. ____ (Attends to task): pupil is actively engaged in the task with her/his eyes focused directly on assignment.
5. ____ (Fights): intimidates other children using physical means to do so.
6. ____ (Hits): strikes other children with a closed fist.
7. ____ (Noncompliance): continually defies the teacher.
8. ____ (Out of seat): child is physically not sitting in her/his assigned seat during periods when the classroom rules say all children should be in their seats.
9. ____ (Disturbs others): creates a disturbance that disrupts classroom atmosphere.
10. ____ (Unmotivated): doesn't seem interested in school work.
11. ____ (Destructive): prefers to destroy creations of others or his/her own creations.
12. ____ (Lies): tells contrary to fact statements.
13. ____ (Cheats): attempts to obtain answers to a test or assignment in an unauthorized manner, e.g., from other classmates.

Answers to Task 1

1.	NO	5.	NO
2.	O	6.	O
3.	O	7.	NO
4.	O	8.	O

9. NO 12. O

10. NO 13. O

11. NO

TASK 2

Instructions: Complete the tasks and exercises below. Answers are provided at the end of the exercises.

1. Compute the social interaction rate for each session and the overall rate across all sessions in the following example. The teacher records the number of social interactions a child has in four free play sessions. Session #1 was 10 minutes in length and the child had 4 interactions; session #2 was 22 minutes in length and contained 7 interactions; session #3 was 15 minutes in length and contained 2 interactions; session 4 was 25 minutes in length and contained 12 interactions.
2. A teacher records the amount of time an acting-out child follows the rules with a stopwatch. She finds that the child's behavior was appropriate for 24 minutes out of the 40 minutes it was observed. Compute the proportion of time the child spent engaged in appropriate behavior.
3. An acting-out child's out of seat rate is .24 per minute. The teacher wishes to compute the peer rate for comparative purposes. The entire class is observed for a 30-minute period. A total of 7 children were out of seat during this period. There are 24 children in the class. Compute the average out of seat rate per child per minute.
4. A teacher observes and records an acting-out child's talk outs during a 15-minute reading and a 20-minute math period daily. The frequencies for reading were 8, 4, 13, 2, 11 and 3, 7, 5, 3, 2 for math.
   a. What are the individual and overall rates of talk outs for reading and math?
   b. Is the rate higher for reading or for math?
   c. Is there a trend in the reading or math rate?
5. During a daily 20-minute activity period, an acting-out child's number of hits was 4, 7, 2, and 9 on four consecutive days.

There are 21 children in the class, excluding the acting-out child. Their frequency of hits was 10, 8, 5, and 4 during the same period.

a. What is the rate of hitting for the acting-out child for each 20-minute period and overall?
b. What are the comparable rates for peers?
c. Would you say the acting-out child's hit rate is deviant when compared to that of peers?

6. A teacher records an acting-out child's attending to task for 30 minutes on five consecutive days. She uses a stopwatch and records the following times on task: 4 minutes, 10 minutes, 8 minutes, 14 minutes, and 11 minutes. A treatment program designed to increase attending is implemented following the fifth day of recording. Another five days of data are recorded. The times are 18 minutes, 21 minutes, 20 minutes, 28 minutes and 26 minutes.
   a. Was the treatment program a success?
   b. Was there a change in the level of the behavior from baseline to intervention?
   c. Was there a trend in either the baseline or intervention data?

Answers for Task 2

1. Session #1 = .40; Session #2 = .32; Session #3 = .13; Session #4 = .48. Overall rate = .35.
2. 60 percent.
3. .01.
4. a. Reading–Individual = .53, .27, .87, .13, .73. Overall = .51.
   Math–Individual = .15, .35, .25, .15, .10. Overall = .20.
   b. Higher for reading.
   c. Decelerating trend for math.
5. a. .20, .35, .10, .45. Overall rate = .28.
   b. .023, .019, .011, .009. Overall rate = .016.
   c. yes.
6. a. yes.
   b. yes.
   c. yes; an accelerating trend in both the baseline and intervention data.

REFERENCES

O'Leary, K. D. & Drabman, R. Token reinforcement programs in the classroom: A review. *Psychological Bulletin*, 1971, *75*, 379–398.

Walker, H. M. & Hops, H. Use of normative peer data as a standard for evaluating classroom treatment effects. *Journal of Applied Behavior Analysis*, 1976, *9*, 159–168.

CHAPTER

4

Behavior Management Techniques for the Acting-Out Child

This chapter describes and illustrates the use of proven treatment techniques for effectively managing the acting-out child. Up to this point, we have discussed the primary behavioral characteristics of the acting-out child, the rules that govern his/her classroom behavior, and procedures for observing and recording the acting-out child's performance. This chapter will teach you how to effectively change the behavior of acting-out children so as to improve their social adjustment and academic achievement and generally to manage the classroom more effectively.

A series of individual treatment techniques are presented and discussed. These include: (1) setting rules, (2) contracting procedures, (3) stimulus change, (4) verbal feedback, (5) teacher praise, (6) reinforcement procedures, (7) modeling plus reinforcement of matching responses, (8) shaping, (9) timeout, and (10) response cost. Each technique is defined and information and examples are given to illustrate its usage; guidelines for correct application as well as issues to consider in using each technique are presented. Finally, the advantages and disadvantages of each technique are discussed.

Recommended combinations of treatment techniques are described alone with the conditions appropriate for their use. Finally, some perspectives are presented for the reader's consideration on the use of classroom intervention procedures with the acting-out child and with children in general.

INDIVIDUAL TREATMENT TECHNIQUES

Setting Rules

1. Defined. Setting rules refers to the process of defining the teacher's expectations concerning classroom behavior in explicit, behavioral terms.

2. Illustrative Examples. Not all children listen carefully when teachers present the instructions and requirements for assignments. The result can be numerous repetitions of instructions and directions on a pupil-by-pupil basis before all children are engaged in the assignment and are making progress toward completing it. Much valuable instructional time can be wasted in this process. As a first step in solving this problem, the teacher can set up a rule relating to assignments and how instructions and directions for them will be given. This specific rule would read as follows:

> No instructions or directions for assignments will be given until all children in the class are listening and paying *close* attention.

Another example relates to lining up behavior. Children are usually very difficult to manage when they are organizing themselves for a particular activity. This is especially true when they are preparing to go to lunch or recess. In these situations, the structure is greatly reduced and with it, teacher control over child behavior is concomitantly reduced. Acting-out children are even more difficult than usual to manage during these periods.

One reason for disruptive, out-of-control behavior in such situations may be a lack of clearly defined rules that communicate the teacher's expectations and behavioral standards. Rule(s) for lining up behavior are presented below:

> Before going to lunch or recess, all assigned work for the preceding period must be completed satisfactorily.

When you are sitting quietly at your desks and your work has been put away, you can be dismissed.

Dismissal will be in rows, with one row dismissed at a time.

Hitting, yelling, pushing, shoving or fighting while lining up will result in loss of recess or lunch period.

Child behavior in the hallways and on the playground is also difficult to manage for all the reasons mentioned in Chapter 1. However, carefully defined rules governing appropriate behavior in these settings can be of assistance in reducing disruptive child behavior.

Rules for hallway behavior might be as follows:

Walk at a reasonable pace. *No running* in halls.

No loud talking or yelling.

Do not disturb other children in classes as you walk by.

Stop when the teacher tells you to stop.

Playground rules might include:

Follow the rules of whatever game you are playing.

Follow general school rules for the playground.

Follow instructions of the playground supervisor.

No hitting, shoving, or fighting on the playground.

Cooperate with others and take your turn on the playground.

The rules above are presented simply to illustrate the characteristics of rules in general. They are not intended as the only rules that would be appropriate in such situations or settings.

3. Guidelines for Correct Application. There are certain guidelines that should be followed in the development and communication of rules to children. For example, rules should be clearly defined and stated in behavioral terms. Vague rules relating to ambiguously defined behavior are probably no more effective than a complete absence of rules. Examples of both clearly defined, behavior specific rules and vague, general rules are presented below:

Good Rules	*Poor Rules*
1. Raise your hand before asking a question.	1. Be considerate of others.

2. Listen carefully to teacher instructions.	2. Behave in class.
3. Pay attention to the assignment and complete your work.	3. Do what you are told.
4. Do not talk to others during work time.	4. Don't disturb others.
5. Take your turn in group activities.	5. Work hard.

A good rule identifies a specific behavior or activity in very precise terms. Remember that the correct interpretation of a rule's meaning should require as little inference on the part of the child as possible.

It is usually a good idea to involve the children in the process of developing rules for both classroom and nonclassroom areas. However, this is primarily a matter of teacher discretion. Children *may* be more committed to the rules if they participate in their development, although this has not been proven.

Rules should be developed at the start of the school year so children have a clear idea of the difference between appropriate and inappropriate behavior from the beginning of their association with the teacher. This is not to say that rules cannot be developed at any time during the year. However, they are likely to be more effective if developed at the start of the school year.

The teacher should be absolutely sure that *all* children in the class understand the rules that are developed. Each rule should be thoroughly discussed with the class. Specific children should be asked to explain what the rule means. It is also helpful to have children role play the behavior or activity identified by the rule. The rules should also be reviewed on a daily basis until class members are thoroughly familiar with them.

Finally, the rules should be posted where all children can readily observe them. Rules are commonly posted on a bulletin board or blackboard. They should be written on construction paper, approximately 2 feet × 3 feet, and written in large letters using a magic marker so that they stand out. The rules should be visible from anywhere in the classroom.

4. Issues to Consider in Setting Rules. It is very important that rules be developed to serve as guidelines for appropriate child behavior.

However, a class of children should not be overwhelmed with so many rules they cannot remember them all, much less follow them. There is no magic figure governing the number of rules that should be developed for any setting. However, each child should be able to at least remember the rules that exist for any setting.

Rules should be fair, reasonable, and within the children's capacity to conform to them. If the rules are perceived as unfair or unreasonable, they will not be effective in controlling the behavior of children in the class.

Finally, the rules should be applied equally to all members of the class. Rules are really standards that establish behavioral goals for the entire class. Even though some children will break them much more than others, it should be understood, on both a conceptual and behavioral level, that they apply to everyone.

5. *Advantages and Disadvantages of Setting Rules.* The advantages of setting rules are obvious. They communicate the teachers' expectations regarding child conduct in both classroom and nonclassroom areas. Rules serve as standards or goals for appropriate child behavior. Consequently, they can prevent the occurrence of deviant/disruptive behavior which is due to a lack of knowledge concerning appropriate versus inappropriate behavior. In this respect, rules can be viewed as antecedent events that actually reduce the probability of inappropriate child behavior. Rules are very easy to construct and their long term benefits usually far outweigh the effort invested in their development.

However, it should be noted that the effectiveness of rules is dramatically affected by the consequences that back them up. Rules alone usually produce only a minimal effect or no appreciable effect upon child behavior. However, if rules are backed up consistently by appropriate consequences (rewards for following the rules and no rewards for not following them), then they can be of great assistance to the teacher in managing child behavior (Greenwood, Hops, Delquadri, & Guild, 1974).

Rules alone generally have *no effect* upon the behavior of acting-out children (Madsen, Becker, & Thomas, 1968; O'Leary, Becker, Evans, & Saudargas, 1969). The behavioral repertoires of acting-out children are usually so strongly developed that rules alone have almost no chance to significantly change their behavior. This is not to suggest that acting-out children should not have a clear understanding of the rules governing appropriate behavior. However, rules alone are more likely to produce a behavioral effect with normal children and with the entire class than with the acting-out child.

Contracting Procedures

1. Defined. A performance contract is usually a two-party agreement between, for example, a teacher or parent and the child, which specifies the role each will perform in achieving a certain goal. The contract may also specify consequences occuring to one or both parties for meeting terms of the contract.

2. Illustrative Examples. Classroom rules designed for the entire class provide only a generalized form of classroom control. A contract is a method for individualizing classroom rules for the acting-out child and for specifying consequences that backup the rules. An example of a contract is provided below.

Contract

________________________ agrees to do the following:

1. Listen to instructions from the teacher.
2. Complete work neatly, accurately, and on time.
3. Comply with teacher directions.
4. Take part in group discussions.
5. Raise hand before asking a question.
6. Cooperate with others during group activities.

The teacher agrees to:

1. Check ______________'s behavior at regular intervals during the day.
2. Award a point on a point record form if ________________ has been following the rules.
3. Sign a *good day card* at the end of each school day indicating whether ______________'s behavior has been satisfactory.

Consequence:

If ________________ earns 80 percent or more of the points available, then the teacher will sign a *good day card* indicating his/her

behavior was satisfactory. __________________ can exchange the card for a privilege at home. One card can be earned for each school day.
Signed:

______________________	______________________
Child	Teacher/Parent

In this contract, the teacher evaluates the child's behavior at regular intervals throughout the day and makes an overall judgment as to whether the child has complied with the terms of the contract. If yes, a point is awarded on a point record form kept on the child's desk or carried by the teacher. If no, the point is withheld and the child has an opportunity to earn a point during the next interval.

A contract can specify a series of behaviors, tasks or terms a child must comply with or it can be built around a single behavior or task. For example, the contract below deals only with a child's academic performance.

Contract

__________________ agrees to:

1. Complete all assignments with a 90 percent level of accuracy.

Consequence:

One minute of free time will be earned for each assignment completed with a 90 percent level of accuracy.

Signed:

______________________	______________________
Child	Teacher

This is a very simple contract. However, it communicates very precisely the teacher's academic expectations for the child and specifies the consequence available for meeting its terms.

Contracts can be as simple or as complex as the teacher chooses to make them. Further, more than one contract can be developed for a given child. The teacher's objectives, the child's ability and performance level, and the classroom (or nonclassroom) situation to which the contract applies must all be considered in determining the type of contract that is to be developed.

3. Guidelines for Correct Application. As with classroom rules, the terms of the contract should be perceived as fair, equitable, and reasonable. Individual contracts should be negotiated with the child and discussed thoroughly. Both parties should agree to carry out their responsibilities and to certify this by signing the contract.

The consequences to the child for following terms of the contract should be specified within the contract. It is absolutely essential that these consequences be made available as prescribed.

As with classroom rules, the child should not be overwhelmed with the terms of the contract. It is better to write a series of contracts than to construct one that is so complex it becomes unwieldy and possibly ineffectual.

Finally, the child's ability to meet the requirements of the contract should be carefully monitored. For example, if the terms are not met for two to three days in succession, the teacher should check to see whether the terms are too difficult. If so, they should be readjusted accordingly. Inappropriate consequences could also be the cause of a failure to meet the terms of the contract. Therefore, the backup consequences should also be evaluated regularly and varied as indicated.

4. Issues to Consider in Using Contracts. There appear to be no deleterious effects associated with the use of contracts to motivate children to achieve and behave better. The primary caution to be considered with contracts is that they should not be too complex and that an individual child should not be overwhelmed with too many contracts.

5. Advantages and Disadvantages of Contracting Procedures. Contracting procedures give the teacher a means of individualizing rules for the acting-out child and arranging consequences tailored to his/her preferences. They make it possible for the teacher and child to enter into a meaningful negotiating process concerning teacher expectations and child behavior. After agreement has been reached, each party is formally committed to the terms of the contract by signing it. All of these factors increase the chances that the child in question will behave more appropriately; however, they by no means guarantee it.

There are few disadvantages associated with contracts. Perhaps the primary disadvantage is the amount of time required to develop a good contract. It is obvious that individual contracts cannot be developed for all members of the class. It would simply take too much of the teacher's time to develop twenty-five to thirty individual contracts and monitor them effectively. Further, some children would likely require more than one contract.

Consequently, if contracts are to be used, they should be applied to small numbers of children on an individual basis. As a general rule, they should be applied to the performance of children who are experiencing difficulties in their academic achievement and/or behavioral and social adjustment.

Contracting procedures may or may not be effective in changing the behavior of a given acting-out child. Contracting procedures are likely to be more powerful than rules alone in changing behavior. However, for some acting-out children, contracting procedures will have to be supplemented with more powerful procedures.

Stimulus Change

1. Defined. Stimulus change is the alteration of controlling antecedent events or conditions for the purpose of changing child behavior.

2. Illustrative Examples. One of the most common examples of stimulus change is the case where two children who often talk to each other during class time are split up and moved to different parts of the room. In this case, it is impossible for them to talk to each other from across the room. However, it does not mean they cannot talk to other children who are sitting near them. In this specific instance, splitting them up may not solve the problem.

A child who does not always comply with teacher commands and instructions may be deliberately noncompliant. However, it is possible that the child may not hear all the teacher's commands or instructions. If this were the case, the teacher would perceive the child as disobedient when in fact the noncompliance is attributable to the hearing problem. If an audiological examination revealed a significant hearing loss, then a hearing aid could possibly solve the problem. If the noncompliance stopped after the child's hearing capacity was improved to within normal limits, then the changed behavior could be attributed to the hearing aid, e.g., changed stimulus conditions that made it possible to hear clearly.

A child who is experiencing reading problems is referred to a reading specialist for a diagnostic/prescriptive evaluation. After a thorough evaluation and analysis of the child's performance, the specialist discovers that the child has no knowledge of phonics. An intensive training program in phonics is developed and applied to improve the child's skills. Noticeable improvement in reading performance is immediately apparent as a result. In this instance, the phonics instruction represents a change in stimulus conditions which improves reading performance.

A teacher has a bad habit of giving out vague, poorly organized instructions for assignments. Consequently, many children are confused and do the assignments incorrectly. The teacher decides to change and develop very precise, carefully defined instructions for each assignment given. As a result, the rate of confusion about assignments is dramatically reduced and the number of children who complete the assignment correctly increases substantially. The changed stimulus conditions in this instance were the improved instructions for assignments.

3. Guidelines for Correct Application. To use stimulus change techniques effectively, the teacher must have a good idea about which classroom conditions and/or events are controlling the child's behavior. Second, these conditions and events must be capable of being changed. Thus, the teacher must have both keen observing skills and good engineering skills to take advantage of stimulus change techniques.

Often the teacher does not know in advance which conditions or events are controlling the child's behavior. Only by carefully noting the circumstances that exist when the behavior occurs, is the teacher in a position to identify causal factors that may control it. After careful observation, the teacher may conclude there are as many as four or five associated events or conditions that could control the behavior in question. If these events or conditions can be changed, then the teacher can begin by altering the one that he/she considers most probably controls the behavior. If there is no corresponding change in the behavior, then the next most probable condition or event can be altered until one is identified that actually controls the behavior. If none of them work, then the teacher may conclude that no antecedents can be identified that will effectively control the behavior. At this point, it would be appropriate to consider consequences that could be manipulated to change the behavior.

Another alternative would be to identify a second set of potentially controlling conditions or events and test them out as before. However, the teacher has a limited amount of time and energy to invest in the process of changing an individual child's behavior. In the process of changing child behavior, there is always a trade-off between the response cost of a particular technique to the teacher or parent and its effectiveness in producing the desired result. This is usually a judgment that must be made on a case-by-case basis.

4. Issues to Consider When Using Stimulus Change Techniques. Stimulus change techniques can be used in both a preventive and a remedial sense. Based on her/his previous teaching experience and on a knowledge of good teaching techniques, the teacher can arrange classroom conditions or events that will optimally facilitate academic performance and appropriate classroom behavior. This can result in the actual prevention of much inappropriate behavior and in a higher rate of academic achievement than would otherwise be the case.

On the other hand, stimulus change techniques can be used to modify inappropriate behavior and to eliminate learning problems after they have developed. This is a remedial use of the technique and can be quite effective if controlling antecedents can feasibly be identified and changed.

As mentioned earlier, stimulus change techniques and the manipulation of antecedent events or conditions should be the first approach considered in changing child behavior. However, it is not always possible to identify a controlling antecedent or to identify one within a reasonable amount of time. Further, it is often not feasible to change antecedents even though the teacher suspects they may actually control the behavior or learning process in question. In cases such as these, the teacher should consider other methods for changing the child's behavior.

5. Advantages and Disadvantages of Stimulus Change Techniques. There are two primary advantages associated with stimulus change techniques. These are cost effectiveness and permanence of treatment effects. If a controlling antecedent(s) can be identified fairly easily, and if it can feasibly be changed, then permanent changes in behavior may be achieved with a minimum investment of teacher time and energy. As a rule, once the teacher has identified and changed the controlling antecedent event(s) or condition(s), no further investment of time and effort has to be made in order to maintain the changed behavior, provided that it is controlled exclusively by the changed antecedent(s).

As mentioned earlier, some child behaviors are not responsive to changed antecedents. Other behaviors are so strongly developed that they require the manipulation of both antecedents and consequences in order to be effectively changed.

Stimulus change techniques should be viewed as a valuable tool for facilitating the occurrence of appropriate classroom behavior. However, it is important to remember that while stimulus change can be a highly cost effective management technique, it may not be sufficiently powerful in isolation to change the acting-out child's behavior.

Verbal Feedback

1. Defined. Verbal feedback refers to the process of giving children information concerning the appropriateness of their academic performance or classroom behavior.

2. Illustrative Examples. Classroom teachers rely heavily upon verbal feedback in teaching children academic concepts and skills in managing their behavior. Feedback concerning the correctness of academic responding is instrumental to effective and efficient learning. Instruction is essentially a process of arranging antecedents carefully, eliciting child responses in relation to the structured antecedents and providing feedback as to the correctness or appropriateness of child performance.

Programmed instruction incorporates feedback into its teaching routines in a very efficient way. One of the reasons programmed instruction is so effective as a teaching device is that the learner can supply answers to stimulus items and then check immediately to see whether they are correct. Computer assisted instruction is another teaching system that makes use of instantaneous feedback to facilitate acquisition of new concepts and skills.

Verbal feedback is used constantly by teachers in managing child behavior in the classroom. Feedback in this context can be positive, negative, or neutral. Unfortunately, most teachers are more likely to reprimand inappropriate child behavior than to praise or give neutral feedback to appropriate behavior. Studies have shown that reprimands can actually increase rates of the behavior to which they are directed (Madsen, Becker, Thomas, Koser, & Plager, 1968).

As mentioned earlier, stating rules and giving children feedback when they are not following the rules may have only a minimal effect upon their behavior. Several studies have shown this to be the case (Madsen, Becker, & Thomas, 1968; O'Leary, Becker, & Evans, and

Saudargas, 1969). These studies suggest that rules are much more effective when they are backed up occasionally by consequences.

Verbal feedback from teacher consultants has proven to be highly effective in assisting teachers in the process of changing their classroom management behavior. For example, Cossairt, Hall, and Hopkins (1973) found that a combination of instructions, feedbacks, and social praise was highly effective in increasing teacher praise for student attending behavior. Similarly, Hops, Greenwood, and Guild, (1975) found that feedback supplied by a teacher consultant in the classroom was instrumental in teaching teachers to increase their praise rates to appropriate child behavior.

3. Guidelines for Correct Application. Feedback during the instructional process should be given immediately following child responses whenever possible. During individual seatwork periods, it is obviously impossible for the teacher to give children feedback regarding their academic performance except after the assignment or occasionally during its completion. There are simply too many children involved to make continuous or semicontinuous feedback practical.

However, in small group, large group, or one-on-one instructional situations, the teacher does have an opportunity to give immediate feedback following the child's oral or written responses. It is extremely important that children receive feedback following both positive and negative responses in these situations. The type and immediacy of feedback given children in these situations have a significant bearing upon how well they learn.

If a child's response is correct or appropriate, the teacher should confirm it verbally and praise the child for giving the right answer. If the response is incorrect the teacher should communicate in a neutral, *nonpunitive* way that the answer is wrong. The child should be given another chance to supply the answer with the teacher providing prompts where appropriate. If the child cannot produce the answer, it should be given by the teacher or another child should be called upon, depending on the instructional situation.

A good rule to remember is that feedback should be delivered in such a way that the child learns something and the chances are increased that a correct response will be given by the child in a similar situation.

4. Issues to Consider in Giving Verbal Feedback. If used correctly, verbal feedback can be valuable for the teacher in helping children acquire complex academic skills and concepts. However, in the management of child behavior, verbal feedback can be a trap for the teacher which, over the long term, can do more harm than good.

Unfortunately, in the management of child behavior, most teacher feedback is of a negative nature and is expressed in the form of reprimands. This is almost invariably true with disruptive, acting-out children.

Although several studies have provided suggestive evidence that teachers' reprimands may have a minimal to moderate effect in reducing disruptive child behavior (Jones & Miller, 1974; O'Leary, Kaufman, Kass, & Drabman, 1970) most experts in the field of behavior management would agree that this is a very inefficient and costly method of controlling child behavior. Further, it may be that the effectiveness of teacher reprimands in the above studies was only of a short term nature. It is possible that with some children, particularly children who are only minimally disruptive, teacher reprimands may produce a short term suppression of the behavior in question but actually strengthen it over the long term. As a general rule, teachers should not rely upon warnings or reprimands to manage child behavior in the classroom.

The author was observing in a classroom for emotionally disturbed children where the teacher was using a system of warnings, backed up by a timeout, for inappropriate behavior. The children were allowed three warnings for each of a series of disruptive classroom behaviors before the consequence of timeout was applied. One of the children came over to the teacher and inquired as to how many warnings he had accumulated for disturbing others. The teacher told him he had already had two warnings and that he had one left. The child then promptly walked over to a classmate who was working on an assignment and engaged him in an argument. This episode illustrates how children, particularly acting-out children, will take advantage of a classroom situation where the teacher relies primarily upon warnings and reprimands to manage child behavior.

If warnings and reprimands are to be used in the classroom, they should be backed up consistently with consequences which are effective in controlling child behavior. It may not be possible or even necessary to pair each warning or reprimand with a backup consequence, however children should not be taught that warnings and reprimands have no meaning beyond their delivery by the teacher.

5. Advantages and Disadvantages of Verbal Feedback. Verbal feedback can be invaluable in the instructional process. However, its use as a behavior management technique can be very risky for the reasons outlined above (and discussed in Chapter 1). As long as the teacher is assured that his/her feedback is having a positive, therapeutic effect on child behavior, then its use is justified. However, the teacher should be extremely sensitive to the consequences of using this technique to manage child behavior.

Teacher Praise

1. Defined. The delivery of a positive verbal, physical, or gestural stimulus for the purpose of increasing the behavior to which it is applied is what is meant by teacher praise. The teacher's affective tone and general attitude in delivering praise is warm, approving, and positive. Praises can be expressed in a variety of forms such as tousling a child's hair, winks, hand and facial gestures, as well as verbal compliments.

2. Illustrative Examples. Praise is one of the most positive, most natural, and for many children, one of the most powerful techniques available to the teacher for managing child behavior. Teachers who have mastered the correct application of this technique are often amazed at how effective it is in increasing the appropriate behavior of normal and minimally disruptive children.

Some sample praise statements, commonly used by teachers, are presented below.

> Jim, you and Fred are really playing and talking nicely.
> Susan, I like the way you're working hard on your math assignment.
> Marsha is listening to directions for the assignment very well.
> Allen, your math problems are 100 percent correct! Very good work!
> Sarah, you read that passage very well!

A more complete list of sample praise statements is presented at the end of this chapter.

3. Guidelines for Correct Application. There are a number of rules that should be followed carefully in order to maximize the effectiveness of praise. For example, the timing of praise is of crucial importance. The praise should be delivered *immediately* after the behavior in question (target behavior) has occurred. Through this process, the child learns to discriminate between appropriate and inappropriate behavior or correct and incorrect performance. Proper timing also insures that the desired target behavior(s) will be reinforced and strengthened. If the delay between the occurrence of the target behavior and praise delivery is too long, it is possible that an intervening behavior could occur. If this behavior were inappropriate or undesirable, then praise could not be delivered and the appropriate target behavior would go unreinforced.

If certain behaviors are ongoing over time, it may be possible to deliver praise unobtrusively while the behavior is being engaged in. For example, if a child has difficulty attending to task and completing assignments on time, the teacher can observe the child's performance carefully during the assignment and deliver praise for attending as it occurs. In certain types of social interactions, particularly on the playground, the teacher can praise children for interacting positively with each other during the ongoing social exchange. This procedure should be used for continuous stream type behaviors that extend for relatively long periods of time, e.g., attending to task, working on assignments, cooperating with others during joint task activities, and so forth.

The quality of praise is also extremely important to its overall effectiveness. Praise should be both positive and sincere. Children are very sensitive to the teacher generally and will quickly sense a lack of sincerity or artificiality in the teacher's praise. The delivery of praise should be accompanied by genuine enthusiasm on the teacher's part.

Teacher praise should be behavior descriptive, that is, as part of the praise statement, the child should be told precisely what behavior she/he is being praised for. Behavior descriptive praise helps the child to make a discrimination between appropriate and inappropriate behavior.

Finally, teacher praise should be varied whenever possible so that it doesn't become monotonous. The list of praise statements at the end of this chapter should help you in this task.

4. Issues to Consider in Using Praise. Praise is generally a rewarding and powerful stimulus for most children since adult approval has often been accompanied by the delivery of positive consequences in the past. Teacher praise derives much of its power from this conditioning process.

As mentioned earlier, teacher praise is not effective for all children. It seems that praise, for largely unknown reasons, is not effective for very deviant children and is not sufficiently powerful to change their behavior.

When such children are encountered, it is important to try and make teacher praise more rewarding for them. This can be done by consistently pairing teacher praise with positive consequences. After continued pairings, teacher praise may begin to take on the rewarding characteristics of the accompanying positive consequences. If this occurs, then teacher praise alone may be eventually powerful enough to control the child's behavior. This pairing procedure will be described later in this chapter.

Praising does not seem to be a "natural" activity for most adults. As mentioned earlier, adults (parents and teachers) are likely to communicate their expectations to children, either verbally or nonverbally and then respond to them only when these expectations are not fulfilled. In general, praise for appropriate and desired behavior is a rare event, particularly between adult and child. Studies of natural rates of teacher praise and approval to individual children have shown them to be extremely low in an absolute sense and also in relation to other categories of teacher behavior (White, 1975; Greenwood & Hops, 1976). Therefore, in learning to use praise effectively, the teacher must also insure that it is applied with a sufficient level of frequency to have an effect on the child's behavior. When using praise to teach children specific skills or to teach them new patterns of behavior, it is important that praise be given often when the appropriate behavior is exhibited. In the early stages of learning, the child should be praised at least once every ten minutes, with the frequency of praise gradually being reduced as the behavior or skills are acquired. Keeping track of the number of praises using a golf wrist counter or some other recording method is a good way to monitor one's frequency of praising.

5. Advantages and Disadvantages of Teacher Praise. There really are no disadvantages associated with the use of praise other than it may not be effective with some children and that it does not seem to be a "natural" activity for most adults. Praise is one of the most convenient, most natural (as opposed to artificial) and potentially effective techniques available to the teacher. The correct use of praise can have a very desirable positive effect upon child behavior in the classroom. Considering its potential benefits, the relatively low response cost to the teacher of using praise makes it a highly cost-effective technique.

Reinforcement Procedures

1. Defined. Reinforcement refers to the presentation of a rewarding stimulus or event for the purpose of increasing a behavior. A stimulus or event is said to be rewarding when its presentation increases the frequency or magnitude with which the reinforced behavior occurs.

2. *Illustrative Examples.* There are different *types* of reinforcement as well as different *methods* by which it can be delivered, and there are different *schedules* that control the frequency of reinforcement and the nature of its delivery. As to type of reinforcement, there are both social and nonsocial forms of reinforcement. Teacher praise is a form of social reinforcement. Social rewards include verbal praise, hugs, kisses, pats on the back or head, winks, and so forth. Nonsocial rewards include *tangibles* (toys, games, trinkets), *edibles* (food, drink, candy), and *activity* rewards such as free time, classroom games, movies, recess, helping the teacher, working on tasks with others, and so forth.

There are a wide variety of rewards available at both school and home that can be used to motivate children and to teach them essential skills, concepts, and appropriate patterns of behavior. The classroom teacher is in a unique position to take advantage of these sources of reinforcement in teaching children and in managing the classroom. A list of rewards available at school, outside the classroom, and at home is presented at the end of this chapter.

The two primary methods of *delivering* reinforcers are *token versus nontoken reinforcement* and *group versus individual reinforcement.* Tokens in the form of points, stars, checkmarks, or poker chips, which are exchangeable for backup rewards, can be a very effective method of reinforcement delivery. There are a number of advantages associated with token reinforcement. For example, children differ greatly in the things or activities they find rewarding. Further, the preferences of individual children change over time. With token reinforcement, a variety of backup rewards can be provided that may appeal to a broader range of individual preferences. Second, the cost of backup rewards can be arranged according to their market value, e.g., their cost in dollars and cents or according to the value assigned to them by the teacher. Thus, an item that costs fifty cents could be assigned a cost of fifty points. Similarly a less expensive item, with a market value of twenty cents, could be assigned a reduced cost of twenty points. By providing a range of backups from relatively inexpensive to more expensive, children can be given an option of exchanging their accumulated points early or saving them toward a more expensive item. Finally, token reinforcement makes it possible to gain considerable mileage out of each individual backup reward. For example, an item that costs 35 points can result in 35 separate reinforcements, that is, the child must earn 35 separate points before they can be exchanged for the backup reward. Similarly, the teacher can charge one point for each minute of free time. Consequently, if a child wanted fifteen minutes of free time, it would cost fifteen points. In this way, the reinforcing power of individual backup rewards is maximally utilized.

Nontoken reinforcement is used by many teachers and parents on an informal and sometimes unsystematic basis. In this type of reinforcement, there is usually a one-to-one relationship between the reward and the behavior that earns it. For example, parents often set up contingencies such as the following. "When you clean up your room, you can watch TV;" "You have to finish your homework before going out to play;" or "When you take out the garbage and help with the dishes, we'll discuss your request to use the car." Similarly, classroom teachers frequently set up arrangements in which children are free to talk quietly with each other or engage in free time after completing their assigned work.

A form of nontoken reinforcement that has been especially adapted for classroom use is called *contingency contracting*. This system was developed by Homme, de Baca, Devins, Steinhorst, and Rickert (1963) and is based upon a very simple idea. Basically, it says that what a person likes to do can be used as a reward for what they do not like to do. In most classroom applications of this system, free time (a preferred activity) has been used to reward academic work (not a preferred activity). In this system, a portion of the classroom is designated as a free time area and children are allowed to spend time in it after completing designated amounts of academic work. As a rule, small amounts of time spent in free time activities can be used to reward larger amounts of time spent in appropriate academic work.

Contingency contracting is a formal, systematic application of what has been referred to as grandma's law (Homme et al., 1963): "You get to do what you want to do after you do what I want you to do." Children can be motivated to work hard, even in content areas they don't especially like, through the correct use of contingency contracting. It can be used with individual children, with small groups, numbers of children, or with the entire class. However, the complexity of operating the system greatly increases as the number of children it is applied to within the classroom increases. Teachers wishing to learn how to use this system should consult *How to Use Contingency Contracting in the Classroom* by Lloyd Homme published by Research Press Company (1969).

The second method of *delivering* reinforcement concerns *group versus individual* reinforcement procedures. Individual reinforcement is essentially a private arrangement between the teacher and a pupil. That is, the teacher defines target behaviors a child is expected to engage in or establishes rules for the child to follow and then systematically reinforces the child on an individual basis for doing so. At the other extreme, the entire class can be handled as a single group; that is, rules or target behaviors are defined for the class as a whole, the teacher reinforces the class for either following or not following the rules, and the entire class earns a group reward. Essentially, the entire class is treated as if it were an individual child. This is known as group reinforcement.

There are many variations and possible combinations of group and individual reinforcement. Greenwood, Hops, Delquadri, and Guild (1974) have suggested that reinforcement procedures consist of at least three key components. These are (1) behavioral criteria for determining when and how reinforcement is to be given, (2) procedures for dispensing or awarding reinforcement, and (3) backup consequences. Each of these components can be established for a single individual or for a group of individuals in a particular setting such as the classroom.

Table 4.1, reprinted from Greenwood, Hops, Delquadri, and Guild (1974), summarizes the possible combinations of individual and group reinforcement procedures ranging from a completely individualized program (e.g., *individual* behavioral criteria, *individual* dispensing procedures, and *individual* backup consequences) to a completely group operated program (e.g., *group* behavioral criteria, *group* dispensing procedures, and *group* backup consequences).

There have been a number of reported studies in the literature which illustrate the application of combinations of group and individual reinforcement procedures. Greenwood et al. (1974) summarize these studies and show how they relate to the various cells of Table 4.1.

The effectiveness of both *group* reinforcement procedures (Packard, 1970; Sulzbacher & Houser, 1968; Bushell, Wrobel, & Michaelis, 1968; and Schmidt & Ulrich, 1969) and *individual* reinforcement procedures (Walker & Buckley, 1968; Birnbrauer, Wolf, Kidder, & Tague, 1965; O'Leary & Becker, 1967; and Ayllon & Azrin, 1968) has been well documented. There have been only a limited number of studies directly comparing group versus individual reinforcement procedures. Studies by Hamblin, Hathaway, and Wodarski (1971), Jacobs (1970), Herman, and Tramontana (1971), Elam and Sulzer-Azaroff

TABLE 4.1. *Possible Combinations of Individual and Group Reinforcement Procedures*

	Behavioral Criteria Established for			
	Individuals		*Group*	
	Dispensing and/or Recording for		Dispensing and/or Recording for	
Backup Consequences for	*Individual*	*Group*	*Individual*	*Group*
Individual	1	3	5	7
Group	2	4	6	8

(1973), and Walker and Hops (1973) have looked directly at this question. Results of these studies seem to indicate that group contingencies, and combinations of group and individual contingencies, are at least as powerful as individual contingencies and perhaps more so.

There are issues to consider in using both individual and group reinforcement procedures. For example, O'Leary and Drabman (1971) have suggested that group contingencies should be monitored carefully because of: (1) the possibility that a particular child in the group is not able to perform the required target behavior(s), (2) the resulting possibility of undue pressure on a particular individual, and (3) the possibility that one or two individuals may find it rewarding to try and subvert the program or to "beat the system." There are appropriate ways of responding to each of these issues. Group reinforcement procedures should never be applied to the behavior of a group of children unless the teacher is certain that *all* members of the group can produce the requisite target behavior(s) or can follow the established classroom rules. If one or more group members cannot meet the reinforcement criterion, the teacher should either (1) lower the reinforcement criterion by making it easier to earn reinforcements, (2) redefine the target behavior(s) or change the classroom rules involved so all group members can produce the required behavior, or (3) consider using other procedures if alternatives 1 and 2 are not feasible.

As to undue pressures mounting up on a particular child, it is unlikely that this will happen if the teacher insures beforehand that all children can perform the requisite behavior(s) or can follow classroom rules. When group reinforcement procedures are used, they should be monitored carefully to determine that the children are working together in a cooperative way to achieve the reward criterion. As a rule, when children are working together to achieve a common goal that is highly valued, they are most cooperative and will even help or tutor each other in order to achieve the goal more quickly.

When using group contingencies, it is unlikely, but possible, that one or two individuals may try to subvert the system because they find it more rewarding to do so than to participate in earning the reward. When this happens, the individuals involved should not be included in either the group reinforcement procedures or the resulting classroom rewards. A separate reinforcement system of lower value and with less attractive backup consequences should be established for these individuals. This has the effect of preventing the disruption of the group reinforcement procedures for the group as a whole and of teaching the individuals involved that such behavior will result in a reinforcement system of reduced value.

With individual reinforcement procedures, the question of fairness and equitable treatment of all children in the classroom inevitably arises. The argument is often raised by teachers and parents alike that a child should not be rewarded on an individual basis for what other children are doing naturally and without rewards. Further, teachers are sometimes concerned that if other children see a child being rewarded on an individual basis for behaving appropriately or for performing academically, they will misbehave or stop working in order to be put on a reinforcement system. These arguments may be valid and they are real and vital concerns of classroom teachers and parents. However, it is the author's impression that these issues are of much greater concern to adults than they are to the children involved. Children are usually quite accepting of peers, who are less skilled or more deviant, receiving special assistance, including the use of reinforcement procedures, to help them succeed in school. If other children inquire as to why a particular child is receiving special assistance or treatment, a fair explanation of the reasons will usually suffice. The teacher can suggest that some children need temporary help and special assistance to help them learn academic skills, to get along with others, and to follow classroom rules.

Some teachers object to providing individual rewards for children at school but do not necessarily oppose reinforcing children on an individual basis to help them succeed. In this situation, an arrangement can be worked out in which the child's parents can provide appropriate rewards at home when the child brings home a slip or card indicating he/she met the reinforcement criterion at school. This arrangement can work out quite satisfactorily for all parties concerned, including the child.

A combined individual/group reinforcement procedure can be used to respond to concerns raised about individual reinforcement. For example, the target child can earn a reward for himself and his classmates by achieving and behaving well in class. The child earns the reward on an individual basis which is then shared equally with the peer group. This contingency has been used successfully in numerous studies reported in the literature (Hops, Beickel, & Walker, 1976; Patterson, 1965) and is quite effective. It has the following advantages: (1) all children share equally in the reward, (2) the target child's peers are usually *very* supportive of her/his efforts to achieve the reward criterion, and (3) it represents a powerful motivational system and teaching device for instructing children.

There are three basic *schedules* for dispensing reinforcers (Ferster & Skinner, 1957). These are (1) continuous, (2) ratio, and (3) interval schedules. A continuous schedule of reinforcement means that a target behavior or response is reinforced continuously; that is, each time it occurs. Continuous schedules are used most frequently in the early stages of learning when a new skill or behavior is being acquired. Continuous schedules are used to build in new behavior(s) in a rapid fashion.

A ratio schedule means that a certain ratio of responses to reinforcers exists and that reinforcement is dispensed according to this schedule. For example, a ratio schedule of 1:5 means that one reinforcer will be dispensed for each five responses; similarly a ratio of 1:8 means that one reinforcer will be awarded for each eight responses produced. Ratio schedules are commonly used to reinforce academic responses in classrooms. For example, teachers often demand that so many math problems be completed or a certain number of pages be read before a reward such as free time is made available.

An interval schedule refers to an arrangement in which a reinforcer is delivered after an interval or period of time has passed. In classroom settings, interval schedules are often used to reinforce social behavior(s) and/or behavior that facilitates academic performance, e.g., attending to task.

In its strictest sense, an interval schedule means that the *first* response occurring after passage of a specified interval of time is reinforced. However, in most classroom applications of interval schedules, reinforcers are usually delivered to a continuously occurring behavior after predetermined time intervals. Reinforcing a child occasionally for following classroom rules is an example of an interval schedule.

Ratio and interval schedules can be either fixed or variable. Table 4.2 summarizes properties of each of the four types of intermittent schedules. Intermittent ratio schedules (fixed and variable) can be arranged so as to produce very high response rates. As a general rule, the higher the ratio of responses to each reinforcer, the higher the response rate. Thus, a 1:15 ratio schedule would produce a higher overall rate of responding than a 1:5 ratio schedule.

Intermittent interval schedules (fixed and variable) produce very predictable patterns of responding and tend to generate lower response rates than ratio schedules. Fixed interval schedules produce what is referred to as scalloped responding. That is, after each reinforcement, the response rate tends to drop off and then it gradually builds up again as the end of the fixed interval approaches and another reinforcer is delivered. The resulting response pattern acquires a configuration that is scalloped.

A variable interval schedule, on the other hand, produces a moderate and steady level of responding. Because of its intermittent nature, it is impossible to predict exactly when reinforcement will occur. Thus, to maximize one's chances for reinforcement, it is necessary to respond at a moderate, relatively stable rate over time.

Fixed interval schedules have relatively limited applications within classroom settings. Sometimes, children are rewarded for spending fixed amounts of time for persisting at certain tasks. For example, a negative, uncooperative child could be reinforced with one minute of free time for each five minutes of constructive behavior produced during a joint activity with other children. Fixed interval schedules used in this way are essentially a performance contract between the teacher and child where the child is informed, in advance, of the fixed units of responding required to earn each reinforcer.

TABLE 4.2. *Properties of Four Types of Intermittent Reinforcement Schedules*

Name Schedule	*Definition of Schedule*	*Effects on Behavior*	
		Schedule in Effect	*Schedule Terminated (Extinction)*
Fixed Ratio (FR)	Reinforcer is given after each X responses	High response rate	Irregular burst of responding. More responses than in continuous reinforcement, less than in variable ratio.
Fixed Interval (FI)	Reinforcer is given for first response to occur after each X minutes.	Stops working after reinforcement. Works hard just prior to time for next reinforcement.	Slow gradual decrease in responding.
Variable Ratio (VR)	Reinforcer is given after X responses on the average.	Very high response rates. The higher the ratio the higher the rate.	Very resistant to extinction. Maximum number of responses before extinction.
Variable Interval (VI)	Reinforcer is given for first response after each X minutes, on the average.	Steady rate of responding.	Very resistant to extinction. Maximum time to extinction.

Fixed ratio schedules are used much more frequently by classroom teachers, particularly in the area of academic performance. It is a common occurrence for a teacher to assign a child ten to fifteen math problems that must be completed correctly before a reward of some kind becomes available. Again, this is essentially a performance contract between the teacher and child.

Variable ratio and variable interval schedules are both used very frequently in classroom settings. In fact, most teachers, because of heavy time pressures, are only able to reinforce children on an occasional basis. Occasional reinforcement that is unpredictable and whose exact delivery cannot be anticipated is truly variable. A variable schedule means that a response or behavior is reinforced, *on the average*, for a predetermined amount of responding. For example, in a variable ratio schedule 1:5, the child is reinforced on the average once for every five responses. Thus, the child could be reinforced after the second, tenth, fourth, seventh, and third responses. Although the child in this instance was never reinforced on the fifth response, reinforcement was delivered on the average following each fifth response.

Precise variable ratio/variable interval schedules can be constructed that would account for the entire range of potential human responding. However, it is usually not necessary to reinforce children in classroom settings according to a strict and preprogrammed variable ratio or variable interval schedule. In using these schedules, it is usually sufficient to reinforce an arbitrarily determined percentage of the child's responses. However, to take advantage of the positive characteristics of these schedules, it is extremely important to make the actual reinforcement delivery unpredictable so the child is not able to anticipate it in advance.

In teaching new behavior/skills or in strengthening responses that occur at a low level, it is advisable to begin with a continuous schedule of reinforcement. However, once the target behavior or response has been acquired and occurs at an acceptable level, one should shift to a variable schedule to maintain it over the long term. Reference to Table 4.2 shows that both variable ratio and variable interval schedules build in greater resistance to extinction than do continuous or fixed schedules.

It should be noted that it is nearly impossible for classroom teachers to reinforce children on a continuous basis for *any* target behavior given their time constraints and responsibilities. However, when teaching any new skill/response, every effort should be made to reinforce the child as often as possible when acceptable forms of the target behavior are produced.

3. Guidelines for Correct Application. There are a number of guidelines that should be followed in using reinforcement procedures. Adherence to these guidelines will make your use of reinforcement both effective and productive.

For example, it is extremely important that the reinforcement system used have incentive value for the child or children to whom it is applied. If it does not, the reinforcement system will not be effective in changing the child's behavior or in motivating him/her to achieve. It is important to provide an array of reinforcing activities and/or events for children to earn. The greater the variety of backup reinforcers available, the more likely it is there will be something to appeal to each child to whom reinforcement procedures are applied.

There are several ways to go about gathering information on a child's reinforcement preferences. For example, the teacher can simply ask the child to suggest a list of activities or events that she/he would like to work for. It may be advisable to build two lists; one for reinforcers available at school and one for those available only at home.

Second, the teacher can put together a reinforcement menu and have the child select events or activities from it. The menu should contain a list of activities/events as inclusive as possible in order to appeal to the varied reinforcement preferences of children in general. Space should be provided for children to add to the menu.

Third, the teacher can observe the activities a child engages in during free time periods and/or the toys he/she chooses to play with. A careful recording of this information will provide clues to the child's preferences for different backup reinforcers.

None of these methods are foolproof. For example, what a child verbalizes he/she would like to work for is not always what is actually chosen. Children will often select a backup reinforcer in advance to work for and then later change their minds and exchange for something else, thereby indicating that the original backup reinforcer had lost its incentive value. Similarly, children will sometimes exchange a number of times for a favorite event or activity and then grow tired of it. Teachers should keep careful records of the backup reinforcers children choose or exchange points for. In this way, a determination can be made as to which reinforcers are effective in motivating children and which are not. If the reinforcement system suddenly loses its effectiveness, the first thing that should be checked is whether the backup reinforcers available coincide with the children's preferences.

Backup reinforcers should also be arranged in sequential order according to: (1) their actual market value, (2) their magnitude, or (3) the degree to which they are preferred by the children. In this way, higher quality performance or greater amounts of work can be demanded for the more preferred/more valuable reinforcers. Consequently, children can be taught to delay exchanging and accumulate credits toward more expensive items. As a general rule, children should have the option of exchanging for a backup reinforcer at least once every day, provided their behavior has been appropriate.

A third rule for the correct use of reinforcement concerns who controls the reinforcement system. In the early stages of learning or acquisition, the teacher should maintain control of the reinforcement system, particularly with highly deviant children. Child determined reinforcement and self-control are long term goals that should be considered. However, substantial and durable changes should be achieved in a given child's behavior before the teacher relinquishes control of the reinforcement system.

Teachers should not argue with children over how much work should earn the various backup reinforcers. Clear rules governing the ratio of amount of work required for various backup reinforcers should be established and communicated to the child or children involved. Once developed, these rules should not be altered.

Sometimes children will approach the teacher and say, for example, "If I do ten math problems correctly, may I have some free time?" Under no circumstances should the teacher agree to such a request. If he or she does, then the child is, in effect, in control of the reinforcement system by virtue of being able to dictate reinforcement contingencies to the teacher. It is far better to carefully define the reinforcement contingencies in advance and to remind the children about details of them if confusion develops.

Whenever a reinforcement system is established, careful attention should be given to what constitutes a reinforceable response or behavior. This is a relatively complex area since the criterion for a reinforceable response is likely to change over time. For example, an initial goal for an extremely deviant, hyperactive child might be to simply sit still for brief periods and listen carefully to teacher instructions. After this has been mastered satisfactorily, the reinforceable response can be changed, e.g., the child may now be required to sit still for longer periods of time, listen to teacher instructions, and attend to the assigned task. In this fashion, the reinforceable response can be gradually increased until the child is achieving and behaving satisfactorily.

It should be noted that this is a gradual process. It is extremely important that the initial reinforceable response be one that the child can reasonably produce. If the initial response is too difficult or beyond the child's capability, then the reinforcement system will not have a chance to work effectively. The rule to remember is begin with an appropriate reinforceable response and then gradually increase it until the child has progressed to a satisfactory level of performance. The teacher should insure that the child has mastered each level within the chain of reinforceable responses, from initial to final response, before the criterion for reinforcement in increased.

When a response or behavior is selected for reinforcement that meets the reinforcement criterion, the reinforcer should be delivered *immediately* after the behavior/response occurs. Immediate reinforcement delivery serves several purposes. For example, it builds in a clear discrimination as to which response or behavior results in reinforcement. Immediate delivery also has a greater effect in strengthening or building in the target behavior. If reinforcement delivery is delayed after the target behavior occurs, it is possible that another behavior could occur in the interim resulting in reinforcement of the wrong behavior!

Some target behaviors occur in a continuous stream fashion. Attending to task and cooperating with others in joint activities are examples of such behaviors. It is difficult to single out discrete examples of such target behaviors and to deliver reinforcement immediately after they occur. Instead, reinforcement has to be delivered *as* the behavior is occurring. This can be done in an unobtrusive way so that the target behavior is not disrupted. Observing the on-going behavior carefully and selecting a time in which reinforcement can be delivered unobtrusively is the key to making this approach work.

Consistency is an important part of the teaching-learning process. Similarly, consistent application is an extremely important part of correct reinforcement delivery. If a child is reinforced for engaging in a given behavior in one situation and then either ignored or punished for engaging in that behavior in another situation or at another time within the same situation, the child's learning and behavior will reflect this lack of consistency. It should be mentioned that while a teacher may not be able to reinforce each occurrence of a given target behavior, under no circumstances should it be deliberately ignored or punished.

It is also important that teacher praise be paired with reinforcement delivery whenever possible. Pairing behavior descriptive praise with reinforcement delivery has a number of advantages. For example, the praise clearly communicates the teacher's approval of the child's behavior and simultaneously informs her/him what the praise and reinforcement are being delivered for. Second, by virtue of being consistently paired with reinforcement delivery, praise can take on the reinforcing properties of the actual reinforcer(s) used. This is especially important since teacher praise is not always initially effective with many deviant children. By systematically increasing the incentive value of praise through pairing, the teacher is in a position to gradually reduce the frequency of reinforcement and to substitute praise. After systematic pairing, the teacher's praise may be much more effective in maintaining the child's appropriate behavior.

Frequency of reinforcement delivery is a variable that has to be carefully attended to in the correct use of reinforcement procedures. In teaching new behaviors or skills, it would be desirable to reinforce each occurrence of the target behavior. However, except with behaviors that occur at a very low rate, this is usually impossible for the classroom teacher. Instead, the teacher must usually reinforce a percentage of the target behaviors that occur.

In the early stages of teaching a skill or behavior that can occur either continuously or at a relatively high rate, it is desirable to reinforce the behavior at least once every five minutes. After the behavior has been strengthened and is occurring at a higher rate, the reinforcement delivery can be reduced. At this stage, once every ten minutes would be a reasonable frequency. It would also be desirable to occasionally fill in with unpaired praises once the reinforcement frequency is reduced. The reinforcement frequency can be gradually reduced over time as the child's behavior indicates it is possible.

If a behavior occurs at a relatively low rate, then a much larger percentage of the child's target behaviors can be reinforced. As the behavior increases in rate, this percentage will decrease unless the reinforcement frequency is concomitantly increased. As a general rule, it is a good idea to increase the frequency of reinforcement as a low rate behavior increases until it can be assured that the behavior has been acquired and is occurring at an acceptable level.

As to the frequency of exchanging (e.g., credits or points toward a backup reinforcer), a general rule is that a child should have an opportunity to exchange for a backup event or activity at least once per day *provided* his/her behavior has been appropriate for most of the day. Some room should be allowed for errors and mistakes. A good criterion for reinforcement is that if the child's behavior has been eighty percent appropriate or better for the entire day, then he/she would be able to exchange for the least expensive item or activity on the list of backup reinforcers. If the program is not in effect for the entire day, the eighty percent criterion can still be used regardless of whether academic performance or appropriate behavior is being reinforced.

When points or credits are used as units of reinforcement, exchangeable for backup consequences, a problem can develop with hoarding—the accumulation of large amounts of points. Sometimes, children will accumulate points just for the sake of accumulating them. When this happens, the reinforcement system may lose some of its effectiveness for the child or children involved. One way to prevent this problem is to set up a rule where the children must cash in all their points at the end of each week and start fresh the next. In this way, children usually do not build up enough points to reduce the effectiveness of the reinforcement system.

4. Issues to Consider in Using Reinforcement Procedures. The question of moral and ethical objections to the use of reinforcement inevitably arises in connection with the establishment of reinforcement systems. It is argued, for instance, that reinforcement (1) restricts a child's choices and behavioral diversity by teaching her/him to engage in a very limited response pattern so as to achieve reinforcement, (2) teaches him/her to respond appropriately only when reinforcement is available and not at other times, and (3) undermines a child's natural intrinsic interest in activities. Logical arguments can be developed both for and against each of these issues. Unfortunately, it is not currently possible to prove or disprove either side of these issues.

However, there is no question that reinforcement works and that it *is* effective in teaching children to achieve and behave better. It is a valuable tool available to the teacher for helping children acquire needed academic and social skills. Reinforcement procedures should be viewed as a short term remedial tool for teaching children new skills and response patterns. After such skills and behaviors are acquired, the reinforcement procedures can be gradually withdrawn, while maintaining the newly acquired skills/behavior.

The term *reinforcement procedures*, as used above, refers to external reinforcement of either a tangible (points, free time, objects of interest) or intangible nature (praise, physical or verbal gestures of approval, and so forth). It also refers to a system or schedule of reinforcement that is manipulated by someone else, usually an adult, for the purpose of teaching specific skills or for encouraging the child to behave in a different way. It is not feasible to expect that adults can maintain such systems indefinitely in order to insure that children follow established rules or continue to display specific skills. At some point, such externally managed systems tailored specifically for a single child must be removed. The challenge is to remove them in a way that preserves as much of the achieved gains as possible. In this context, the hope is that the changed behavior or skills taught will become a permanent part of the child's repertoire and will be maintained by natural reinforcers available in the school and/or home environment (feelings of mastery and achievement, spontaneous expressions of approval from the teacher, peers, or parents for improved performance, and so forth).

Self-control is the ultimate goal of interventions based upon external reinforcement procedures. However, it is not an easy task to get children, especially deviant/disruptive children, to the point where they can or will accept responsibility for maintaining changes produced by externally managed reinforcement systems. Given that the time, expertise, and resources are available, it is recommended that a three-stage behavior change process be considered, i.e., an externally managed reinforcement procedure is implemented initially to produce desired changes, and control of the system is then transferred to the target child who is taught to manage and control his/her own behavior. When the child is successful in doing so, the system is gradually faded out, with control shifting to naturally occurring reinforcers available in the child's social environment. The reader is referred to Thoresen and Mahoney (1974) for an excellent presentation of behavioral self-control issues and procedures.

Acting-out children place such intense pressures upon the management skills of teachers and upon school personnel in general that they are usually receptive to techniques and procedures that will teach acting-out children appropriate academic and social skills. Reinforcement procedures, if used properly, can be of invaluable assistance to school personnel in managing the acting-out child.

While reinforcement procedures can be instrumental in producing powerful changes in an acting-out child's behavior, they are by no means magical. The procedures must remain in effect long enough for the changed behavior to become a permanent part of the child's repertoire. Building in changes that become permanent is a very complex process and one that we are just beginning to understand. Chapter 7 is devoted to this topic.

5. Advantages and Disadvantages of Reinforcement Procedures. The advantages of reinforcement procedures are obvious and have been reviewed indirectly in earlier sections of this chapter. The primary disadvantages concern the response cost accruing to the person implementing the reinforcement system and the general tendency for behavioral changes not to generalize to those settings in which the reinforcement procedures have not been implemented.

The use of reinforcement is essentially a trade-off between their cost to the implementer, usually the teacher or parent, and their effectiveness in producing the desired changes in child behavior. If the procedures are applied correctly, reinforcement is usually a highly cost-effective procedure. However, it should be obvious that the correct use of reinforcement requires the investment of time and effort by the teacher (or parent). The majority of the time and effort that has to be invested is expended initially in setting up the system. The actual daily operation of a reinforcement system requires a surprisingly small amount of the teacher's time and effort.

The tendency for treatment effects produced by reinforcement procedures not to generalize to nontreatment settings is a more troublesome problem. A number of studies have been conducted on this issue and most show an overall lack of generalizability (O'Leary & Drabman, 1971). This means that if it is expected that a child's behavior will change across a number of settings (e.g., different classrooms, playground, lunchroom, home, etc.), then the treatment program or a variation of it must as a general rule be implemented in those settings.

In summary, the potential benefits of reinforcement procedures seem to far outweigh their disadvantages. It should be noted that the precision with which reinforcement procedures are applied will usually be reflected directly in the behavior of children to whom they are applied.

Modeling Plus Reinforcement of Matching Responses

1. Defined. Modeling plus reinforcement of matching responses refers to a teaching procedure in which a behavior or skill is demonstrated by a model (usually a teacher or parent), and the child is reinforced for producing correct matching responses.

2. *Illustrative Examples.* Modeling plus reinforcement of matching responses is an extremely powerful teaching device. It combines the instructional precision of modeling with the motivational properties of reinforcement. Bandura (1969) has suggested that the combined use of modeling and reinforcement procedures is perhaps the most effective method available for teaching response patterns. The procedure is most often used when the instructor is not sure the child can produce the desired response or skill on demand.

For example, the technique is often used by speech therapists to improve the enunciation skills of children who have articulation problems. Sounds which the child has difficulty pronouncing correctly are identified. The therapist then models the correct pronunciation of each of these sounds and asks the child to produce the sound. Feedback as to correctness is given following each attempt by the child. Child responses which closely approximate those of the therapist are positively reinforced. Usually, after the child has demonstrated a reasonable mastery of the sounds involved, words are identified which contain them and the teaching procedure is repeated.

Modeling plus reinforcement is also very useful in teaching children social skills and appropriate patterns of social behavior. Many children are rejected by their peers because they do not have the necessary social skills to either initiate or maintain positive social relationships with classmates. Some children are highly negative and their initiations to others are often characterized by aggression and hostility. Consequently, peers tend to avoid them whenever possible. Other children are generally unresponsive and thereby do not reinforce children for initiating to them.

In cases such as these, the teacher can model appropriate social skills for the child in private rehearsal sessions and then reinforce the child for matching them in social interactions with classmates. Another option would be to involve a classmate in the modeling/roleplaying sessions and have each child take turns matching the demonstrated social skills in their interactions with each other. Reinforcement could be delivered as each child displayed the appropriate social skills. If necessary, the reinforcement system could be extended to the target child's social interactions with classmates in the classroom, on the playground, in the lunchroom, and so forth.

While consulting at a residential school for the deaf, the author observed an ingenious demonstration of the use of modeling plus reinforcement in teaching a deaf child correct sign language.

The child in question was a male adolescent with very limited communication skills and equally deficient social skills. His teachers were only minimally successful in teaching him sign language so he could communicate more effectively with others. A psychologist at the institution designed a teaching routine for him that used modeling plus reinforcement of matching responses.

Three individuals were involved in the procedure. These were the boy, one of his peers, and the dorm counselor. The teaching procedure was carried out daily in a private area and went as follows: (1) The counselor asked the peer a simple question using sign language such as "What is your name, please?" (2) The peer responded with "My name is ____________________." (3) The peer was rewarded with a piece of candy each time she responded correctly using sign language. (4) The counselor then asked the boy the same question in sign language. (5) If he responded correctly, he was rewarded; if not, he received no reward. This proved to be a highly effective teaching procedure; however, a number of learning trials were required before the boy would respond appropriately to the counselor.

In this instance, the target skill was modeled for the boy by one of his peers. Further, he was able to observe her being rewarded for responding appropriately. After each trial, he was given an opportunity to respond in the same fashion and to be rewarded. This teaching routine combined excellent instructional procedures with a powerful incentive system. As a result, dramatic growth in the boy's mastery of sign language was apparent within a short period of time.

3. Guidelines for Correct Application. Although modeling plus reinforcement is perhaps most appropriate in direct instructional situations where the teacher is not sure whether the target response or skill is within the subject's behavioral repertoire, it can be used across a variety of tasks and teaching situations. Because of its power and precision, it can be a highly cost-effective technique for teaching children complex social, language, and academic skills.

The first rule to consider in using this technique is that the target skill be modeled *correctly* for the child. It is literally true that the child will learn what is demonstrated and selectively reinforced by the model. Secondly, the target skill should be modeled *consistently* from trial to trial; that is, there should be a high degree of similarity between correct demonstrations of the skill by the model. Thirdly, the instructor should insure that the child is attending very carefully to what is being modeled. Attending is a very powerful component of the modeling process. Skill acquisition and mastery will be greatly impaired if the attending response is not well developed and executed during the modeling sessions. Fourth, the child should be given precise and descriptive feedback concerning her/his performance following *each* modeling trial. Fifth, correct matching responses should be selectively rewarded with either praise and/or tangible rewards. It is extremely important that correct, rather than almost correct, matching responses be selectively rewarded since the responses that are rewarded will be the ones that are learned and acquired. If less than correct forms of the responses are rewarded, the goal(s) of the instructional procedure will not be realized. It should be noted that prompts and cues can and should be used to assist the learner in correctly discriminating and reproducing the target skill being taught.

4. Issues to Consider in Using Modeling Plus Reinforcement. As mentioned above, modeling plus reinforcement is a very powerful and potentially cost-effective technique for directly teaching children needed skills and behavioral responses. The teaching routine must be carefully designed and usually it must be operated by the teacher or some other adult. As a rule, it is carried out in a private or semi-private area where direct observation, communication, and modeling demonstration are feasible.

Whenever possible, it is desirable to involve a peer or peers in the teaching process, especially peers who are already competent in producing the skill or response that is being taught. In this way, the target child can observe the adult modeling the skill or response, can observe a peer(s) correctly reproducing it and receiving positive feedback or consequences for doing so, and then can attempt to reproduce it himself/herself with the encouragement and assistance of both the instructor and the peer(s).

Involvement of a peer(s) can also facilitate generalization of the learned response from the private teaching situation to the classroom or playground. Too often children are taught complex social language or academic skills in intensive tutoring sessions with generalization to other settings being assumed rather than programmed. It is extremely important that such skills be selectively identified, reinforced, and thereby strengthened within the *natural* setting (e.g., classroom, playground) where they are expected to occur. Peer(s) involved in the original teaching situation can be of great assistance to the teacher in this process, especially if they are prompted occasionally by the teacher to do so.

5. Advantages and Disadvantages of Modeling Plus Reinforcement. The power, instructional precision, and potentional cost-effectiveness of modeling plus reinforcement are its most salient advantages. There really are no disadvantages associated with the technique. It does require the involvement of an adult and must be implemented in a tutorial fashion. Further, skills/responses taught in private sessions must be strengthened within the natural setting(s) where they are expected to occur. However, these minor limitations and constraints are more than offset by the potential benefits of the technique's correct application.

Shaping

1. Defined. Shaping is used to build in totally new responses that did not previously exist in the subject's behavioral repertoire. Shaping is an appropriate teaching technique to use when the target response or behavior does not currently exist in the child's repertoire and he/she is not initially capable of producing a reasonable approximation of it. Shaping uses a combination of positive reinforcement and extinction procedures to build in totally new responses/behavior that did not previously exist.

In using shaping, one begins by reinforcing a form of the behavior that may bear only a remote resemblance to the final target response. This is called reinforcing an *approximation* to the final target response or behavior. Shaping is simply the process of successively reinforcing ever closer approximations to the final desired forms of the behavior or the target response.

The process of successively reinforcing closer and closer approximations is a delicate one. Initially, a relatively crude approximation to the target response is selected and reinforced. After this form of the behavior is strengthened and occurs reliably, reinforcement is then withheld and the behavior is placed in extinction. When this occurs, the subject's behavior becomes more varied and a number of responses are produced in an attempt to meet the reinforcement criterion. During this process, a form of the behavior is selected for reinforcement that represents a closer approximation to the final target response. This form of the behavior is then strengthened and, once it occurs reliably, is also placed on extinction. New forms of the behavior are produced and an even closer approximation is selected for reinforcement. In this way, the criterion for reinforcement is gradually increased until the final target response is acquired. This process is called shaping.

2. Illustrative Examples. The acquisition of language is a good example of how shaping techniques are used to build in new behavior. The language repertoire of infants is largely undifferentiated at birth and consists of randomly produced sounds that bear little resemblance to any spoken language. However, as the child matures and interacts with family members, the repertoire of sounds increases and becomes more varied. Parents listen to the child's verbalizations carefully and begin to pay attention to sounds that approximate spoken language. In this process, the correct sound or word is repeated for the child and parental approval is given for the child's attempts at producing it. As a result, the child learns to listen carefully to spoken language and to try to reproduce it. Over the long term, highly complex language patterns are acquired through this basic process.

In viewing a film on the use of behavior management procedures within an institutional setting, the author once observed an ingenious application of shaping to teach a developmentally delayed child to walk. The subject of the demonstration was a four-year-old girl who was physically capable of walking, but for some reason had not learned to do so. One of her favorite pastimes was eating ice cream.

Two child care workers set up an arrangement where they positioned themselves opposite each other, seated in chairs, with the chair backs facing each other. Initially, the chairs were only two feet apart or so with the girl stationed in between. Each attendant had an ice cream cone. The girl was taught to go from one attendant to the other, and each time she did, she was allowed one lick on the ice cream cone.

As the child's motor skills improved and she gained confidence, the chairs were gradually moved further away from each other until her outstretched arms would barely reach from one chair to the other. To facilitate the child's walking from one chair to the other as the chairs were gradually moved even further apart, the experimenters set up a pulley attached to the ceiling with a rope which had a handle on the end of it. There was tension on the rope and the child held on to the handle and quickly learned to walk from chair to chair using the rope as an aid. After the chairs were moved approximately fifteen to twenty feet apart, the tension on the rope was gradually released until the child was in effect carrying the rope from chair to chair. The rope was clipped off into a ten-foot length or so and gradually shortened until the child was carrying only a small piece of rope in her hand. One day she eventually dropped the rope and apparently thought no more of it.

Once the child developed her walking skills through this procedure, they generalized beyond the experimental situation. There were a sufficient number of naturally occurring reinforcers to maintain her walking so that she did not regress to a nonwalking state when the ice cream and shaping procedures were terminated.

This is an example of a very successful and quite ingenious use of shaping techniques to gradually build in a new behavior. The attendants gradually increased the criterion for gaining access to the ice cream, but at the same time provided the necessary prosthetic aids (chairs, rope pulley) that were necessary in this case to facilitate progress from one approximation to the other.

Child care workers and psychological personnel in school settings often use shaping procedures to gradually teach withdrawn children new patterns of social behavior. Many withdrawn children are extremely limited and suppressed in both their verbal and nonverbal interactions with peers. This may be because of a traumatic fear of social interaction, because they have not developed the necessary social interactive skills, or because they have been punished when initiating to peers. Whatever the reason(s), social skills cannot develop in the absence of opportunities to interact with others. Thus, the first step in modifying social withdrawal is to make it possible for the withdrawn child to interact with others.

This is no simple task. However, shaping techniques which initially reinforce only approximation to social interactions with peers can be used in this process. For example, as a first step, the withdrawn child could be reinforced for being in closer and closer proximity to peers on the playground. If the child could manage this, she/he could be reinforced for participating in group games or activities that require no verbal interaction. Next, the criterion could be raised to the point where the child was required to simply acknowledge a previously arranged and prompted initiation by a selected classmate. Eventually, the child could be required to initiate to a peer. As a next step, the withdrawn child could be assigned to a joint activity or game that requires no interaction or only limited interaction, e.g., chess or checkers.

As the child's skills developed, minimal verbal interaction could be required as part of the criterion for achieving reinforcement. The child could be gradually required to interact, both verbally and nonverbally, with more and different peers as his/her social skills developed. In this instance, shaping would be a very appropriate teaching technique for moving a child from a position of noninteractive behavior to positive social interaction with a variety of peers.

3. Guidelines for Correct Application. Given a working knowledge of how to use reinforcement and extinction procedures correctly, shaping is not a difficult technique to master. Shaping is basically the alternate application of reinforcement and extinction procedures in conjunction with a gradually increasing criterion governing what is a reinforceable response. However, there are some cautions that one should consider when using the technique.

For example, one should be certain that the form (approximation) of the target behavior selected for reinforcement at any point in the shaping process is clearly distinguishable by the child from other nonreinforceable forms of the behavior. This discrimination is apparent when the child consistently engages in the desired form of the behavior when reinforcement is available and other competing forms of the behavior extinguish. Only when this form of the behavior occurs consistently and reliably should the reinforcement criterion be raised and a closer approximation demanded before reinforcement is again made available.

Finally, when raising the reinforcement criterion to a new approximation, one should be sure that the new form of the behavior is in fact a closer approximation to the final form of the target behavior or response, and that it is sufficiently different from the previously reinforced approximation to be discriminated by the child. In the application of shaping procedures, one should progress in sequential fashion through ever closer approximations to the final desired form of the behavior. If this is not achieved, the shaping process will be disrupted and skill acquisition will be delayed.

Related to this problem, one should also insure that once a given form of the target behavior has been placed on extinction, it is never again reinforced. If this were to occur, the now undesired form of the behavior would likely reappear and possibly at a higher rate than before!

When reinforcing a given form of the target behavior in a chain of approximations, it is important to reinforce *each* occurrence of the form of the behavior that meets the reinforcement criterion. There are several reasons for this. First, immediate and continuous reinforcement builds in response acquisition at the maximum rate; that is, learning is usually fastest with this type of reinforcement schedule. Second, responses that have been reinforced on a continuous schedule will extinguish more quickly. Thus, a continuous schedule produces rapid acquisition *and* extinction of responses. Consequently, this is an ideal schedule to use in shaping since the goal is to teach new forms of a target behavior rapidly and also to extinguish those forms quickly when the reinforcement criterion is changed.

4. Issues to Consider When Using Shaping. Shaping is a highly effective but complex teaching procedure. It is time consuming and generally demands a one-on-one teaching arrangement. It requires an ability to monitor a child's behavior very carefully on a moment-to-moment basis, and also to use reinforcement and extinction procedures in a very precise fashion. One should be certain therefore that shaping is actually necessary to teach the target behavior in question.

Sometimes a close approximation of the target behavior is within the child's repertoire but is not apparent from casual observation. If this were the case, a reinforcement alone, or modeling plus reinforcement of matching responses procedure would be more appropriate and more cost-effective. As a general rule, shaping should be used as a last resort in teaching new skills and behavioral responses after it has been determined that other methods would be either inappropriate or ineffective. Whenever possible, other, less costly methods should be considered first.

5. Advantages and Disadvantages of Shaping. There are no disadvantages associated with shaping other than its cost effectiveness in certain situations.

TIMEOUT

1. Defined. Timeout is a behavior management technique in which the child is temporarily removed from a reinforcing situation immediately following the occurrence of a deviant or inappropriate behavior. It is a form of mild punishment and its purpose is to decrease the occurrence of behavior(s) to which it is applied. It differs from extinction in that extinction removes a rewarding stimulus or consequence from a previously reinforced behavior, while timeout removes the child from a reinforcing situation. Both timeout and extinction effectively deny access to reinforcement.

2. *Illustrative Examples.* Timeout generally involves removal from a reinforcing situation for anywhere from three to thirty minutes. Timeout, in various forms, has traditionally been a very popular behavior management technique. Parents are probably the most frequent users of timeout procedures. It would be rare to encounter parents who have not sent a child to her/his room at one time or another for misbehaving.

Wahler (1969) trained two sets of parents in the systematic use of differential attention and timeout in controlling their children's oppositional behavior. The children involved were aged six and five, respectively, and were described as stubborn, negative, destructive, and unwilling to obey parental requests and commands. Parents were trained to be especially sensitive to and approve of instances of cooperative child behavior. A five-minute timeout period was applied immediately after each instance of oppositional child behavior. The child was sent to his bedroom for five minutes of isolation following each instance. If the child threw a tantrum while in timeout, the period of isolation was extended until the tantrum behavior had subsided. The combination of parental approval for cooperative behavior and a brief timeout period for oppositional behavior proved highly effective with both children. As a general rule, it is likely that the combination of differential approval/timeout would be more effective than timeout alone in changing child behavior.

Bostow and Bailey (1969) used a combination of tangible reinforcement procedures and timeout to reduce the disruptive and aggressive behaviors of two retarded patients in a state hospital setting. One patient was a 58-year-old female resident who was confined to a wheelchair. The other was a seven-year-old boy who had recently been admitted to the hospital.

The female patient frequently used loud and abusive language with other patients and engaged in tantrum-like behavior(s) until her demands were met. For cooperative, nonaggressive behavior, the patient was allowed brief access to preferred activities or objects, e.g., a second cup of coffee, a special treat, or time to use a favorite object. For disruptive and/or abusive behavior(s) the patient was placed into a two-minute timeout period within a corner of the hospital day room.

This treatment procedure proved to be extremely effective in reducing the patient's abusive and disruptive behavior. When treatment was in effect, the patient's frequency of inappropriate vocalizations was reduced to near zero levels.

The same treatment procedure was applied to the aggressive behavior of the seven-year-old patient. The results were similar, with his aggressive responses reduced to near zero levels during treatment periods. As in the previous example, the effectiveness of timeout was no doubt enhanced by the precise use of reinforcement procedures for the patient's appropriate behavior.

Wasik, Senn, Welch, and Cooper (1969) used timeout from social reinforcement as part of a treatment procedure designed to teach culturally disadvantaged children new patterns of behavior within a primary level classroom setting. The two subjects of the study were seven-year-old girls enrolled in a second-grade classroom. The goal of treatment was to reduce their levels of inappropriate, unacceptable classroom behavior and to teach behavior patterns that would facilitate positive social and academic development. Treatment consisted of teacher praise for appropriate behavior, withholding teacher attention and praise for inappropriate behavior, and timeout (five minutes in a quiet room) for aggressive and disruptive behavior. The treatment package proved to be highly effective in reducing the occurrence of inappropriate and unacceptable behaviors and in increasing the occurrence of appropriate classroom behavior.

Numerous examples of the successful application of timeout procedures have been reported in the professional literature. The procedures have been used effectively in home, institutional, and classroom settings.

3. Guidelines for Correct Application. The effectiveness of timeout rests on the assumption that removal from ongoing activities is a form of mild punishment. Therefore, if timeout is applied to certain inappropriate or undesirable behaviors and their frequency is substantially reduced as a result, then we can assume that timeout is being applied correctly and that the setting from which the child is being removed is reinforcing.

The first rule to consider in the correct application of timeout is that the setting or activities from which the child is being removed are in fact reinforcing for her/him. If not, timeout will have only a limited effect, if it has any effect at all, in reducing the occurrence of the behavior(s) to which it is applied.

Second, the area to which the child is removed should be relatively isolated; that is, the child should be effectively removed from ongoing activities which she/he values. However, it is very important that the proper supervision is available for the child during the timeout period. Most states have laws relating to the supervision of children in school settings. One should be sure that timeout does not conflict with such laws.

Third, if a timeout room is used, it should be well lighted, well ventilated, and meet fire code regulations. Areas within the classroom or in other parts of the school, such as the health room or office, can be designated as timeout areas. If a within classroom timeout area is used, a desk can simply be placed behind a portable folding screen that is commonly found in schools. If the child engages in disruptive behavior while in timeout thereby disturbing the rest of the class, he/she can be removed to a timeout room or another suitable area of the school.

Fourth, the timeout period should be a relatively dull and uninteresting experience if it is to be effective. In other words, timeout should not represent an escape from an unpleasant situation nor should it be something one looks forward to. Consequently, when a child goes into timeout, he/she should not be allowed to take along reading materials, objects to play with, or assignments to work on.

Finally, it has been the author's experience that children tend to be ignored by teachers for relatively long periods of time after emerging from timeout. Thus, the child's appropriate behavior following timeout may be ignored and could eventually extinguish. It is important, therefore, that the child's behavior be observed closely following timeout and that an instance of appropriate behavior be selected and reinforced, if possible, within ten to fifteen minutes after the timeout period is over.

4. Issues to Consider in Using Timeout. Timeout is an effective technique for controlling deviant or inappropriate child behavior. However, it is a technique that can be easily abused if it is applied incorrectly.

In recent years, several cases have come to attention where timeout has been used incorrectly. For example, in one instance, an old wooden crate was stood on end, bars were installed and a padlock used to lock children inside. The parents involved were not informed that timeout procedures were being used to control their children's behavior.

This example raises a number of issues that should be considered in using timeout. For instance, parents should be informed in advance if timeout is to be used on their children, and the rationale for and correct application of timeout should be discussed with parents as part of this process.

It is not necessary to lock children in enclosed areas in order for timeout to be effective. In fact, within school settings, there is *no* reason for locking children within any area. Timeout simply removes a child from an ongoing activity for a brief period of time. As mentioned earlier, timeout can be used effectively within the classroom by simply blocking off a small area with a portable screen. If the child becomes disruptive while in timeout, she/he can be removed to another area for a time, such as the office or health room.

Finally, the length of time a child spends in timeout should be carefully considered. White, Nielsen, and Johnson (1972) carried out a study on timeout duration in a residential setting for retardates. They compared the effectiveness of one, fifteen, and thirty minutes of timeout in suppressing such behaviors as aggression, self-destruction, and tantrums. Overall, they found timeout to be effective for controlling deviant behavior. However, there were some subjects who were relatively unaffected by the timeout procedure. Each of the timeout durations was effective in controlling deviant behavior. However, the sequence in which the one-minute duration was presented affected its power. When it preceded the use of longer timeout durations, the one-minute duration was most effective. When it came later in the sequence, it was less effective, as would be expected. There was no difference in effectiveness between the fifteen- and thirty-minute timeout durations.

Most classroom applications of timeout use five- to fifteen-minute timeout durations. It would be possible to program longer durations for relatively more serious or disruptive behaviors. However, there have been few studies in which this has been done. More typically, a class of disruptive or inappropriate behaviors are defined (e.g., teacher defiance, swearing, fighting, disturbing others, and so forth) and a standard timeout duration of five to fifteen minutes is applied to them. As a general rule, a standard timeout of five to fifteen minutes is recommended unless special circumstances indicate otherwise.

5. Advantages and Disadvantages of Timeout. There is no question that timeout can be effective in controlling inappropriate/deviant child behavior. However, in the author's opinion, it should be used only as a last resort in changing child behavior. There are several reasons for this. First, timeout removes the child from classroom activities and deprives him/her of the opportunity to engage in appropriate or productive behavior while in timeout. Second, timeout is an easily abused technique and its use must be supervised and monitored very carefully. Third, when timeout is applied to nondisruptive relatively innocuous classroom behaviors, it represents a form of overkill. Finally, other methods such as response cost are equally as effective as timeout, but are easier to manage and less subject to abuse.

Response Cost

1. Defined. Response cost refers to the removal of previously awarded or earned reinforcers for the purpose of reducing behavior that is considered deviant or inappropriate. Research evidence suggests that response cost can prevent as well as suppress the behavior(s) to which it is applied (Kazdin, 1972).

In the application of response cost, reinforcers are removed whenever instances of undesirable behavior(s) occur. Consequently, a "cost" is incurred each time the target child or adult produces an undesirable behavioral response(s).

2. Illustrative Examples. There are numerous examples of response cost in everyday life. Parking tickets and fines for traffic violations are two very good examples of response cost. In addition to providing city traffic departments with needed revenues, such fines discourage traffic and parking violations. Football games represent another area in which response cost is used to discourage undesirable behavior. Yardage fines are assessed against the offending team for such infractions as clipping, unnecessary roughness, offsides, and interference. These penalties are highly effective in controlling behavioral excesses in football games.

In recent years, response cost has been used in a variety of settings (laboratory, institutional, clinic, and school) to control undesirable behavior of a deviant or inappropriate nature (Kazdin, 1972). It has proven highly effective in suppressing the behavioral responses to which it has been applied.

There are two forms of response cost (Weiner, 1962, 1963). In one, points or tokens are awarded at the beginning of the session and the subject can only lose points, for engaging in the inappropriate/deviant behavior, during the session. In the second, the subject can earn points or tokens for appropriate behavior during the session and can also lose the earned reinforcers for inappropriate behavior. Although there is some suggestive evidence that a combination of positive reinforcement and response cost is more effective than response cost alone (Phillips, Phillips, Fixsen, & Wolf, 1971), a recent study by Hundert (1976) found no difference in effectiveness between positive reinforcement procedures, response cost, and a combination of positive reinforcement and response cost upon the attending rates and academic performance of a group of special class children. At this stage, it seems fair to conclude that no clear evidence exists as to whether response cost alone is either more or less effective than a combination of positive reinforcement and response cost.

Response cost, either alone or in combination with positive reinforcement procedures, has been applied to a large variety of behaviors in applied settings. These include *violence and loud noise* (Winkler, 1970), *deviant classroom behavior* (Walker, Hops, & Fiegenbaum, 1976), *rule violations* (Upper, 1971), *aggressive verbal behavior* (Phillips, 1968), *out of seat behavior* (Wolf, Hanley, Lachowicz, & Giles, 1970), *an obscene gesture* (Sulzbacher & Houser, 1968), *nonattending and academic errors* (Hundert, 1976), *cigarette smoking* (Elliot & Tighe, 1968), and *speech disfluencies* (Siegel, Lenske, & Broen, 1969). The utility and effectiveness of response cost have been amply demonstrated in the studies reported above and in others reported in the professional literature.

The author has used response cost extensively in the process of modifying the behavior of disturbed children in both special and regular classroom settings. Walker, Hops, and Fiegenbaum (1976) applied a combination of teacher praise, points (exchangeable for backup reinforcers), and response cost to the classroom behavior of five acting-out children. The combination of praise, points, and response cost was extremely effective in changing their behavior to within normal limits (Walker & Hops, 1976). Moreover, this combination was substantially more effective than praise alone or the combination of praise and points.

In the above study, the children were required to earn points for appropriate behavior which were then subtracted whenever instances of inappropriate behavior occurred. In a subsequent study, Walker, Street, Garrett, and Crossen (1977) used a response cost point system to control the aggressive and socially negative behavior of a primary-grade boy in playground settings. In pretreatment observations, approximately 30 to 40 percent of his social interactions with peers were of an aggressive or negative nature. At the start of each playground period, he was given one point for each minute of time in the period, e.g., 15 points for a 15-minute recess. His goal was to keep the points.

Five points were subtracted for each instance of aggressive or negative social behavior and two points were subtracted for playground rule violations. If all points were lost, the remainder of the recess period was forfeited. The child could exchange the number of points remaining at the end of the playground period(s) for special privileges at home. In addition, if no episodes of aggressive/negative social behavior occurred in the playground periods, he could earn a special group activity for himself and his classmates at the end of the school day.

This treatment procedure was effective in almost totally eliminating aggressive/negative behavior from the child's repertoire on the playground. Further, there was clear evidence of generalization of the child's improved behavior to playground periods in which the treatment program was not in effect.

3. Guidelines for Correct Application. If applied correctly, response cost can be an extremely effective therapeutic technique. However, to take maximum advantage of its considerable therapeutic benefits, particular attention must be paid to how response cost is implemented.

For example, response cost and how it operates should be carefully explained in advance before it is applied to the behavior of children. Each specific behavioral or academic response to which response cost will be applied should be identified, explained, and if necessary role-played for the child or children involved. Further, the number of points, tokens, or units to be lost for each type of behavioral response should also be communicated in advance. Walker, Hops, and Fiegenbaum (1976) ranked inappropriate classroom behaviors according to their relative seriousness as percieved by two experimental classroom teachers and assigned higher point loss values to the more serious behaviors, e.g., foul language cost four points while talking-out cost two points.

It is extremely important that a delivery/feedback system be developed that tells the child: (1) when response cost has been applied, (2) which behavior it has been applied to, and (3) how many points have been lost as a result. Unless this information is communicated effectively, response cost will not have a chance to impact on behavior. There are a variety of ways to construct an effective delivery/feedback system for response cost. The author developed one that worked quite well for individual children within an experimental classroom. It was based on a card system and is illustrated in Figure 4.1.

One card was used per child per week. The card was approximately 4 × 6 inches and was taped to the corner of the child's desk.

Behaviors	*Point Values*	*Days*				
		M	*T*	*W*	*Th*	*F*
Out of Seat	2	• •				
Talk Outs	2	•	• •			
Nonattending	1	• • •	•			
Noncompliance	3		•			
Disturbing Others	2	•				
Foul Language	4		•			
Fighting	5					

FIGURE 4.1. *Response Cost Delivery/Feedback System*

The behaviors listed on the card were described and explained to the children as was the operation of the card system. During the week, whenever a given child engaged in one of the inappropriate behaviors, the teacher simply walked over to the child's desk and, using a specially colored pen, placed a dot in the box corresponding to the day of the week and the inappropriate behavior to which cost was applied. As a rule, no verbal interaction occurred between the teacher and child during this transaction. However, the child was immediately informed of the inappropriate behavior to which cost was applied, as well as the number of points lost.

In the sample card above, the child lost 11 points on Monday and 12 points on Tuesday. On Monday, cost was applied once each to *talk outs* and *disturbing others*, three times to *nonattending*, and twice to *out of seat*. On Tuesday, it was applied once to *nonattending*, *noncompliance*, and *foul language*, and twice to *talk outs*. As is obvious, the card provides a permanent record of the application of response cost for individual children.

The author used a second point card to deliver points for appropriate academic and social behavior (Walker & Buckley, 1974). However, opposite sides of the same 4 × 6 inch card could be used to implement positive reinforcement and response cost procedures.

A third factor that greatly affects the impact of response cost on behavior is the ratio of points earned or awarded to points lost. This ratio affects the degree to which cost functions as a punishing stimulus. For example, if a child has a total of three points and loses one of them, the magnitude of cost is substantial; however, if he has twenty-four points accumulated and loses one, the magnitude of cost is much less substantial and may not be as effective in suppressing the undesirable behavior. Kazdin (1972) reports studies using response cost where the fines ranged from 10 to 10,000 tokens in a system where each child could earn 1,000 points per day versus fines ranging from 3 to 15 tokens for each violation where 65 tokens could be earned each day. Walker, Hops, and Fiegenbaum used a system where point losses ranged from one to five points per violation and thirty-five points could be earned per day. There are no standard rules for determining the ratio of fines per behavior to the total number of points available each day; however, if the child is going to produce the behavior, he/she should learn that it will be costly in terms of points lost. A related issue concerns the relationship of cost magnitude to the severity of deviant behavior. As a rule, the more severe or deviant the behavior, the more it should cost in points, tokens, or units lost. The greater magnitude of cost applied to these behaviors should reduce the probability of their occurrence relative to less serious or severe inappropriate behaviors.

Probably the most important rule to remember in implementing response cost is that *the child's point total should never be taken below zero.* If the child is allowed to go in the hole, effective control of his/her behavior via response cost will likely be lost. This is especially true of a response cost only procedure where the child does not have an opportunity to earn additional points. Even in a point earning/point loss system, the effectiveness of response cost will be greatly reduced if a child realizes that she/he must earn "x" amount of points just to get back to zero. If a child should lose all accumulated or awarded points, some other consequence such as timeout should be used to consequate further instances of inappropriate behavior until additional points have been earned or the period is over.

Consistency in the application of response cost is also extremely important to its overall effectiveness. Cost should be applied *every time* an identified deviant behavior occurs. If the application of cost is inconsistent, the child may not form a clear discrimination between appropriate and inappropriate behavior and may be inclined to risk engaging in deviant behavior on the presumption that response cost might not be applied.

Verbal interaction in the delivery of response cost should be held to an absolute minimum, particularly since the delivery system tells the child which behavior precipitated the application of cost. Sometimes children are inclined to argue or protest the application of cost in a given instance. Under no circumstances should the teacher argue with the child over the justifiability of cost in a given instance, nor should the teacher ever be talked out of cost or intimidated into not using it in a given situation because of tantrum behavior on the part of the child. If this happened, the child would learn to engage in deviant/disruptive behavior in order to prevent the application of response cost when it was warranted.

Response cost is one of the most powerful and effective techniques available for controlling inappropriate behavior in classroom and playground settings. However, it is very important that the implementation guidelines described above be followed carefully in the application of response cost so that its full potential will be realized.

4. Issues to Consider in Using Response Cost. Like timeout, response cost is considered to be a mild form of punishment. The question arises as to whether undesirable side effects associated with punishment (e.g., avoidance, escape, emotional effects) are also side effects of the use of response cost. In his review of the use of response cost in applied settings, Kazdin (1972) suggests that the available studies on escape/avoidance in connection with the use of response cost indicate that response cost tends not to elicit these behaviors. As to emotional effects, he concludes that the available evidence is too limited to draw a conclusion.

In the author's use of the technique, he has never observed attempted avoidance or escape from the therapeutic situation as a consequence of the application of response cost. Even when response cost is used to control aggressive social behavior in playground situations, it does not reduce the frequency with which the target child interacts with other children, e.g., even though the child will lose points for episodes of aggressive/negative social behavior, he/she still continues to interact socially.

However, unless response cost is carefully explained and set up and implemented according to the guidelines described earlier, its application can elicit emotional behavior. In the author's experience, response cost has very rarely, if ever, generated emotional responses from children when applied correctly.

5. Advantages and Disadvantages of Response Cost. The advantages of response cost are obvious from the foregoing discussion. It is also a highly cost-effective technique, given the minimal amount of effort required in its implementation. It has an added advantage over timeout in that the child does not have to be removed from ongoing classroom or playground activities in order to experience consequation for inappropriate behavior.

The disadvantages of response cost appear to be minimal. The possibility of emotional side effects was described earlier. Given what is currently known about response cost, its advantages appear to far outweigh its disadvantages.

COMBINATIONS OF TREATMENT VARIABLES

Various combinations of the treatment variables described earlier are presented below along with a discussion of (1) the situations appropriate for their use, (2) relevant implementation details, and (3) their probable effects. It should be noted that any of the described treatment techniques can be applied singly and with effectiveness to achieve specific therapeutic or educational goals in situations where their application is appropriate. However, the combined use of some of these techniques can produce extremely powerful treatment effects that are far more effective than those that could be achieved with any single technique.

Drabman and Lahey (1974) have argued persuasively that school psychology personnel are probably often guilty of using more powerful techniques to change child behavior than are required. The more powerful the technique(s) involved, the more costly and more time consuming they are likely to be. They suggest that therapists and intervention specialists should first attempt to change behavior without major environmental manipulations, and that more radical techniques be implemented only when their application is clearly called for.

The position of Drabman and Lahey is probably applicable to the treatment of many children who are experiencing behavioral and academic problems in school. However, it is no doubt much less applicable to acting-out children whose repertoires of deviant behavior are strongly developed and have been acquired over a number of years. Such children almost invariably require massive intervention procedures and major environmental manipulations over a fairly extensive period of time in order for their behavior to be permanently changed. It is unlikely that simple treatment techniques or environmental changes would significantly alter the behavior of acting-out children.

This is not to suggest that stimulus change procedures, rules and instructions, and behavioral feedback should not be used with acting-out children. While important to the overall change process, these procedures by themselves are unlikely to change appreciably the behavior of most acting-out children.

Therefore, it is recommended that for most acting-out children, unless circumstances clearly indicate otherwise, a powerful treatment program be implemented as a first step in changing their overall behavior pattern. As the child's behavior changes and gradually comes under control of the treatment procedures, components of treatment can be gradually removed as the child's behavior warrants it.

The most powerful treatment available for changing the behavior of acting-out children in school settings consists of a combination of positive reinforcement procedures and mild punishment (Bostow & Bailey, 1969; Holz, Azrin, & Ayllon, 1963; Patterson & Gullion, 1968; Walker, Hops, & Fiegenbaum, 1976). Several combinations of positive reinforcement and mild punishment procedures are available. These are (1) teacher praise for appropriate behavior and brief timeout for inappropriate behavior, (2) teacher praise and token reinforcement for appropriate behavior and timeout for inappropriate behavior, (3) teacher praise for appropriate behavior and response cost for inappropriate behavior, and (4) teacher praise and positive reinforcement for appropriate behavior and response cost for inappropriate behavior. In the author's opinion, these four treatment combinations are ranked from least to most powerful. Although direct comparisons of the effectiveness of these four treatment combinations have not been carried out, the author's own research experience (Walker & Buckley, 1974; Walker, Hops, Greenwood, Todd, & Garrett, 1977) plus studies reported in the literature on these treatment variables, provide suggestive evidence that this may be the case.

The choice as to which of these treatments to apply to a given acting-out child's behavior depends upon the severity of the behavior problem(s) involved and the teacher's preference as well as willingness to implement the procedures involved. Given that the teacher is willing to implement any one of the three combinations for a given child, the severity of the child's repertoire of inappropriate behavior and its relative intractability should determine which combination is to be selected.

If an acting-out child spends more than fifty percent of the time engaged in inappropriate behavior, a combination of teacher praise, positive reinforcement (token or point system), and either response cost or timeout should be implemented in the form of a comprehensive treatment program. Unless there are special reasons for using timeout as the primary technique for consequating inappropriate behavior, the author recommends response cost because of its equal power and greater ease of implementation. However, timeout should be used as a backup to response cost whenever the child has zero points.

If an acting-out child spends less than fifty percent of the time in inappropriate behavior, the behavior problems involved are not overly severe and the child's behavioral repertoire appears reasonably tractable, a combination of teacher praise for appropriate behavior and timeout for deviant behavior should be implemented. This treatment combination is relatively easier to implement but it is also less powerful.

Before implementing any combination of treatment techniques, it is essential that careful attention be given to antecedent events that might be maintaining the child's inappropriate behavior. For example, the teacher should insure that academic programming for the child is at an appropriate level and that his/her inappropriate behavior is not limited to certain academic or social situations during the day. If it is, it may be possible to isolate a causal event or factor that is common to those situations. One should also be sure that the child can clearly discriminate between appropriate and inappropriate classroom and/or playground behavior. It is possible, but not likely, that the acting-out child is behaving inappropriately because she/he is not aware of the rules governing appropriate behavior. After these steps have been taken, a comprehensive treatment program should be implemented to change the child's behavior.

Teacher Praise and Timeout

The treatment combination of teacher praise and timeout can be implemented in approximately the same fashion for acting-out children in either regular or special classroom settings. The first step in implementing this treatment procedure is to decide which inappropriate behaviors to simply ignore and which to consequate with timeout.

If a given behavior is minimally disruptive of academic performance, if classroom atmosphere is not seriously disrupted and there is a possibility that it is maintained primarily by teacher attention, ignoring would be an appropriate consequence. On the other hand, if the behavior is serious, is disruptive of classroom atmosphere and achievement, and its consequences cannot be tolerated, timeout should be applied. Once this decision has been made, the child should be informed as to which behaviors will result in timeout *before* the program is implemented.

After this has been accomplished, a systematic treatment program should be implemented on a daily basis where the child's appropriate behavior is carefully and frequently praised, minimally disruptive attention getting behaviors are ignored, and more serious disruptive behaviors are consequated with timeout.

In a treatment program of this type, the teacher's management of his/her attention to the acting-out child is extremely important. The purpose of treatment is to teach the child that inappropriate behavior will result in either no response (ignoring) or a mildly unpleasant consequence (timeout), while appropriate behavior will result in a pleasant consequence (positive teacher attention and approval). Achieving this goal is much easier said than done. It is not easy for a teacher to, in a sense, turn her/his attention around in relation to the acting-out child's behavior, particularly if prior interactions between teacher and child have been of a hostile, aversive nature.

The teacher must learn to observe the child's behavior very carefully and to withhold and deliver attention as the child's behavior warrants it. At first glance, this may seem incompatible with teaching; however, numerous studies of teacher attention in modifying child behavior indicate this is not so (Hanley, 1970). In fact, the overall amount of teacher attention given the child may not change appreciably in this process. The difference is that teacher attention becomes differential and is much more responsive to the quality (appropriate or inappropriate) of the child's behavior.

It is obvious that a teacher cannot observe an acting-out child's behavior continuously and still teach effectively. Therefore, some compromise has to be developed that will provide for effective teaching *and* careful monitoring of the acting-out child's behavior. A good rule to remember in this regard is that you should try to "*catch the child being good!*" and deliver your positive attention to her/his appropriate behavior as is feasible. Rather than focusing upon the acting-out child's inappropriate behavior, the teacher should try to find an episode of appropriate behavior, or at least an approximation of it, during each interval in which the child's behavior is evaluated. This may be difficult to implement at first, but focusing upon the child's appropriate behavior and praising it as often as possible is extremely important in teaching a new pattern of behavior.

The author (Hops, Walker, & Fiegenbaum, 1976) and other researchers as well have found that regular classroom teachers can observe, evaluate, and either praise or ignore a child's behavior at least once every five minutes while carrying on normal teaching duties. When implementing the treatment program being described here, it is essential that the teacher observe, evaluate, and consequate the acting-out child's behavior at least once every five minutes during the first part of the treatment program. After the child's behavior has been changed effectively, has stabilized, and the child has adjusted to the treatment program and the new behavior pattern, the frequency of observing, evaluating, and consequating can be reduced to once each ten-minute period. By building upon increments of five minutes, this interval can be gradually extended until the acting-out child is receiving a normal amount of teacher attention; that is, approximately the same amount as received by his/her peers.

Before implementing this treatment program, you should review the sections on the correct application of praising and timeout procedures described earlier in this chapter. It is also helpful to monitor the frequency of your praising and to record each instance of timeout. Recording praise will tell you how well you are doing in achieving the frequency goals you have established for praising the child's behavior. A record of timeouts, including the behaviors to which timeout is applied, will give you an indication of how well the overall treatment program is working. Wasik, Senn, Welch, and Cooper (1968), for example, found that the frequency with which timeout had to be used to control the disruptive classroom behavior of two primary-grade children decreased significantly over time.

There are several ways to record your praise. Perhaps the most efficient method is to divide the school day into continuous five- or ten-minute intervals and then to make sure that at least one praise is delivered per interval. A form similar to the one in Figure 4.2 can be used for this purpose.

As each praise is delivered, a notation is made in the appropriate interval. The form can be kept on a clipboard for use when the teacher is away from his/her desk.

	M	*T*	*W*	*Th*	*F*
8:30– 8:40					
8:40– 8:50					
8:50– 9:00					
9:00– 9:10					
9:10– 9:20					
9:20– 9:30					
9:30– 9:40					
9:40– 9:50					
9:50–10:00					
10:00–10:10					
10:10–10:20					
10:20–10:30					
10:30–10:40					
10:40–10:50					
10:50–11:00					
11:00–11:10					
11:10–11:20					

FIGURE 4.2. *Recording Teacher Praise*

A less precise method makes use of a golf counter worn on the wrist. Most counters will go up to at least ninety-nine and can be readily used for counting praises each time they are delivered. Their disadvantage is that they do not provide for delivery of praise within equally measured units of time.

A third method uses a 3 × 5 index card taped to the child's desk. Each time a praise is delivered, a notation is made on the card. An additional limitation of this method is that it is unsuitable for free play or playground periods when the child is not at her/his desk.

The form below was used by the author to record timeout episodes within an experimental classroom.

Timeout Record

Date	*Precipitating Behavior*	*Duration*	*Child*
1/19/76	Hitting	10 min.	Jeff
1/23/76	Noncompliance	5 min.	Jim
1/24/76	Fighting	10 min.	Fred & Jim
1/28/76	Foul Language	10 min.	Elliot

The form provides a daily record of timeout and allows the teacher to track the behaviors that timeout is being used to suppress. The entries in the above form are a typical example of the behaviors to which timeout is usually applied.

Wasik, Senn, Welch, and Cooper (1968) used a combination of differential positive reinforcement, dispensed by teachers, and timeout to control the disruptive behavior of two seven-year-old children in a demonstration school setting. The teachers were carefully trained by the authors to use reinforcement procedures correctly. The praise procedures were applied to both social and academic classroom behaviors. Teacher attention was carefully withheld from inappropriate child behavior. Timeout was used to control three classes of behavior. These were aggressive, resistive, and disruptive classroom behaviors.

Figure 4.3 below shows the effect of the treatment program upon one of the children's classroom behavior.

Inspection of Figure 4.3 shows that the treatment program had a positive impact upon all three types of behavior. Desirable, appropriate behavior increased from a level of approximately 50 percent in baseline to approximately 85 percent during treatment. Both inappropriate and unacceptable behaviors showed clear decreases from baseline to treatment phases.

When the treatment program was terminated, there was some recovery in the level of inappropriate behavior. Reinstitution of the program quickly produced treatment effects equal to those in the first treatment phase.

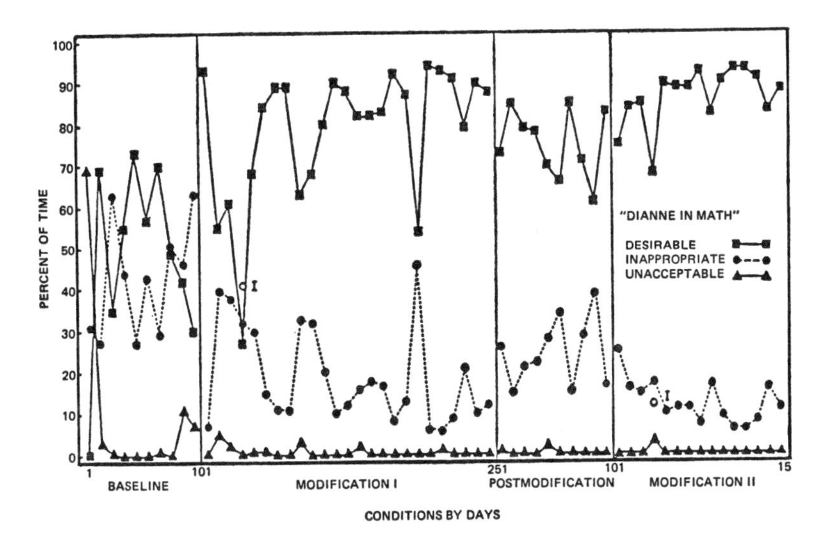

FIGURE 4.3. *Desirable, Inappropriate, and Unacceptable Behavior for Dianne in Math Period across Baseline and Treatment Phases*

Figure 4.4 shows Diane's performance in reading. Initially, her behavior was much more variable than in math. Interestingly, her rate of unacceptable behavior was much higher in math, her rate of inappropriate behavior much lower, and her desirable behavior much higher.

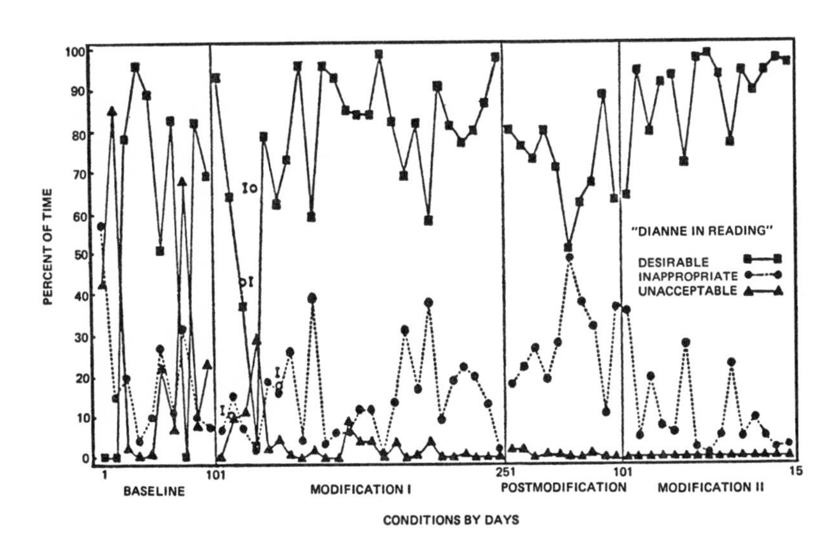

FIGURE 4.4. *Desirable, Inappropriate, and Unacceptable Behavior for Dianne in Reading across Baseline and Treatment Phases*

Overall, the treatment program had a relatively powerful impact upon desirable and unacceptable behavior, but essentially no effect upon her inappropriate behavior rate.

The treatment program implemented by the authors would have to be judged a success. However, it is possible that stronger and more powerful treatment effects would have been achieved had a token reinforcement system been established along with the praise and timeout procedures. The effectiveness with which timeout suppressed the child's unacceptable behavior was quite impressive.

Further, once suppressed, these behaviors tended to stay suppressed even during the post modification phase. Results of this study are highly encouraging and demonstrate that a combination of teacher praise and timeout can be effective in modifying certain types of classroom behavior.

Teacher Praise, Token Reinforcement, and Timeout

The addition of positive token reinforcement to the teacher praise and timeout procedures used in the Wasik, Senn, Welch, and Cooper (1968) study would, in the author's opinion, have created a more powerful intervention program. A powerful treatment combination such as this would be appropriate for deviant, disruptive children who engage in inappropriate behavior more than fifty percent of the time.

The type of token reinforcement system selected should be determined in part by the setting in which the treatment program is to be implemented. If the system is being implemented in, for example, a special classroom for behavior disorders with an enrollment of six to twelve pupils, then an individual reinforcement system can be established for each child. In a system of this type, a certain number of points (and teacher praise) can be earned each day for appropriate social and academic behavior. The number of points each child earns depends upon the teacher's judgment of her/his performance.

In a special class setting, it is also possible to set up overlapping group contingencies that operate in tandem with the individual system. For example, one of the problems behavior disordered children in general and acting-out children in particular have is in group instructional situations. Such children often encounter difficulties in meeting the behavioral requirements of group situations which usually include

(a) paying attention, (b) listening carefully, (c) following instructions, and (d) responding when called upon. It would be possible to set up group situations during the school day and have the children earn group points toward a group activity for meeting the behavioral requirements of the situation. *All* children would have to meet the behavioral requirements simultaneously in order to earn the group points.

Walker, Mattson, and Buckley (1971) used a group reinforcement procedure to teach appropriate group behavior to six behavior problem children enrolled in a special class setting. The group system operated in addition to an individual system for each of the six children. For thirty minutes each day, the children were required to listen to a teacher led activity and to answer questions on the material presented. For each five-minute period in which all children were engaged in appropriate group behavior, the group as a whole was awarded one point. If one or more of the six children did not follow the rules during the five minute period, the point for that interval was not awarded. When the group had earned thirty points (six were available each day) they could be exchanged for a preferred group activity such as a field trip, class party, or special film. This procedure proved highly effective in teaching and maintaining the children's appropriate group behavior. It should be mentioned that the children's individual reinforcement systems did not operate during the daily thirty-minute periods in which the group contingency was in effect.

If a combination of teacher praise, token reinforcement, and timeout is applied to the behavior of an acting-out child in a *regular* classroom setting, it is strongly recommended that a dual group and individual contingency be implemented. In past classroom applications, the author has found a group contingency at school and an individual contingency implemented at home to be a highly effective combination (Hops, Walker, & Fleischman, 1976; Walker, Street, Garrett, & Crossen, 1977). For example, a contingency is established wherein the acting-out child has an opportunity to earn a daily group activity reward for him/herself and classmates if the reward criterion is achieved at school (e.g., her/his classroom behavior was judged to be appropriate in eighty percent or more of the intervals in which it was evaluated). Group activities include such things as extra recess time, special educational cartoons, and classroom games such as Seven-up, Simon Says, and Flying Dutchman. When the group reward is earned at school, the acting-out child earns a special individual reward at home, accompanied by parental praise for the appropriate school behavior (Hops, Walker, & Fleischman, 1976).

Another variation of this combined group and individual contingency was implemented by Walker, Street, Garrett, and Crossen (1977). In their studies, acting-out and socially aggressive children could earn a group activity reward for themselves and classmates at school for suppressing their negative rule-breaking behavior and for retaining a minimum proportion of the total number of points available each day, e.g., eighty percent or greater. The children could take home the number of points retained and earned each day in school and exchange them for a variety of options preselected by the child and her/his parents. Options included such things as extra TV time, movies, snacks, special food treats prepared at home, trips to the park, bowling, and so forth.

Both of these variations proved to be highly effective in motivating and teaching children to behave differently. Further, it was observed that some children tended to respond primarily to the individual reward at home, others primarily to the group reward at school, and still others to both systems equally. Consequently, providing a combination of school and home rewards probably increases the effectiveness of most positive reinforcement systems and increases the likelihood that they will have an impact on the behavior of most children.

Providing combined group rewards at school and individual rewards at home has a number of other potential advantages that make them worthy of careful consideration. For example, teachers are usually concerned about the issue of fairness when one child is singled out and treated in a special or unique way because of behavior and/or academic problems. When a given child is allowed to earn rewards for behaving in approximately the same way as are normal children in the class, teachers are concerned (and justifiably so) that other children might learn to act out or disrupt the class in order to gain access to the reward system. There is no clear evidence at present that this occurs, but such an outcome seems well within the realm of possibility.

A contingency wherein the child earns a group activity reward that is shared equally with classmates has a number of features that reduces the probability of this situation occurring. For example, peers do not see the target child as one who is being treated in a special way, but rather, as an individual whose appropriate behavior can earn special privileges for the entire class. It has been the author's experience that the classmates of target children in such situations are highly motivated for him/her to achieve the reward criterion. Instead of providing attention and support for the child's inappropriate behavior, classmates usually encourage and attempt to facilitate the target child's attempts at appropriate classroom behavior under such contingency arrangements since it is in their interest to do so. Although it has not been documented as yet, this type of contingency may also have an impact upon the appropriate behavioral level of the entire class (Walker, Hops, & Greenwood, 1977).

It *is* possible to set up group contingencies designed to have an impact upon the behavior of all children in a regular classroom setting (Packard, 1970; Greenwood, Hops, Delquadri, & Guild, 1974). However, it is comparatively more difficult to implement them in regular classrooms than in special classroom settings because of the much larger number of children involved. Yet such contingencies can be highly effective in regular classrooms if implemented correctly and monitored carefully. It should be noted though that group contingencies of this type are usually not powerful enough to control the behavior of acting-out children effectively. If teachers wish to implement group contingencies and there is an acting-out child or children in the classroom, it is recommended that a treatment program be applied to the target child's behavior beforehand, followed by implementation of the group contingency. If this is not done, the acting-out child may seriously reduce the potential effectiveness of a group contingency applied to the behavior of the entire class.

Walker, Mattson, and Buckley (1971) implemented a treatment combination consisting of teacher praise, positive token reinforcement, and timeout for six disruptive children enrolled in a special class setting. Table 4.3 provides an overview of the treatment program implemented for the children in the special class.

The six children were enrolled in grades four, five, and six. They were able to earn individual points on a daily basis for appropriate social and academic behavior. Points were exchangeable for a variety of backup rewards ranging from inexpensive school supplies (pencils, paper, erasers) to the purchasing of free time to build model airplanes which were also purchased with earned points. Group rewards, available on a weekly basis, could be earned for engaging in appropriate group behavior at certain times during the day.

Three types of consequences were applied to the children's inappropriate classroom behavior. These were *ignoring* for such minimally disruptive behaviors as asking for help without raising one's

TABLE 4.3. *Overview of Treatment Program Consisting of Teacher Praise, Positive Token Reinforcement, and Timeout*

I. Consequences of Deviant Behaviors
   A. Immediate removal from ELP building for the following behaviors—(If expelled during a.m. the *S* will stay out for the remainder of the day and return the following morning. If expelled during p.m. will remain home following day.)
      1. Disobedience and/or defying teacher
      2. Fighting
      3. Leaving building without permission
      4. Foul language, lewd gestures
      5. Creating a disturbance during isolation period (time out)
   B. Immediate exclusion from the classroom area for 10 minutes (minimum for the following operants: (*S* decides when he will return to classroom area.)
      1. Talking out of turn
      2. Unauthorized standing or walking
      3. Talking or standing without raising hand and securing permission
      4. Throwing objects
      5. Other, nontolerated operants falling within this class of behaviors

II. Reinforcement
   A. Individual Basis
      1. Social:
         —raising hand
         —not talking
         —remaining in seat
         —beginning work without talking upon entering room
      2. Academic:
         —task-oriented
         —completion of tasks
         —correct answers on assignments
   B. Group Basis
      1. Clock timer will be set at preselected time intervals each day provided all *S*'s are present in the classroom area and are engaged in task-oriented behavior.
      2. A group payoff will be instituted when the group accumulates a preselected number of points.

III. Behaviors to Be Ignored
   —asking for help without raising hand
   —irrelevant questions
   —tapping pencils (unless disturbing class)
   —pouting and crying

hand, asking irrelevant questions, pencil tapping, and pouting and crying. Timeout (ten minutes) was applied to such moderately disruptive behaviors as talking out of turn, out of seat, and throwing objects. A one-half- to one-day suspension from the classroom was applied to more severe child behaviors such as fighting, teacher defiance, leaving the building without permission, and so forth. This overall treatment program proved to be highly effective in modifying the classroom behavior of the six children to whom it was applied.

Figure 4.5 (Parts A and B) provide a record of the effects of the treatment program upon the children's appropriate classroom behavior. Individual graphs of the children's task-oriented behavior during baseline in their respective regular classrooms and during treatment in the special classroom are contained in Figure 4.5. The six children averaged thirty-nine percent of the time spent in appropriate task-oriented behavior when observed in their respective regular classrooms. While assigned to the special classroom, a period of approximately three months, the six children averaged approximately ninety percent of the time spent in appropriate behavior.

Inspection of Figure 4.5 shows that there was a very powerful treatment effect achieved for each of the six children. As a group, the children also made some impressive academic gains while assigned to the special classroom. Figure 4.6 presents pre- and post-test results for the six children on the Wide Range Achievement Test and on the Gray's Oral Reading Test.

All six children showed gains on either one or both of the tests. Thus, the overall impact of this combination of treatment variables upon the children's social and academic behavior was substantial.

This treatment combination can be applied effectively to the behavior of acting-out children enrolled in regular classroom settings. However, it requires some minor adaptations in order to be maximally effective in the regular classroom. For example, it is recommended that the child be allowed to earn a group reward at school and an individual reward at home for all the reasons outlined earlier. This requires parental cooperation and occasional monitoring to insure that parents follow through and actually provide the agreed to rewards at home. If not, the effectiveness of the program may be greatly reduced.

The author has used good day cards, point cards, or tickets to facilitate the delivery of home rewards. Good day cards are used whenever an either/or judgment is made at school as to whether or not the child earned an individual reward to be given at home. A good rule to remember is that if a child's behavior has been eighty percent appropriate at school or better, the child earns a group reward for her/himself at school and an individual reward at home. At the end of the day, a good day card containing a smiling face and signed by the teacher is sent home with the child if she/he met the reward criterion at school. If the criterion is not achieved, then no card is

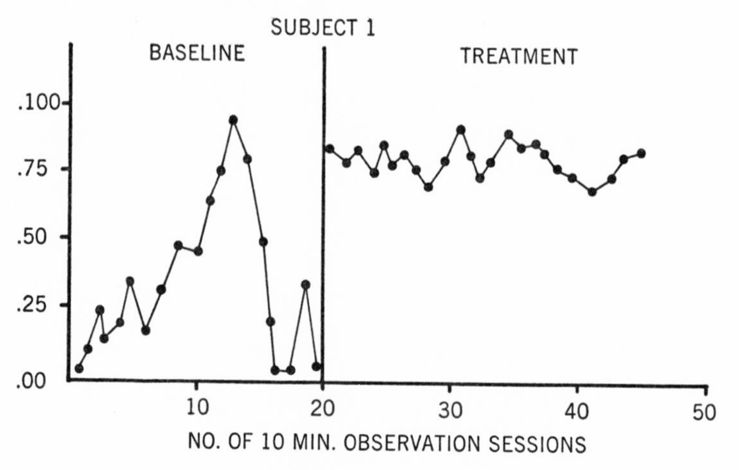
SUBJECT 1
BASELINE
TREATMENT
.100
.75
.50
.25
.00
10
20
30
40
50
NO. OF 10 MIN. OBSERVATION SESSIONS

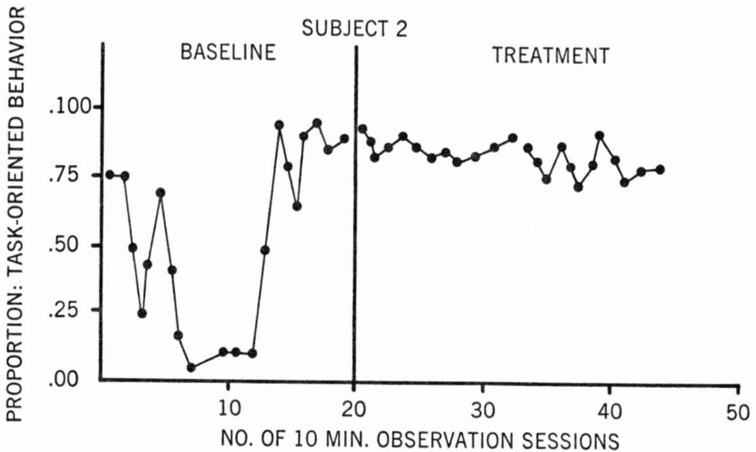
PROPORTION: TASK-ORIENTED BEHAVIOR
SUBJECT 2
BASELINE
TREATMENT
.100
.75
.50
.25
.00
10
20
30
40
50
NO. OF 10 MIN. OBSERVATION SESSIONS

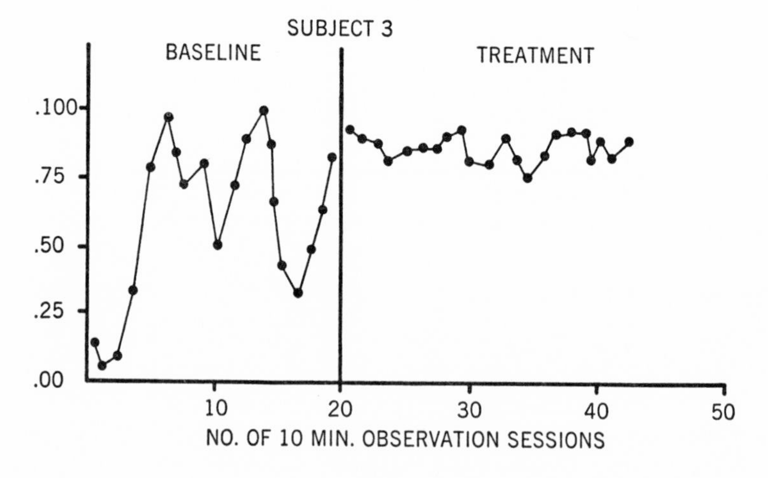
SUBJECT 3
BASELINE
TREATMENT
.100
.75
.50
.25
.00
10
20
30
40
50
NO. OF 10 MIN. OBSERVATION SESSIONS

A.

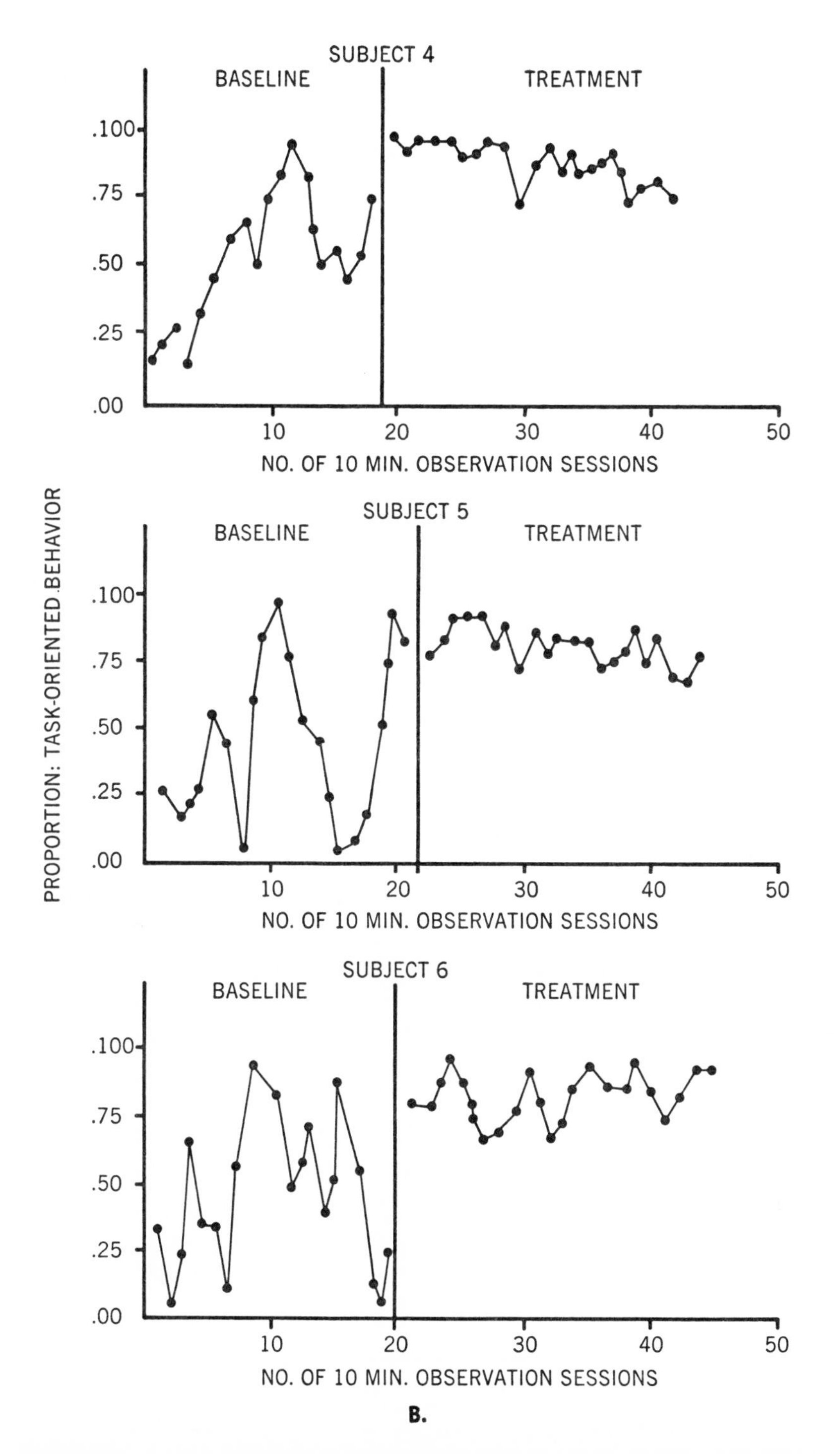

FIGURE 4.5. *Proportions of Task-Oriented Behavior for Deviant Subjects during Baseline and Treatment Conditions*

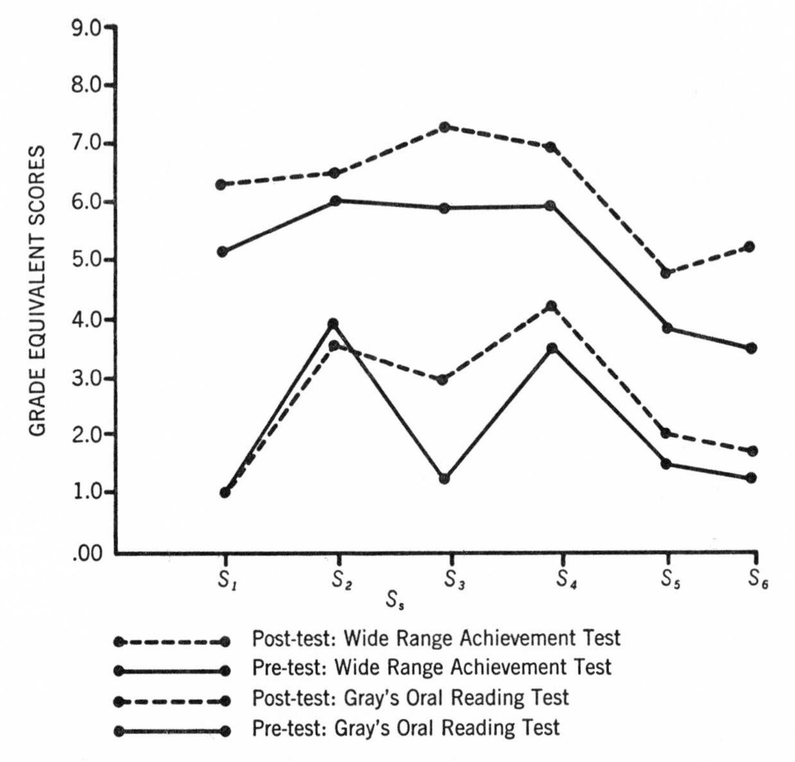

FIGURE 4.6. *Academic Gains during Treatment as Measured by the Wide Range Achievement Test and the Gray's Oral Reading Test*

sent home, and parents withhold home rewards for that day. A sample good day card is provided below.

Sample Good Day Card

Good Day Card

__________ earned a home
privilege for today.
______________ Teacher Signature
______________ Date

Good day cards acquire considerable value for children over time as they signal success at school and are exchangeable for privileges at home.

Point cards have been used by the author in situations where children earn a group reward at school for earning eighty percent or more of the available points at school and then take their earned points home at the end of the day to be counted toward individual rewards. In this situation, a reinforcement menu is worked out between the teacher, child, and parents wherein the child can purchase privileges or tangibles varying from inexpensive to expensive.

Point cards are very simple to make and use. A sample is presented below.

Sample Point Card

Point Card

__________ earned ______
points at school today.
_______________ Teacher Signature
_______________ Date

The author has also used tickets in this situation. Instead of sending points home, the child exchanges his/her points for tickets at school and then exchanges the tickets for home privileges or tangibles. An ordinary roll of theater tickets can be used for this purpose. Any ratio of points to tickets can be used. As a matter of convenience, the author has used a 5 to 1 ratio in past work. As a rule, children respond positively to tickets, see them as valuable, and seem to enjoy earning them.

The use of timeout sometimes creates special problems in regular classroom settings. Most regular schools and classrooms do not have built in timeout rooms so timeout presents something of a logistical problem for the classroom teacher. It is possible to send a child to the office or to an unused room in the school, however there may be problems with both of these alternatives. For example, some children may actually enjoy going to the office, thus making the use of timeout in this situation highly inappropriate. When a child is sent to an unused room, he/she must be properly supervised to insure the child's safety and to comply with the public supervision school laws. Even if a special timeout room were available, problems would arise when more than one child was sent to timeout at the same time.

If timeout is to be used in the regular classroom, it is recommended that a part of the classroom be designated as a timeout area so that children in timeout can be properly supervised and the relative ease with which timeout can be implemented is maximized. The important ingredient in timeout's effectiveness is that the child is temporarily removed from a situation which he/she finds reinforcing. If the activity from which the child is removed is rewarding, timeout is an aversive experience for the child generally and will suppress specific child behaviors to which it is applied.

If the regular classroom is a pleasant and reinforcing place to be, and even temporary removal from it is unpleasant for the child, a simple screen with a desk behind it in a corner of the classroom can serve as the timeout area. A portable blackboard or ordinary screen can be used for this purpose. It is *extremely important* that the child not have visual contact with the rest of the class while in timeout. Visual contact with the class would greatly reduce the effectiveness of timeout in the classroom.

If the child creates a disturbance in timeout or refuses to go into the timeout area, it is important to have a backup alternative. The author has used a one-day suspension from school for this purpose. While suspended, the child cannot earn points or teacher praise and must complete all work missed during the suspension period. This therapeutic use of suspension has proven to be quite effective in past research (Walker & Buckley, 1974; Brown & Shields, 1967).

It is extremely important that teacher praise be systematically paired with the delivery of points in regular classroom applications of this treatment combination. In regular classrooms, it is both likely and desirable that the positive token reinforcement system will be eventually faded out. When this occurs, the child's behavior must be maintained by teacher praise. As noted earlier, teacher praise may not be all that effective initially in changing or maintaining the behavior of acting-out children. By systematically pairing the delivery of praise and points, praise may take on some of the incentive properties and value of points. If so, praise will be more effective in maintaining appropriate child behavior over the long term in the absence of a point system.

As mentioned, the author considers a combination of teacher praise, points, and timeout to be a highly effective treatment combination—one that is sufficiently powerful to modify the behavior of acting-out children who engage in appropriate behavior an average of less than fifty percent of the time. However, its effectiveness depends greatly upon the precision with which it is implemented. In this regard, there are certain guidelines that should be followed to insure effective application. First, in the early stages of the program (at least for the first month) the child's behavior should be evaluated for purposes of reinforcement at least once every ten minutes. If the child's behavior was appropriate, praise and a point should be awarded; if inappropriate, nothing should be awarded. Second, praise should always be awarded first, followed immediately by a point(s). This type of pairing increases the chances that praise will take on some of the incentive value of points. Third, daily group and individual rewards should be made available, if earned, for at least the first month of the program. Fourth, ignoring, timeout, and/or suspension should be applied *every time* an inappropriate behavior occurs that warrants their application. This is an extremely important point to remember. Fifth, after a month has elapsed, an evaluation should be made to determine whether fading of the program can be initiated. If the child's behavior is stable and he/she is responding well, fading can begin. If not, the program should be maintained as is until a reasonable level of stability and responsiveness is achieved. Systematic fading procedures are discussed in Chapter 7.

Teacher Praise, Token Reinforcement and Response Cost

In the author's opinion, this treatment combination is the most powerful and potentially effective system available for changing the behavior of acting-out children. It is also much easier to implement in regular and special classrooms than a combination of teacher praise, points, and timeout. If applied correctly, a combination of teacher praise, points, and response cost (cost contingency) can be extremely effective in modifying the classroom behavior of the most deviant children that can be tolerated in regular classroom settings, including acting-out children.

Walker, Hops, and Fiegenbaum (1976) used this treatment combination with a group of acting-out children in a special classroom setting. The five children were enrolled in grades one, two, or three and were selected because of their high rates of disruptive classroom behavior such as noisy, aggressive, yelling, inappropriate peer interaction, and out of seat.

The children were able to earn points for appropriate social and academic performance which could later be exchanged for a variety of backup rewards ranging from free time to athletic equipment. Each child could earn a maximum of thirty-five points per day delivered via two reinforcement schedules. They could receive points on both a variable interval schedule of reinforcement for appropriate classroom behavior and a fixed ratio schedule for correct academic responses and completion of assignments.

At the end of each day, points could be exchanged for backup rewards. These ranged in value from 25 to 200 points, with occasional special items for 500 points. The point values, which were related to their actual purchase price in cents, were arranged so that sufficient points for the least expensive item could be earned with a very high proportion of appropriate behavior produced within a single day. The children were free to exchange their points for an inexpensive item or accumulate them for a more expensive one. Teacher praise was delivered as described earlier and systematically paired with points.

Response cost was consistently applied to the children's inappropriate classroom behavior. The classroom behaviors of talking back to the teacher, talking out, not attending, out of seat, disturbing others, and playing with objects cost the child one point; teacher defiance cost two points; swearing, three points; and fighting and throwing objects, four points. When a deviant behavior occurred, the teacher placed a mark on a cost contingency record form located on the child's desk. Using this delivery system, the child was immediately aware of the inappropriate behavior to which response cost was applied, as well as the number of points lost. When a child had lost or was about to lose more points than she/he had earned, timeout was used as a backup consequence to control occurrences of inappropriate classroom behavior until additional points could be earned. Efforts were made to insure that the children never "went in the hole" on their individual point systems. Whenever the children's point totals approached zero levels because of their engaging in inappropriate behavior, timeout was used as an alternative consequence. In addition, the teacher discussed with the children in advance the inappropriate classroom behaviors to which response cost would be applied to be sure that they understood the system and how it would operate.

Figure 4.7 contains results of the application of these treatment procedures to the behavior of the acting-out children over a four month period.

Figure 4.7 shows results for all five children combined and for the children individually. A very powerful treatment effect was achieved for all five children. As a group they averaged thirty-eight percent appropriate behavior during pretreatment observations recorded in their respective regular classrooms. In contrast, while exposed

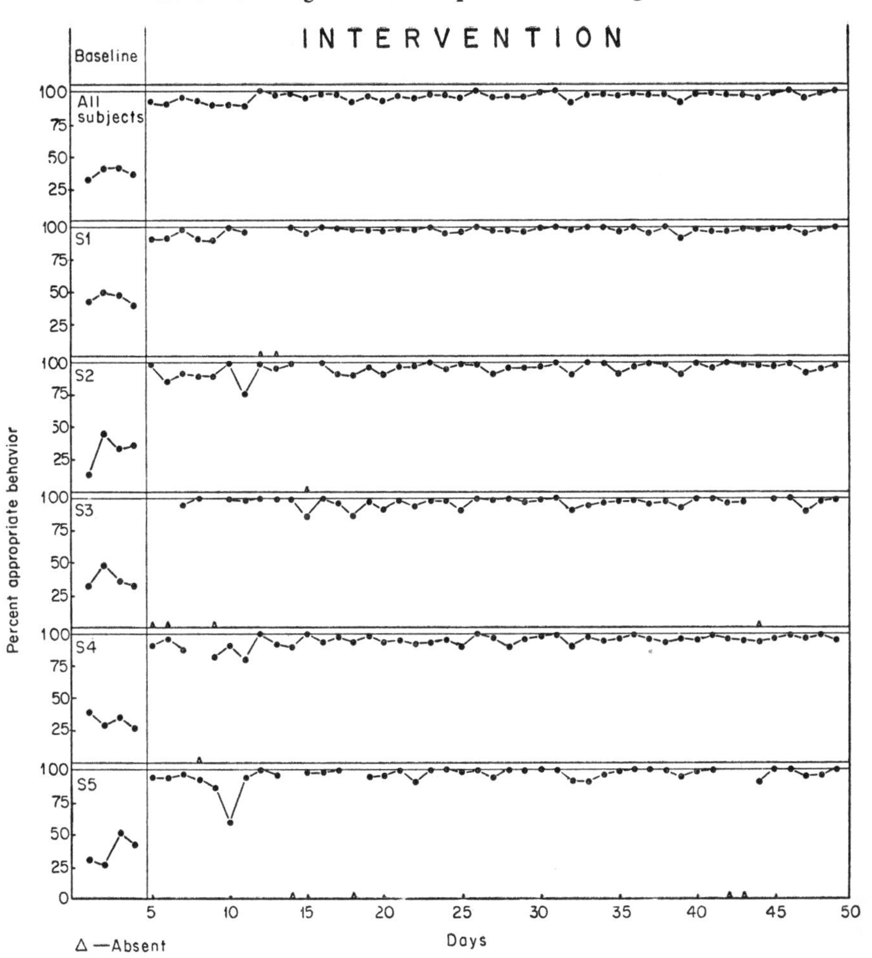

FIGURE 4.7. *Effects of the Application of Teacher Praise, Positive Token Reinforcement, and Response Cost upon the Classroom Behavior of Acting-Out Children*

to the treatment procedures implemented in the special classroom, the children averaged ninety-six percent appropriate behavior.

The effectiveness of this treatment combination was impressive and is at least as powerful as a combination of teacher praise, points, and timeout. It has the added advantage of using response cost instead of timeout for the consequation of inappropriate child behavior. In the author's opinion, response cost is easier for teachers to implement than timeout, it is at least as effective as timeout, and it is more appropriate for use in classrooms since inappropriate child behavior can be consequated without the necessity of classroom removal.

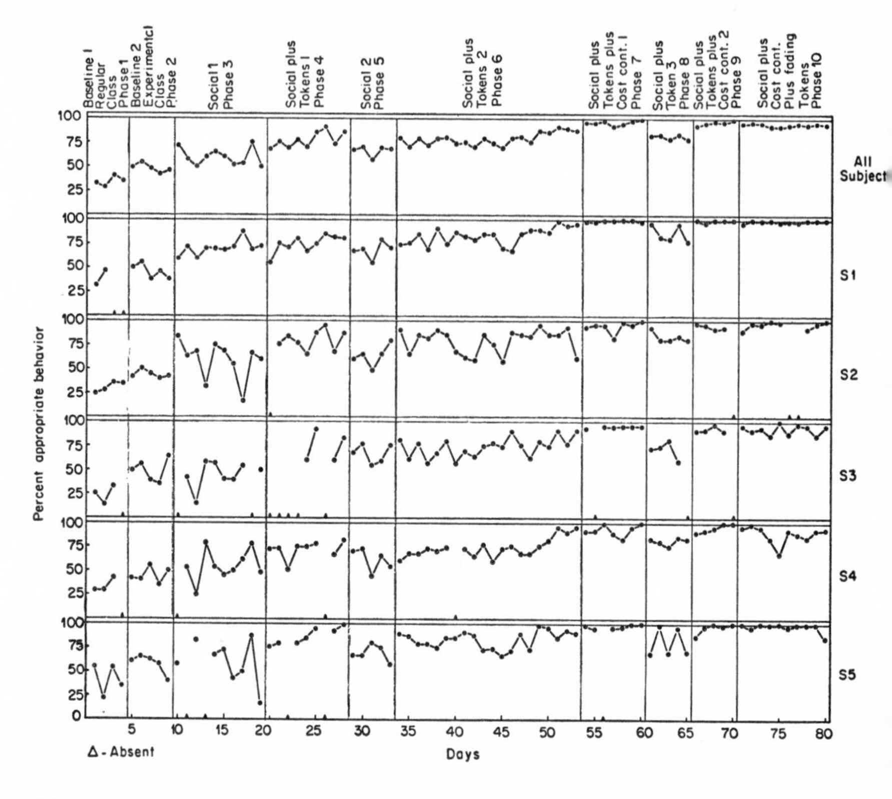

FIGURE 4.8 *Appropriate Child Behavior as a Function of Change in Setting, Teacher Praise, Token Reinforcement, and Cost Contingency*

Figure 4.8 contains results of a second experiment carried out by the authors to evaluate the effectiveness of different combinations of the following four variables: (1) assignment to the special classroom, (2) teacher praise, (3) point system, and (4) response cost.

As in Figure 4.7, results are presented for all five children combined and for the children individually. Figure 4.8 shows that simple assignment to the special classroom resulted in a slight increase in appropriate behavior for each of the five children. This was probably a result of (1) a reduced teacher-student ratio, and (2) individualized instruction and (3) the use of relatively sophisticated programmed instructional materials. When teacher praise for appropriate child behavior was introduced, there was an increase in appropriate behavior for all of the children except one who showed a slight decrease. When a point system was added to the teacher praise, there was an increase in appropriate behavior for all of the children, ranging in magnitude from slight to moderate. With the addition of response cost for *inappropriate* behavior, there was a further increase in the appropriate behavior level of the five children to approximately ninety-six percent.

Results of this study showed that a *combination* of teacher praise, points, and response cost administered within a special class setting produced a more powerful effect upon child behavior than either simple assignment to the special class with no formal treatment procedures implemented or the addition of teacher praise and points. In this instance and with these children, a *combination* of positive reinforcement for appropriate behavior and mild punishment (response cost) for inappropriate behavior was clearly required to produce high levels of appropriate classroom behavior. Without the addition of response cost, these high levels of appropriate behavior could not have been achieved.

As noted earlier, positive reinforcement procedures only can be successfully used to increase the appropriate behavior levels of minimally to moderately disruptive/deviant children. However, for acting-out children and for more deviant/disruptive children generally, a combination of positive reinforcement and mild punishment procedures is usually required to effectively change their behavior.

In a special class or resource room setting, a combination of teacher praise, token reinforcement, and response cost can be implemented as described above. In such an application, it is highly recommended that a visible and tangible delivery system be used for both the positive reinforcement and response cost systems. If all children are being exposed to the same system, its relative obstrusiveness will not present problems. With children in general, and especially with deviant or disturbed populations, it is important that they receive frequent feedback *and* consequences for both their appropriate and inappropriate behavior. A daily point card placed on the child's desk is recommended for the delivery of positive reinforcement, and a weekly response cost form (taped to the child's desk) is recommended for the delivery of response cost. A response cost form of this type was described and illustrated earlier. Figure 4.9 provides an example of a point card used by the author in a special classroom for behavior problem children.

With the card in Figure 4.9, it would be possible to deliver fifty points per day, twenty-five for appropriate classroom behavior and twenty-five for appropriate academic performance. The size of the card can be easily adjusted to accommodate delivery of either a smaller

Academic Performance				Classroom Behavior			

FIGURE 4.9. *Point Card for Delivery of Positive Reinforcement*

or larger number of points. Thus if a teacher were planning to award a child two points each ten-minute period, one for classroom behavior and one for academic performance, and the school day is five hours, a total of sixty points could be earned and a larger card would be required.

A response cost form should be taped securely to the corner of the child's desk and remain there for a week when it is replaced with a new one. A special colored felt-tipped pen should be used to indicate the loss of points on the response cost form.

The number of points on the point record form (Figure 4.9) and the number lost (on the response cost form) should be monitored carefully so that a child is not allowed to lose more points than he/she has earned. When the child's balance approaches zero, timeout or some other consequence should be applied to instances of inappropriate child behavior until additional points have been earned. At the end of the school day, the number of points on the response cost record form is subtracted from the total number earned and the result is recorded on the point card. The child is allowed to keep the net difference and exchange them for whatever backup privileges are available.

A combined positive reinforcement/response cost system could probably be implemented *most* effectively in a regular classroom using the delivery system described above. However, the relative obtrusiveness of this system may be a problem for some classroom teachers; that is, they would be most uncomfortable in implementing a special system for a single child using point cards and response cost record forms.

There are several alternative procedures which can be considered in such cases. For example, instead of awarding and subtracting points on cards at the child's desk, a less obtrusive system can be implemented using a clipboard. That is, the teacher keeps a tally of points earned and lost throughout the day on forms kept on a clipboard. The child's behavior is evaluated every ten minutes, and a point is either awarded or withheld. Points are subtracted whenever inappropriate behavior occurs. However, points are not awarded or subtracted at the child's desk, but on the clipboard at the teacher's desk or whereever he/she happens to be. It is important that the child be informed *each time* points are subtracted for inappropriate behavior. Further, the child should be given a progress report on his/her appropriate behavior (how many points have been earned) at least once each hour and preferably every thirty minutes. It is also important that children be praised frequently when using a system such as this. It should be noted that while this system will be effective in impacting upon child behavior, the reduced obtrusiveness obtained *may* be achieved only at the expense of a slightly less effective system.

A second alternative is to deliver points and response cost via teacher praises and reprimands. In this variation, the child is taught that each time her/his behavior is praised, one point (or x amounts of points) is earned. Similarly, whenever the teacher reprimands his/her behavior, the inappropriate behavior is verbally described and x points are subtracted from the total earned.

This is a very unobtrusive delivery system and if implemented correctly will have an effect upon child behavior. However, it is important that a covert record of points earned and lost be kept using a golf counter, tally, or some other system.

There are several points to consider in using reprimands as a delivery vehicle for response cost. For example, the inappropriate behavior should be identified and described for the child and the number of points lost should be indicated. *Do not* argue with the child about whether she/he did or did not engage in the specific inappropriate behavior; simply describe the behavior and indicate the points lost. Do not criticize the child for behaving inappropriately. Criticism will have no therapeutic or beneficial effects upon child behavior. Finally, attempt to control the expression of active disapproval in delivering the response cost. Your disapproval may actually be a reinforcing consequence for some children and would, in such cases, weaken the effectiveness of the response cost.

As noted earlier, this combination of treatment variables is potentially the most powerful system available for changing child behavior in the classroom setting. It is extremely important that *all* the guidelines for correctly using response cost be followed in the implementation of this treatment combination. It is also highly recommended that the target child be allowed to earn a group consequence only at school where it is shared equally with classmates. If parent cooperation can be achieved, an individual reward system should be set up at home. If this isn't possible, individual rewards can also be made available for the child at school, although this is a less satisfactory alternative than having them provided at home.

Response Cost and Teacher Praise

A combination of teacher praise and response cost can be an easy to manage, effective system for changing child behavior. Its relative ease of implementation makes it especially appropriate for use on playgrounds and in lunchrooms and hallways. It is much easier to implement in the classroom than a combination of teacher praise, positive token reinforcement, and response cost, but it has the disadvantage of being perhaps not as powerful (although, to date, it has not been empirically established that one of these combinations is either more or less powerful than the other). The trade-off between ease of implementation and probable effectiveness is constantly an issue that must be considered by teachers in selecting optimal treatment combinations for changing a given child's behavior.

With this system, the target child is given x amount of points in advance, e.g., at the start of the period, and is allowed to keep them as long as her/his behavior is appropriate. Praise is delivered intermittently throughout the period for appropriate behavior. Whenever inappropriate behavior occurs, points are subtracted from the child's total. At the end of the reinforcement period or school day, the child is allowed to keep whatever points are left and to exchange them for privileges at school and/or home.

The number of points awarded is arbitrary. There is no set rule for determining this in advance. However, several factors should be considered in this decision process. For example, the ratio of points available to backup privileges should be such that a very high proportion of the points available in any day must be retained in order to exchange for the least expensive privilege. A good rule is that eighty percent or more of the points must be retained in order to exchange for the lowest privilege. It is usually quite feasible to tie the number of points available to the passage of time. For example, for playground behavior, one can set up a system where a child earns one point for each minute of recess in which playground rules are followed and the child's interactive behavior with peers is appropriate. In academic settings, e.g., math or reading, the ratio can be one point for each five or ten minutes in which the child is following classroom rules and his/her academic performance is appropriate. The important rule to remember is that the number of points available for the period should be determined *and* awarded to the child in advance as on a point card of some type. It is extremely important that the child understand that (1) the points are her/his to keep as long as rules are followed and classroom and/or playground behavior is appropriate, (2) that points will be subtracted from the total for inappropriate behavior, and (3) that only the net amount of points retained at the end of the period or day can be counted toward the purchase of rewards.

A sample point card for delivery of this treatment combination is presented in Figure 4.10. The author has used a point card of this type in numerous instances and found it to be both effective and easy to implement.

In the classroom, the point card can be placed on the child's desk and points crossed off as the child's behavior indicates. On the playground, the supervisor should carry the card, preferably on a clipboard, and mark off points whenever a playground rule is broken or the child engages in inappropriate social behavior. With this system, the

Name ________________ Date ________________

Recess

<table>
<tr><td>Morning</td><td>| | | | | | | | | |</td></tr>
<tr><td>Lunch</td><td>| | | | | | | | | | | | | | | | | | | |</td></tr>
<tr><td>Afternoon</td><td>| | | | | | | | | | | | | | |</td></tr>
</table>

FIGURE 4.10 *Sample Point Card for a Response Cost Only Intervention*

supervisor should be within close proximity of the child before points are subtracted for inappropriate behavior. Whenever inappropriate behavior occurs, the supervisor should walk over to the child, describe the inappropriate behavior, indicate the number of points lost, and cross off the points on the point card. If all points are lost the child should sit out the remainder of the recess period.

Variable point loss values can be assigned to inappropriate behaviors occurring on the playground or in the classroom, or they can be assigned identical values. As a rule, variable point loss systems are set up according to the severity of inappropriate child behavior. That is, the more severe the inappropriate behavior the greater the point loss. Thus, fighting would be more severe and cost more than a behavior such as out of seat or talks out. Variable systems have the advantage of teaching children about the relative seriousness of differing classroom and playground behaviors.

Walker, Street, Garrett, and Crossen (1977) implemented a response cost only intervention procedure with adult praise to change the playground behavior of a primary-grade boy. The target child's classroom behavior was normal, but his playground behavior in all three recess periods was highly inappropriate. A procedure was set up in which the child was awarded one point for each minute of recess at the start of the period. Five points were subtracted for each instance of negative or aggressive playground behavior and two points were subtracted for each instance of rule breaking. A consultant monitored the child's behavior, subtracted points, and praised the child's appropriate playground behavior. Later, the playground supervisor was trained to operate the program.

Both school and home rewards were made available to the child in this study. If the child had zero negative or aggressive behavior in the recesss periods, a group reward was earned at school that was shared equally with classmates. The child could take home the number of points retained at the end of the school day and exchange them for special privileges. Consequently, even though the group reward may not have been earned, the individual reward system was still available to motivate the child to behave appropriately.

Figure 4.11 presents the target child's proportion of interactive behavior with peers that was positive during the morning, noon, and afternoon recesses.

The program was introduced first in the morning recess, then in the noon recess, and finally in the afternoon recess. As Figure 4.11

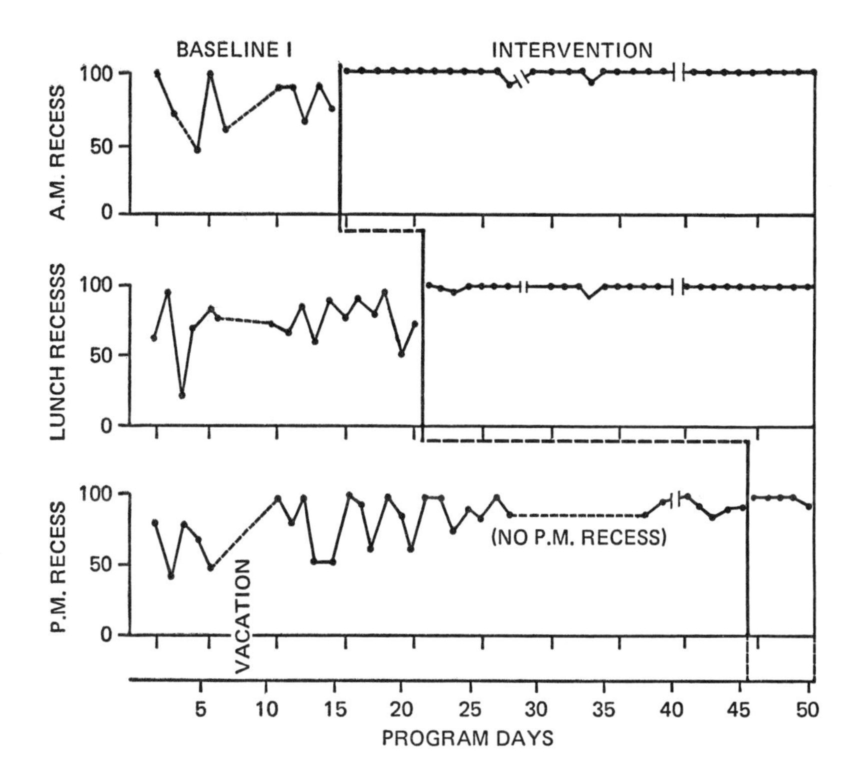

FIGURE 4.11. *Percent of Positive Social Interactive Behavior during Morning, Noon, and Afternoon Recesses for an Aggressive Child*

shows, the program produced immediate and very powerful effects in the child's behavior whenever it was introduced. The program was also very easy to implement and manage.

The most significant advantage of a response cost only point system is ease of management. Points are simply awarded uncontingently and taken away only if inappropriate behavior occurs. A child is much less likely to lose all his/her points in a given period with a system of this type. In contrast, when the child has to earn points *during* the period and can lose them at any time for inappropriate behavior, the risk of going in the hole is much greater. If this occurs, timeout or some other consequence must be used to control additional episodes of inappropriate child behavior.

A disadvantage of this system is that it tends to focus attention on negative child behavior. It is extremely important that the child's positive appropriate behavior be praised frequently when using this system. It is helpful to determine a praise rate in advance, e.g., once every five or ten minutes, and keep a tally during the period to insure that the goal is achieved. Unless the child's appropriate behavior is recognized and approved the overall effectiveness of this system may be substantially reduced.

As is obvious from the foregoing results and discussion, these four combinations of treatment variables are highly effective in modifying child behavior. The choice as to which combination to use depends upon the following considerations (1) the severity of the child's behavior, (2) ease of implementation, (3) the relative effectiveness of the different combinations, and (4) the teacher's preferences.

OTHER COMBINATIONS OF TREATMENT VARIABLES

The treatment combinations described above represent combinations of positive reinforcement and mild punishment procedures. They are designed for modifying the inappropriate behavior of moderately to severely deviant children in school settings. However, there are other combinations of treatment variables that can be used successfully with less deviant children, and for teaching specific social and academic skills. Combinations of this type usually do not involve the use of punishment procedures.

Rules, Praise, and Ignoring

Madsen, Becker, and Thomas (1968) reported a study in which they trained two regular classroom teachers to apply behavior management procedures systematically to children in their classes. Two children in a second-grade classroom and one child in a kindergarten class were selected as targets for the study. From the descriptions of their behavior, it appears that they were mildly to moderately disruptive children. Both children were enrolled in regular, self-contained classrooms. There were twenty-nine children in the second-grade classroom, and twenty children in the kindergarten class.

The purpose of the study was to evaluate, separately and in combination, the effects of rules, praise, and ignoring in changing child behavior from inappropriate to appropriate. The behavior management procedures were applied to the class *as a whole*. The target children were used to document effects of the intervention only. They were not singled out or treated any differently than other children in their respective classrooms. The teachers were also instructed to use the procedures throughout the entire school day, not just when the experimenters and/or observers were present.

The teachers were first instructed to develop a set of classroom rules that would clearly communicate their expectations governing appropriate behavior in the class. Rules were expressed in overt behavioral terms, they were short and to the point, and they were limited in number to five or six. Initially, the teachers went over the rules three or four times with the children and asked them to repeat the rules. During the phase in which rules were evaluated, the teachers were instructed to repeat them at least four to six times per day. They actually repeated them an average of 5.2 times per day during this phase of the study.

The teachers were next trained to ignore inappropriate classroom behavior. Specific instructions for this phase were given to each teacher and conferences were held to explain and discuss the instructions. Ignoring was defined as not attending to child behaviors that interfere with learning or teaching. Examples of ignoring were given and specific child behaviors to which ignoring was to be applied were identified for the teachers. In Classroom A, the teacher was instructed to continue repeating and emphasizing the rules on a daily basis in addition to ignoring inappropriate child behavior. In Classroom B, the teacher was instructed to discontinue repeating or emphasizing rules and to use ignoring only.

In the third phase of the study, both teachers were trained to praise appropriate child behavior. Both teachers were again given instructions on how to praise. Praise was defined and sample praise statements were provided to both teachers. The teachers were instructed not only in which child behaviors to praise, e.g., achievement, prosocial behavior, and following group rules, but also in how to deliver praise correctly. They were given the general instruction to "catch the child being good" in their use of praise. Teacher A was instructed to continue emphasizing rules, to continue ignoring inappropriate behavior, and now, in addition, to praise appropriate child behavior. Teacher B was also given the same instructions for this phase of the study.

At the end of this phase, Teacher A only was given instructions to discontinue emphasizing rules, ignoring, and praising. The purpose of this phase was to re-establish preintervention baseline conditions in

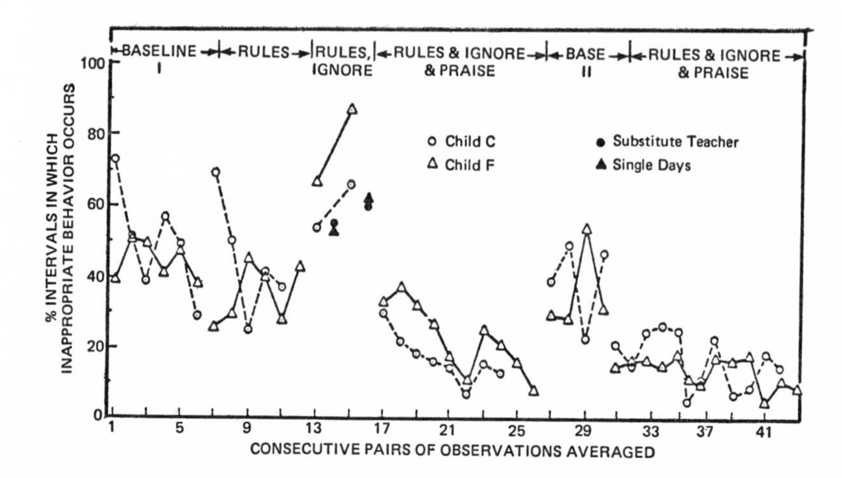

FIGURE 4.12. *Inappropriate Behavior of Two Problem Children in Teacher A's Classroom as a Function of Study Phases*

order to demonstrate the functional role of the intervention program in producing the observed changes in child behavior. Rules, praise, and ignoring were later reinstated and remained in effect for the remainder of the study. No such reversal was implemented for Teacher B.

Figure 4.12 presents the results of the program for the children in Teacher A's classroom. The results show that rules had no effect upon the children's rates of inappropriate classroom behavior. Under the rules and ignore condition in phase two, the children actually became *worse*, that is, levels of inappropriate behavior increased for both target children. However, when praising appropriate behavior was added to rules and ignoring, there was a substantial immediate and very clear decrease in inappropriate behavior for both children. When baseline conditions were reinstated, the children's behavior returned to original baseline levels. When rules, ignoring, and praising were put back into effect, there was an immediate return to the behavioral levels occurring in the previous phase (three) in which these components were in effect.

Figure 4.13 presents the results of the program for the target child in Teacher B's class. Rules alone and ignoring alone had no effect whatever upon the target child's behavior in Teacher B's class. The combination of rules and ignoring was not evaluated in Teacher B's room. It would have been interesting to see whether this combination would also have made this target child worse, as was observed in

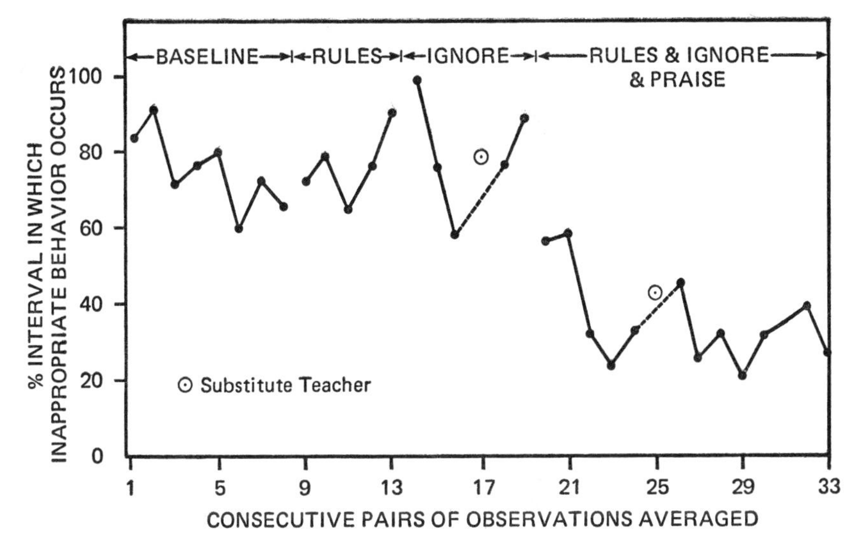

FIGURE 4.13. *Inappropriate Behavior of One Problem Child in Teacher B's Classroom as a Function of Study Phases*

Teacher A's room. Rules, ignoring, and praising produced very similar results for this child as noted in Teacher A's class. When the combination of rules, praising, and ignoring was introduced, there was an immediate and substantial decrease in inappropriate child behavior as noted in Classroom A.

The conclusions that can be drawn from this study are as follows: (1) rules alone had essentially no effect upon the children's behavior, (2) ignoring alone also had no effect upon inappropriate child behavior, although this effect could only be observed in Classroom B, (3) the combination of rules and ignoring made the two children in Classroom A worse, (4) the combination of rules, praise, and ignore produced almost identical results in both classrooms, e.g., significant and immediate decreases in inappropriate child behavior.

An immediate question that comes to mind with this study is: Would praise for appropriate behavior, by itself, have produced results equivalent to those achieved for the combination of rules, praise, and ignore? The answer is: probably not. The reason for this is that the contrast of praising appropriate behavior and ignoring inappropriate behavior is probably more powerful than the effects of either technique used in isolation. Further, the explicit statement and repetition of classroom rules may have also enhanced the effects of praise once it was introduced. However, it should be noted that these observations are speculative only and are based upon the author's own research experience, and that of others doing research in this area.

A second question concerns the extent to which the target children were representative of other children in Classrooms A and B. In other words, were the same effects produced for other children, both deviant and nondeviant, in the class? Further, were the effects specific only to some children or were they pervasive throughout the two classrooms? Although the authors did not collect or report data that would answer either of these questions, they note that both teachers and classroom observers in the study indicated there were dramatic changes in the atmosphere of the whole class.

If the behavior management procedures had been applied specifically and individually to the three target children involved, the effects might have been even more dramatic. However, it is important to note the magnitude of effects that can be achieved for individual behavior problem children when the teacher simply implements systematic behavior management procedures on a class-wide basis. This demonstration is perhaps the most important contribution of this study.

The study clearly shows that a combination of behavior management techniques is more powerful than the same techniques applied singly and in isolation. Since these children were enrolled in self-contained, regular classrooms, it is unlikely that they would be considered severely deviant or disruptive. The techniques used were effective in changing the children's rates of appropriate behavior to within normal limits. However, the effects of the procedures might have been significantly less dramatic if the children's behavioral and learning problems had been more severe or if there had been a larger number of behavior problem children in the two classrooms.

The study also shows that rules by themselves, and ignoring used in isolation, are extremely weak procedures when used to modify inappropriate classroom behavior. In certain situations, these procedures can be effective in modifying specific aspects of child behavior. However, as techniques for producing global changes in child behavior, their effects will usually be minimal at best.

Rules, Educational Structure, Praise, Ignore, and Token Reinforcement

O'Leary, Becker, Evans, and Saudargas (1969) evaluated the effects of rules, educational structure, praise, ignore and token reinforcement in modifying the inappropriate behavior of seven children in a regular, second-grade classroom. The combinations of these variables that were evaluated were as follows: (1) rules alone, (2) rules plus educational structure, (3) rules plus educational structure plus praising appropriate behavior and ignoring inappropriate behavior, and (4) rules plus educational structure plus praise and ignore plus positive token reinforcement.

These behavior management techniques were introduced in sequential fashion as presented above, e.g., rules first, followed by educational structure, and so on. According to the authors, the four conditions were introduced in the order of their expected relative effectiveness. That is, it was thought that rules would have less effect on the children's behavior than praise and ignore. Similarly, it was felt that rules and praise plus ignore would have less effect than the token reinforcement system with backup rewards.

The classroom teacher had had no previous experience other than student teaching. She indicated there were eight children in the class who exhibited a great deal of undesirable behavior. The teacher selected seven children for observation purposes. Presumably, the most deviant children were selected by the teacher. Neither the criteria used to select the children nor their behavioral characteristics were presented; however, as a group, the seven children averaged approximately fifty-five percent of the time spent in *inappropriate* classroom behavior during baseline observations.

The teacher agreed to cooperate with the authors in carrying out the study. As in the previous study, the behavior management procedures were implemented on a class-wide basis. The seven children selected for observation purposes were not treated any differently with respect to implementation of the behavior management procedures than were any of the other fourteen children in the class.

Rules, and praise and ignore were in effect for the entire school day. Educational structure and the token program were in effect only for a two-hour period during the afternoon.

Nine rules, expressed in overt behavioral terms, were developed and presented to the class. They included such things as "we sit in our seats, we raise our hands to talk, we do not talk out of turn," and so forth. The teacher reviewed the rules twice each day, once in the morning and once in the afternoon.

When token reinforcement programs are implemented in classrooms, they introduce an element of formal structure that may not have existed before. It has been suggested that this structure, rather than the reinforcement contingencies themselves, may account for the program's effectiveness in changing child behavior. To evaluate this variable, the teacher was asked to reorganize her afternoon instructional program into four thirty-minute sessions in which the whole class participated. These were spelling, reading, arithmetic, and science. Thus, the purpose of this phase was to assess the importance of educational structure per se.

Praise and ignoring was introduced in the next phase. The teacher was asked to praise appropriate child behavior and to ignore inappropriate behavior as much as possible. She was also asked to discontinue her use of threats.

In the next phase, token reinforcement was introduced. The children were told they would receive ratings four times each afternoon based on how well they followed classroom rules. The points available at each of these rating sessions ranged from one to ten and were recorded in small booklets placed on each child's desk. The points could be exchanged for a variety of backup reinforcers ranging in value from two cents to thirty cents. Points could be exchanged for backup rewards only at the end of the school day.

The authors assisted the teacher in running the program during the first week. After that, the teacher ran the program by herself.

In the next phase, the token program (and backup rewards) were withdrawn to demonstrate their effect in producing the changes in child behavior. Rules, educational structure, and praise and ignoring remained in effect.

In the final phase of the study, the token program and rewards were reinstituted. They were implemented exactly as before.

Figure 4.14 contains results of the application of these behavior management techniques. As can be seen, rules and educational structure had no effect whatever upon the children's behavior. The praise and ignore condition actually made the children slightly worse. The authors noted that the teacher used the praise and ignoring techniques effectively and that initially a number of children responded well to them. However, two of the seven children, both boys, had been disruptive all year, and they became increasingly unruly during this phase. The effect also spread to other children in the class. Several children were so disruptive that the academic pursuits of the rest of the class became impossible. The classroom situation became intolerable

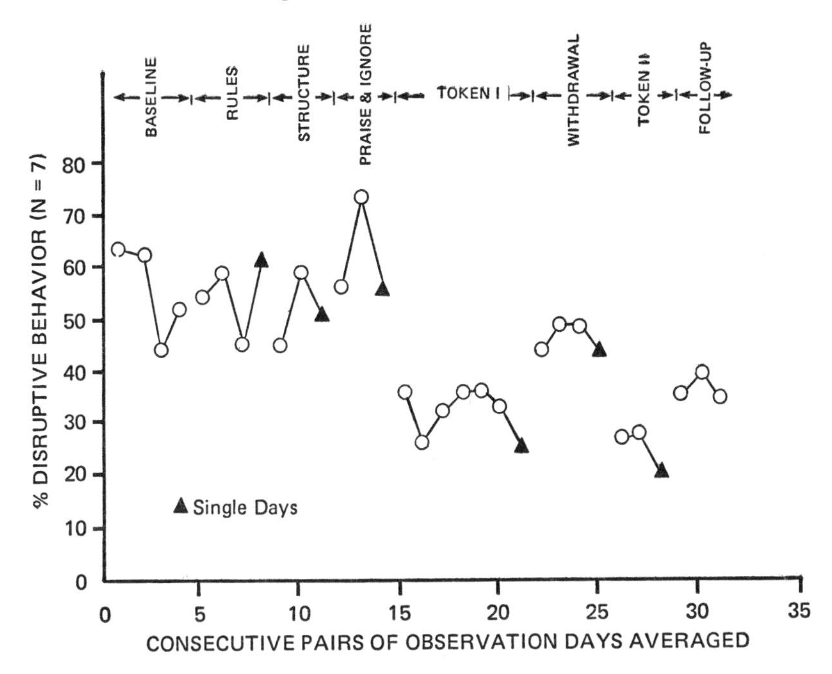

FIGURE 4.14. *Average Percent of Disruptive Behavior of Seven Children during the Afternoon Over the Eight Study Phases*

and the praise and ignore phase had to be terminated much earlier than planned.

This result illustrates some important points about applying relatively weak behavior management techniques to the behavior of disruptive, deviant children. While praise and ignoring may be sufficient to change the overall behavior of minimally to moderately disruptive children, as was noted in the study by Madsen, Becker, and Thomas (1968), or in changing specific aspects of child behavior such as off-task or asking irrelevant questions, they are *not* sufficiently powerful to control the behavior of more deviant children. In this instance, their correct application produced more, rather than fewer, behavior problems for the teacher. A behavioral contagion effect was produced when other children realized that they could be disruptive with impunity. The classroom situation quickly got out of control.

This effect might not have been produced had the children been less disruptive or if there had been a smaller number of such children in the classroom. The author has noted a similar effect with a group of six socially aggressive, primary-level children assigned to an experimental classroom for four months (Walker, Hops, Greenwood, Todd, & Garrett, 1977). All the children in the classroom had much higher rates of negative, socially aggressive interactions with their peers than normal children. The teacher and aide were instructed to praise positive social interactions between children. The results were that the children became substantially *worse;* that is, their proportion of positive interactions with each other was initially reduced by approximately one-half when they were praised for interacting positively.

It appeared that the teacher praise was almost an occasion for the children to become negative and/or aggressive with each other. The author expected praise either to have no effect or only a minimal effect upon the children's behavior. It was totally unexpected that praise would make them worse. Given these children's history of interaction with adults, e.g., threats, criticism, warnings, verbal reprimands, and so forth, it may be that *any* attention from adults is initially perceived negatively.

Identical adverse effects of adult attention on appropriate child behavior have been reported by Thomas, Becker, and Armstrong (1968) in classroom settings and by Herbert, Pinkston, Hayden, Sajawaj, Pinkston, Cordua, & Jackson (1973) with mothers of deviant children who were trained, under supervision, to praise their children's appropriate behavior in a one-to-one teaching situation. It appears that the more deviant the child involved, the more likely it is that adult praise will produce such effects. Praise seems to work extremely well with normal and minimally disruptive children, as evidenced by literally reams of published studies (see Hanley, 1970). It may be that a child's deviance level and history of interaction with adults are the primary determinants of their responsiveness to adult social praise.

Taken together, these results have several implications for changing the behavior of highly disruptive and/or deviant children. As a general rule, praise alone or praise combined with ignoring *should not* be used alone as strategies for changing their overall behavior patterns. It would be highly advisable to use these procedures in combination with token reinforcement and either response cost or timeout to control disruptive behavior. Praise should always be paired systematically with the delivery of points or tokens so that teacher attention can be developed as a generalized reinforcer for such children. If paired consistently and often enough, teacher praise may acquire some of the reinforcing effectiveness of points. Finally, with highly disruptive children, praise or praise and ignoring should only be used to change discrete aspects of child behavior (e.g., dawdling or breaking minor classroom rules).

In the O'Leary, et al. study, only one of the seven children's appropriate behavior was affected positively by the combination of rules, educational structure, and praise and ignore. Either there was no effect or there was an adverse effect for the remaining six children. When the token program was introduced, the disruptive behavior of the remaining six children was reduced. Five of the six showed substantial reductions, while one child showed only a minimal reduction of approximately three percent. For this child, the addition of either response cost or timeout would probably have been required to impact upon the disruptive behavior.

In the phase wherein the token program was withdrawn, the children's behavior returned to the levels observed in the previous rules and educational structure phase. When the program was reintroduced, there was an immediate return to the Token I program levels.

The results of this study, when compared to the previous study by Madsen, Becker, and Thomas (1968), are instructive in several respects. For example, had the combination of rules and praise and ignoring that proved successful in the Madsen study been implemented in the O'Leary, et al. study, it is *extremely* unlikely that the same results would have been achieved. This is because the teacher in the O'Leary, et al. study appeared to have a far more disruptive classroom and a much larger number of deviant children than either of the teachers in the Madsen, et al. study. A token reinforcement program was clearly not required to gain control of the students' behavior in the Madsen, et al. study but it clearly was in the O'Leary, et al. study. In addition, the behavior of one of the seven children in the O'Leary, et al. study was still not controlled effectively by this more powerful behavior management program. These results indicate that the more deviant/disruptive the child behavior involved, the more likely it is that a powerful behavior management system will be required to effectively change the behavior.

Moderately effective gains were maintained in the immediately following followup phase; however, the total program was by no means withdrawn during this phase—only parts of it were changed. That is, the teacher continued to use praise, rules, and educational structure. In addition, a system of stars for good behavior was introduced in followup that could be redeemed on a weekly basis for a piece of candy if a certain performance criterion had been achieved.

In spite of these treatment variations remaining in effect, only three of the six children for whom the program had been effective showed satisfactory maintenance of behavioral gains in the followup period. It would be interesting to know if these three children were more or less deviant/disruptive initially than the three for whom maintenance effects were not achieved. It has been the author's experience that the more deviant the child initially, the less likely it is that satisfactory maintenance effects will be achieved, and the greater the effort that will be required to produce such effects.

No followup data were recorded in the Madsen, et al. study. Thus, we do not know how the behavior of children would have maintained in that study following the rules and praise and ignore program. It is likely that, if the teachers involved had continued to use the procedures on a regular basis, satisfactory maintenance effects would have been achieved.

The O'Leary, et al. study is also valuable in that it demonstrates that a token reinforcement system, implemented on an *individual* child-by-child basis, can be operated by a regular classroom teacher with a total of twenty-one students and produce highly satisfactory results. The teacher was not overwhelmed by the recording and point delivery requirements of operating the system because she only had to do so four times in a two-hour period, or once every thirty minutes. Thus, these requirements were held to a minimum, yet powerful effects were still achieved for a very unruly and out-of-control classroom. This demonstration is highly effective in showing how systematic behavior management procedures can be adapted for successful use in a regular classroom without placing unreasonable burdens upon the classroom teachers.

Rules, Feedback, and Group and Individual Consequences for Appropriate Behavior

Greenwood, Hops, Delquadri, and Guild (1974) evaluated the effects of rules, rules plus feedback, and rules plus feedback plus reinforcement (social praise and backup activity rewards) upon appropriate child behavior in three primary-level classrooms. The classrooms were all located in one school. There was one classroom each at the first-, second-, and third-grade levels. The authors worked with each of the teachers in implementing the procedures. Initially, the teachers were given several inservice training sessions in the procedures to be used, and then they were supervised and given feedback on their implementation of the procedures during the study.

This study is interesting in that the children were given daily feedback on the extent to which they followed classroom rules. In addition, the behavior management procedures were primarily of a group nature, in that the entire class was treated as a single unit in the rating of performance and the earning of units of reinforcement. That is, all children had to be following classroom rules simultaneously in order for the group to earn units toward a backup reward activity. If one or more children were not following the rules, no units could be earned until those children's behavior became appropriate.

As a first step, each teacher developed a set of explicit classroom rules, went over them with the class, and posted them on the bulletin board. The rules were reviewed with the class on a daily basis in this phase.

In the rules plus feedback condition, the teacher operated a clock-light instrument which gave the class continuous feedback on whether all children were or were not following classroom rules. A standard wall clock was equipped with a light in the center and wired to be operated from a hand-held switch so that when the light was on, the clock ran and when the light was off, the clock stopped. Thus, the teacher would let the clock run when everyone was following the rules and stopped it when one or more children were not.

The program operated in daily reading and math periods. During these periods, the class had continuous feedback as to whether the rules were being followed by everyone. At the end of each period, the teacher calculated and posted a percent score which indicated the proportion of time during the period the entire class had followed the rules. Thus, two types of feedback were provided, *continuous* during the session and *overall* at the end of the session.

In the final phase, group activity rewards and social praise were made available for meeting a criterion based on the extent to which class rules were followed. As the class improved its performance, the reinforcement criterion was raised accordingly, e.g., a greater proportion of time following the rules was required in order to earn the group reward. Individual children and the entire class were praised regularly for following the rules during daily sessions.

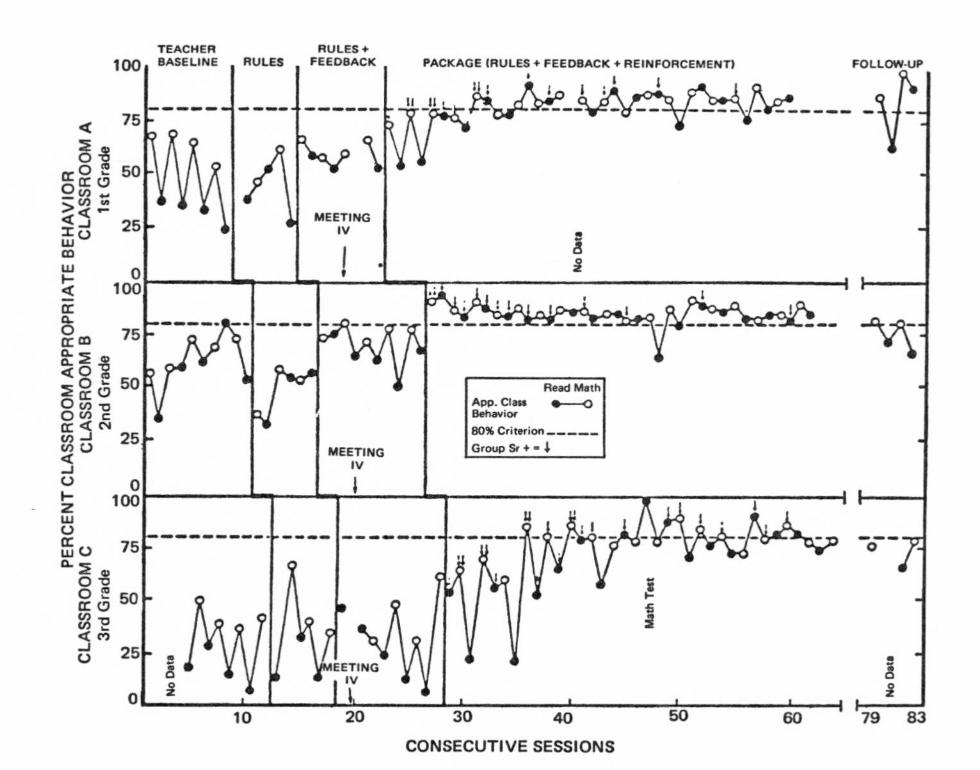

FIGURE 4.15. *Percent Appropriate Classroom Behavior for Three Classrooms during Reading and Math Periods as a Function of Different Management Techniques*

Figure 4.15 contains results of the program.

The results show that rules produced no change in overall classroom behavior. The behavior of the entire class recorded via the clock-light instrument served as the primary outcome measure in this study.

The combination of rules plus feedback produced increases in appropriate behavior in two of the classrooms. However, the increases were only of low to moderate magnitude.

When the full package of rules plus feedback plus reinforcement was introduced, substantial increases in appropriate behavior were achieved for all three classrooms. There was an immediate and very powerful effect for the second-grade classroom, and more gradual but equally powerful effects eventually achieved for the first- and third-grade classrooms.

The program was eventually terminated with *all* program components removed including rules, feedback, and the reinforcement procedures. Three weeks after termination, a series of followup observations was recorded in each teacher's classroom. The short term maintenance effects recorded were quite impressive. The behavioral levels of the three classes appeared to be slightly lower than those during the full program and slightly more variable as well. The ultimate question, as always, is how long into the future these gains would have persisted without support by the program or a variation of it. Data recorded on the teachers' praise rates showed that praise rates maintained well for two of the three teachers during the followup period. The extent to which the teachers continued to praise both the whole class and individual students would in all likelihood have an effect on how long such gains in child behavior would maintain.

This study demonstrates the impact a simple-to-operate group behavior management program can have upon an entire classroom. The great majority of students in the three classes were affected positively by the program. A question arises as to the mechanical nature of the recording/reinforcement delivery system, e.g., the clock-light instrument. While such a device makes implementation of a program such as this easier, it is not essential. Comparable results can be achieved using a simple rating system of pluses and minuses for the entire class recorded on the blackboard.

The study results show that the addition of feedback to the development and posting of rules increases their effectiveness. However, it is clear that without an accompanying reinforcement system, this is an extremely weak intervention procedure.

Teacher Attention and Ignoring in the Control of a Preschool Child's Aggressive Behavior

Pinkston, Reese, Le Blanc, and Baer (1973) carried out an intriguing study in which they demonstrated that a preschool child's aggressive behavior toward peers was (a) being maintained by the attention in the form of verbal admonitions and reprimands that it produced from teachers, and that (b) it could be controlled effectively through a combination of simultaneously ignoring the target child and attending to the victim(s) of his aggression.

The target child was a 3½-year-old boy from a culturally enriched background. He had well developed language skills, but for some reason had acquired an extremely aggressive and destructive style of interacting with peers. His behavior was clearly unacceptable in the preschool setting and a program was developed to control it.

In the initial baseline phase, the preschool teachers were instructed to respond to the target child's aggressive behavior as they normally would. This consisted mainly of verbal reprimands such as "Cain, we don't do that here," or "You can't play here until you are ready to be a good boy."

In the next phase, extinction or ignoring, the teachers did not attend to his aggressive behavior except to separate him occasionally from the peers he was interacting with (to prevent injury). Instead, the teachers ignored Cain whenever aggressive episodes occurred and they attended, in a sympathetic and caring way, to the peer or peers whom Cain was attacking. This attention took the form of such statements as, "I'm sorry that happened to you. Why don't you play with this nice truck?"

In the next phase, the extinction procedures were eliminated and the teachers were instructed to attend to Cain's aggressive behavior by setting limits, reprimanding him, and by attempting to reason with him.

In the next phase, the previous extinction procedures were reinstituted. Procedures in this phase were identical to those in the previous one.

Over the next three phases, spanning approximately thirty-five school days, reinforcement, extinction, and followup conditions were alternated. These phases were implemented to achieve some additional study objectives.

The results are presented in Figure 4.16 below.

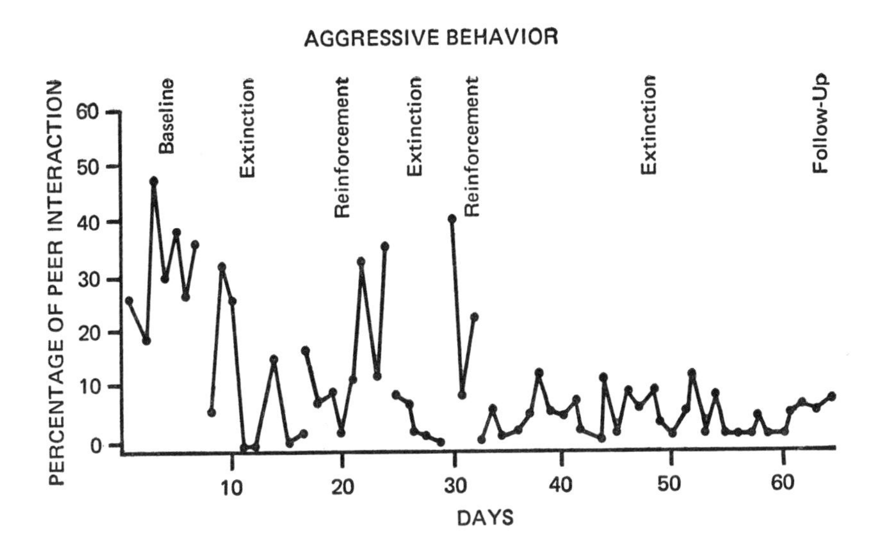

FIGURE 4.16. *Daily Episodes of Aggressive Behavior across Study Phases*

The data in Figure 4.16 show that a combination of ignoring the aggressive child and attending to the child's victim was a highly effective procedure for reducing Cain's aggressive social behavior. These gains were sustained over a thirty-day period and maintained into a followup phase.

Contrary to what one would expect, a combination of ignoring and positive attention to the child's victim produced a very powerful suppression of the target child's aggressive behavior. It is interesting to speculate as to why this effect was achieved.

It may have been that the teacher's praise was more effective in this study because of Cain's age. Preschool children, because of their immature status, are more dependent upon adults. Therefore, adults have greater influence with them, and their praise and approval may be more powerful.

Also, Cain was being deliberately ignored while simultaneously observing the teacher attending, sympathetically, to his victim(s). This particular application could be more powerful than the usual combined use of praise and ignore because of the built in contrast and because of the vicarious learning involved (the teacher was communicating that aggression would be ignored and that nonaggressive behavior would be attended to and positively reinforced).

Finally, whenever an aggressive episode occurred, one of the teachers intervened and terminated it in order to deliver the extinction procedures. This interruptive effect could have also contributed to the overall treatment outcomes.

What this study shows is that an ingenious application of praise and ignore procedures can control the aggressive behavior of a preschool child. However, it is not recommended that these procedures be used to consequate aggressive behavior in older primary or intermediate level children. Much more powerful procedures would be recommended and probably required to achieve this goal with older children.

Prompting and Adult Praise in Modifying Preschool Social Behavior

Strain, Shores, and Kerr (1976) carried out a study in which they evaluated the effects of verbal and physical prompts in combination with verbal praise in facilitating the appropriate social behavior of three handicapped preschool children. Strain et al. carried out the study in an early education center for behaviorally handicapped preschool children. Three boys, ages 4–1 to 4–2, enrolled in the center, served as target children in the study. The three children had a history of behavior problems including delayed speech, tantrums, and opposition to and withdrawal from peers.

A combination of verbal and physical prompts, plus verbal praise contingent on appropriate social behaviors, was used to increase the children's rates of appropriate social behavior. Prompts included such verbal comments as, "Now let's play with the other children;" "Pass the block to Steve;" or "You can play house together." Physical prompts consisted of leading the child into the proximity of other children, modeling play with other children, or moving a child in such a way that he/she joins in a positive interaction with peers. The teachers timed the prompts so as to facilitate the occurrence of positive social behavior in the target children.

Teacher praise was given contingent on a child's positive social behavior. Praise was always preceded by the adult calling the child's name, e.g., "Dan, I like it when you play with friends."

Whenever the procedure was introduced, there was an immediate increase in the child's positive social behavior. In the case of Dan and Hank, there was a corresponding decrease in their rates of negative social behavior as well. In addition, there were spillover effects of the intervention from Dan to Hank when the procedure was introduced for Dan. Similarly, there were spillover effects from Ricky to Hank when the procedure was introduced for Ricky.

Figure 4.17 contains the effects of this procedure upon the children's positive and negative social behavior.

This study demonstrates the practical role verbal and physical prompts can play in facilitating appropriate social behavior. These prompts served as very powerful antecedent events that set the occasion for appropriate behavior to occur. Once it occurred, it was immediately consequated with teacher praise. This can be a highly effective teaching strategy, especially when used skillfully, as it was

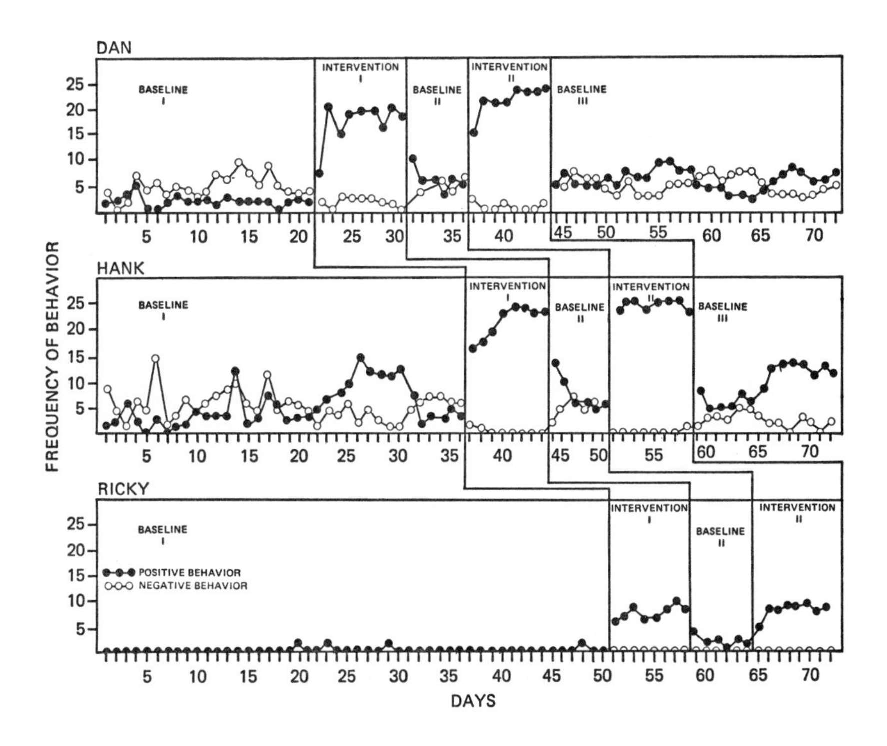

FIGURE 4.17. *Frequency of Positive and Negative Behavior for Dan, Hank and Ricky across Phases*

in this study. In using a combination of prompts and adult praise to increase any child behavior, the recommended procedure is as follows: (1) wait for an appropriate occasion for a prompt to be used, (2) prompt the response, and (3) reinforce it immediately when it occurs.

WHEN TO USE DIFFERENT COMBINATIONS OF BEHAVIOR MANAGEMENT TECHNIQUES

There are no hard and fast rules for using one combination of treatment variables over another within an intervention program. Of the ten techniques presented earlier in this chapter, it would be possible to apply them either singly or in combination with each other. Here are some general guidelines that have been developed out of the author's research experience.

As a general rule, a combination of both positive reinforcement and mild punishment techniques will be required to effectively change the behavior of moderately to severely deviant/disruptive children. Children who spend less than fifty percent of the time engaged in appropriate behavior may fall in this category.

Also, as a general rule, only positive reinforcement (social and/or nonsocial) is required to change the behavior of mildly to moderately deviant/disruptive children. Children who engage in appropriate behavior more than fifty percent of the time may fall in this category.

Sometimes one doesn't know how a child will respond to an intervention program until it is actually implemented. If a positive only system is implemented and the child's behavior does not change effectively, then a mild punishment component can be added to the intervention program. If the child responds satisfactorily, nothing else is required.

Unless special circumstances are indicated, do not use a combination of praise and ignoring to change the overall behavior of highly deviant/disruptive children. They may actually become worse under a program of this type (see Madsen, et al. and O'Leary, et al.).

Whenever possible, use prompts to facilitate the occurrence of appropriate child behavior, whether social or academic. Reinforce the appropriate or correct response immediately as it occurs with either social and/or nonsocial reinforcement. Prompts will greatly facilitate the effectiveness of reinforcement in changing child behavior.

Rules are a very important component of the process of changing child behavior in the classroom; however, by themselves they are an extremely weak behavior management procedure. Rules should be used in conjunction with a feedback and reinforcement program to motivate the children to follow them.

As a general rule, use the simplest and least costly combination of variables necessary to change child behavior. The fewer the techniques involved, the easier to manage the intervention program will be for the teacher. If one has a choice of using praise only or a simple stimulus change or prompting procedure to change behavior, as opposed to a more complex praise and token reinforcement procedure, select the simpler procedure first. A more complex one can always be implemented at a later point if the simpler system proves ineffective.

It has been the author's purpose to illustrate the application of different combinations of treatment variables in the preceding section. Research studies that achieved success in the application of appropriate combinations of such techniques were selected and presented. The studies presented by no means exhaust the possible appropriate combinations of the ten behavior management techniques presented in the first part of this chapter.

SOME PERSPECTIVES ON CHANGING CHILD BEHAVIOR

Research has clearly shown that teachers' expectations can affect both academic performance and pupil-teacher interactions (Anderson, 1971; Meichenbaum, Bowers, & Ross, 1969; Beez, 1970; Rubovits & Maehr, 1971). The research literature, for example, shows that students who are perceived by teachers to be brighter and more competent receive more teacher attention (Rothbart, Dalfen, & Barrett, 1971), are given greater opportunities to respond (Brophy & Good, 1970), receive more praise (Rubovits & Maehr, 1971), and receive more verbal cues (Blakely, 1971). Rest (1972) found that children in lower reading groups had more negative interactions with the teacher than other children. Finally, Firestone and Brody (1975) showed that children who experienced the highest percentage of negative interactions with their kindergarten teacher were also those who demonstrated low levels of competence on the Metropolitan Achievement Test at the end of first grade. These studies provide a great deal of convergent evidence that teacher expectations can have a powerful influence upon child behavior.

If the expectations of teachers relating to child competence and other child characteristics can powerfully influence their interactions with them, then it seems equally plausible that teacher expectations concerning procedures for changing child behavior could affect their receptivity to them. This is precisely what the author has found in numerous behavior management workshops and inservices he has conducted over the last ten years. Teachers will sometimes reject proven behavior management techniques, such as positive reinforcement, because they see them as representing too much work to be practicable, as being forms of bribery, or as involving special treatment of a single child (which the teacher feels is unfair to other children in the class not involved in the program). This is indeed unfortunate since both individual children and their teachers are then deprived of access to highly effective procedures that can (1) improve child learning outcomes, (2) increase appropriate child behavior, and (3) make the classroom a more pleasant place for both teachers and students.

There are some key issues surrounding the use of proven behavior management techniques that teachers continue to raise in inservice training sessions. These include: (1) the issue of reinforcement as a form of bribery, (2) the special treatment of one child whose behavior is inappropriate or incompetent versus the fair and equitable treatment of all children in the class, (3) the fear that if one child is singled out and treated in a special way because of behavioral or learning problems, other children will learn to "act out" in order to be treated in the same way, (4) the amount of work and time required to implement the procedures does not justify whatever changes in child behavior would occur as a result of their application, (5) behavior management procedures do not produce enduring changes in child behavior that are internalized and displayed throughout all aspects of the child's functioning, regardless of setting(s) or conditions, and (6) the issue of powerful behavior management techniques representing an undesirable form of behavioral control which (a) restricts a child's freedom and (b) teaches an artificial set of values. A number of teachers have rejected the use of behavior management procedures based on one or more of the above issues. In the author's opinion, it is important in a book of this type to address each of these issues and to provide some perspective on them.

Reinforcement as a Form of Bribery

Reinforcement is a technique for motivating someone to do something, e.g., to acquire a skill, to learn a task, to behave differently, and so forth. The dictionary definition of reinforcement is "to strengthen by the addition of something new, as new material . . . ." Reinforcement involves the addition of a stimulus or event to a learning situation which is designed to facilitate the learning or acquisition process. In a sense, it strengthens the response or behavior that is being acquired through a differential conditioning process. A reinforcer is made available if the correct form of the behavior/response is produced and is withheld if it is not.

The dictionary definition of a bribe on the other hand is as follows: "A prize, reward, gift, or favor bestowed or promised with a view to pervert the judgment or corrupt the conduct of a person in a position of trust." Given this definition, it is clear that reinforcement is not a form of bribery, but instead it is a technique designed to facilitate the learning process. Reinforcement procedures are not used to corrupt individuals or to induce them to do something illegal. Instead they are used in a therapeutic fashion to help individuals become more competent or to change some aspect(s) of their behavior pattern.

It should be noted that bribery *does* involve the use of rewards dispensed in a contingent fashion, e.g., a building inspector receives an illegal payment for approving a building that is not consistent with the local building code. Reinforcement uses exactly the same principle, that is, the contingent dispensing of rewards, but the similarity ends there. Reinforcement and bribery can perhaps be most clearly distinguished via the purpose for which the principle of dispensing contingent rewards is put in their respective applications. In the case of bribery, it is designed to corrupt and to induce one to act illegally; in the case of reinforcement, it is used to make people more competent or to induce them to change some feature of their overall behavior pattern.

Reinforcement is used in a systematic fashion throughout all levels of our society. The government deliberately sets up incentives to encourage the public to behave in a certain way (e.g., the government frequently uses its vast powers to control the areas in which investors place their money through manipulation of allowable interest rates). This is a systematic use of incentive systems, or reinforcement procedures, designed to control and/or change the way investors behave economically. It is a clear case of behavioral control, of deliberate manipulation, but it is usually accepted without criticism since it is designed to improve the overall economy and to create more economic opportunities for a broad spectrum of the public.

Similarly, parents use reinforcement procedures constantly in the process of socializing children. Most parents apply massive amounts of social, and sometimes nonsocial, reinforcement in the process of teaching their children language, motor, and self-help skills. These procedures are instrumental in helping children achieve essential developmental tasks and in acquiring the behavioral repertoires they need to function effectively in society.

Ironically, many teachers object, sometimes strenuously, to the use of reinforcement procedures in helping children develop educationally and in achieving difficult educational tasks. Our society seems to communicate a generalized expectancy that all children should want to learn, should be motivated to achieve, that they will come to school with a behavioral repertoire that will allow them to consume academic instruction easily and efficiently, and that they will be socially responsive to adults. As everyone knows, this is often not the case. Our tasks as educators would be greatly simplified if it were.

It is apparent that many children do not develop the knowledge and acquire the skills expected of them under normal instructional conditions. Such children, especially handicapped children, will often require *special* instructional and management procedures in order for them to develop at a reasonable rate of progress. The great majority of children do not require such special procedures. However, for those who do, it is incumbent upon the school system to accommodate their needs and to use the most effective methods available for instructing them and for managing their socially and academically related behavior.

A very powerful technology of instruction and behavior management currently exists and has produced truly remarkable gains in the education of children, both handicapped and nonhandicapped, in school settings. Reinforcement is an integral part of this technology. It is the author's hope that teachers will counterbalance the moral, esthetic, and philosophical objections they have raised about reinforcement procedures with an active consideration of the therapeutic child benefits that can result from their effective application in classroom settings.

The Fairness Issue—The Special Treatment of Single Children Via Behavior Management Procedures

One of the most pervasive objections of teachers to the use of systematic behavior management procedures in the classroom revolves around the fairness issue. Teachers, and people in general, are thoroughly trained to be fair and to treat others equitably. Fair treatment is a very powerful value in our society and one that has a broad basis of consensus. Because behavior management procedures are often applied to single children in classrooms and because reinforcement is usually involved in their application, teachers are quite sensitive to interventions that give the appearance of treating children in a special or unique way.

There is nothing wrong with the fair and equitable treatment of all children in a classroom given that they (1) can meet the behavioral requirements of the situation and (2) they do not have special or unique learning problems. However, many children enrolled in regular classrooms, especially handicapped children, have learning, behavioral, and emotional problems that *do* require that they be treated in very special ways if they are going to achieve a normal rate of progress. Cerebral palsied, hearing impaired, partially sighted, learning disabled, physically handicapped, mentally retarded, emotionally disturbed, and behavior disordered children all require special consideration on the part of their teachers in order to perform up to their potential. Even a normal, nonhandicapped child who is not motivated to learn requires special consideration in the sense that efforts should be invested to identify why the child is unresponsive to instruction.

Many of these children require specially designed and adapted instructional procedures. Reinforcement procedures implemented on either a short or long term basis, may be necessary in order for them to learn and achieve. In all likelihood, the teacher will have to invest much greater amounts of time, energy, and effort in the process of instructing such children than he/she does in working with normal children. A cerebral palsied child, for example, requires much greater amounts of teacher assistance and attention to perform, simply because of the nature of the handicap.

With the advent of Public Law 94–142 wherein more and more handicapped children are being placed in regular classrooms, educators are going to have to reevaluate their traditional position that all children must be treated fairly and equitably. These children are going to have to be instructed and treated in very special ways, ways that may appear at first glance to be unfair to other children. If the school does not recognize their unique learning and behavioral problems and attempt to accommodate them, it will be denying such children access to what is for them an equal education.

Legislation now in effect requires that *all* children be given an equal education. It now appears that in order to achieve this goal, a number of children will have to be accommodated in very special or unique ways that may conflict with the posture of fair treatment schools have traditionally maintained in the delivery of educational services.

There are a number of potential responses to this problem. One is to simply explain to other children, when they inquire, that the child involved is going to require some special assistance with schoolwork for awhile. If the child is obviously handicapped, the question may not even arise. If the handicapping condition is more subtle, inquiries from other children are perhaps more likely.

The extent to which children are cognizant of each other's special problems and the acceptance of unique or different procedures for remediating them is truly remarkable. If a reinforcement procedure is being used to teach a given child a specific skill or task, most children will accept it without objection if they are given a logical and rational explanation for its use.

Another alternative is to have the class share in the rewards earned by the target child. This is a most appropriate procedure when working with a behavior problem child who disrupts the class and breaks classroom rules. However, it is not always feasible when working with other types of children.

A third alternative is to simply treat the handicapped child no differently from any other child in the class. In this alternative, whatever special help the child receives would be delivered outside the regular classroom setting via a resource room or one-to-one instructional situation with a specially trained professional.

These alternatives are by no means exhaustive of those potentially available. However, of the alternatives currently available to school personnel for responding to this problem, these appear to be the most feasible. The alternative selected would likely depend upon such things as the teacher's preferences, the nature of the child's problem(s), and the type of classroom situation involved.

If a Single Child Is Treated in a Special Way, Other Children Will "Act Out" in Order to Be Treated in the Same Way

There has been a great deal of rhetoric and concern expressed over this issue in the last ten years. In spite of this, however, no one has empirically documented that this effect actually occurs. This is not to say that it could not happen; for logically, it appears to be well within the realm of possibility. However, the fact that it has not been empirically documented suggests that the problem may not be as pervasive as one might expect. Nevertheless, it is a legitimate and real concern of teachers, and it is one that must be dealt with.

Teachers are quite concerned that children may be given the expectation that they will be rewarded for breaking classroom rules, disrupting the class, or failing to do their schoolwork. If a child who displays these behavioral characteristics is placed on a behavior management program where she/he is reinforced for appropriate behavior, many teachers fear that other children would then learn to act out in order to be put on a similar program.

There are a number of ways in which this potential problem can be circumvented, some of which have been discussed earlier. For example, an unobtrusive, private program can be developed and implemented so that it is not known to anyone but the child, the teacher, and his/her parents. The teacher can rate the child's behavior covertly during the day, and praise and give feedback where appropriate. However, reinforcers are awarded only at the end of the day based upon a global assessment of the child's performance. This type of program would not be obvious to other children in the class, and would not produce the undesirable modelling effects described above.

Another method, also described earlier, is to have the target child earn a group reward at school via her/his appropriate behavior that is shared equally with classmates. The target child is still singled out and treated in a special way, however the rewards earned are shared equally. Thus, other children would not be motivated to act out in order to gain access to the available rewards. However, with this system, children will occasionally ask if they can have a turn at earning rewards for the rest of the class. As a matter of fact, the opportunity to earn a group reward could be used as a special privilege to motivate children to improve their classroom performance, although the author has not used this particular system in this fashion.

A third alternative is to set up a group contingency in which all children in the class are treated as a single unit. Thus, *all* children must be following class rules and behaving appropriately in order to meet the reinforcement criterion. A potential problem with this contingency is that it may be too general to control the behavior of individual children who have deviant or disruptive behavior patterns. It may be necessary to develop individual programs for such children first and get their behavior under some form of reasonable control before introducing a class-wide group contingency.

A fourth alternative uses a combination of group and individual contingencies to circumvent this problem. The teacher sets a timer for varying intervals of time such as 10, 15, 5, 30, 22 minutes, and so forth. Instructions to the class are that whoever is behaving appropriately, working, and following class rules when the timer goes off will receive x amounts of points, units, or stars that can be exchanged for backup rewards later. Many teachers have children earn minutes of free time as a backup reward.

This procedure works extremely well in maintaining a high level of appropriate behavior in the classroom. Its effectiveness is based on the intermittent nature of reward delivery. That is, the children do not know when the timer will go off. Thus to maximize their chances of earning reinforcers, they learn to behave appropriately most of the time.

Every child is treated the same in this procedure. All have an equal chance of earning a reinforcer when the timer goes off. Those who are behaving appropriately earn a reinforcer when the timer goes off, and those who are not earn nothing.

There are several potential problems with its use in classroom settings, however. For example, it might be impractical to run the procedure throughout the whole day. Several solutions to this problem would be to (1) start out with small average time intervals such as ten to twenty minutes and gradually extend them to an hour or two, so that the amount of teacher time involved in running it is reduced to manageable proportions or (2) the procedure operates only during certain periods throughout the school day, and the class has to earn the right for it to operate by behaving appropriately in other periods. Either of these alternatives would probably be an effective remedy to this problem.

A second problem concerns the number of children in one's class. The procedure would be simple to operate in a special or resource room setting, but not so simple, in terms of the work involved, in a regular classroom. If there are a large number of children involved, say twenty to thirty, then the teacher can simply assume that most children will earn a point or reinforcer when the timer goes off and note which children are *not* following the rules when the timer goes off (the teacher notes which children do not earn a reinforcer rather than those who do). At the end of the day, a tally is computed for each child.

This change would greatly reduce the work involved in managing the program.

A fifth alternative is a procedure called the "good behavior game" (Barrish, Saunders, & Wolf, 1969). The teacher begins by developing a list of classroom rules that govern the more overt forms of inappropriate classroom behavior such as talk outs, out of seat, off-task, and disturbing others. The class is then divided into two equal teams with labels for each team written on the blackboard.

When the game operates, the teacher simply places a mark next to the team listing for any member of the team who breaks a rule. At the end of the period or day, the team with the fewest marks wins and all members of that team are allowed a special privilege. The game has proven highly effective in increasing the appropriate behavioral level of the classrooms in which it has been implemented.

There are also some problems with using the game in classrooms. For example, it does not seem practical to run the game the entire day. Second, it may not be powerful enough to control the behavior of highly disruptive or deviant children. Third, care must be exercised in making up teams, since it would be possible to easily overload one team with children experiencing learning and behavior problems.

These alternatives give the classroom teacher a great deal of flexibility in responding to the problem of not teaching children to act out in order to be placed on a behavior management program. They involve varying amounts of work and monitoring, and each must be adapted to a given teacher's classroom situation.

The Teacher Effort Involved in Implementing Behavior Management Procedures Does Not Justify the Changes in Child Behavior Produced

It is indeed unfortunate that behavior management procedures have been represented to teachers as involving considerable effort, time, and energy in order for them to be applied effectively. While such procedures *do* require careful planning and monitoring, they can be implemented effectively without becoming a burden to the teacher. In fact, they can result in the teacher having more rather than less time to devote to instruction.

In the training they have been exposed to vis à vis behavior management procedures, many teachers have been taught that elaborate recording requirements are an integral part of their application. These recording requirements include such things as (1) observing and recording child behavior, (2) graphing child behavior on a daily basis, (3) completing elaborate forms used for the purpose of delivering points or other units of reinforcement, (4) counting praise rate, (5) keeping track of the reasons a child is sent to timeout, (6) keeping track on a daily basis of the backup rewards a child selects, and so on. For research purposes, it is valuable to have information on such variables, and on others that can help document the effectiveness of different behavior management procedures; however, much of this information is inappropriate when one considers the teacher's usual goals in applying behavior management procedures (e.g., to improve learning outcomes and to increase appropriate patterns of child behavior at the lowest possible cost to themselves in time, effort, and energy).

Cost-effectiveness is a major issue of concern to teachers in such applications. That is, given the anticipated outcomes resulting from application of a given procedure(s), what is the relative cost to the teacher in terms of time, effort, and energy in the implementation process? Many teachers have rejected the use of systematic behavior management procedures because they view them as cost-ineffective. In the author's opinion, this is often because the recording requirements associated with behavior management procedures are perceived as overwhelming and as simply "not being worth it." The author has received this feedback literally hundreds of times in behavior management workshops with classroom teachers. It is clearly a legitimate concern of teachers and one that must be addressed if behavior management procedures are going to be adopted for effective use in classroom settings.

The recording requirements associated with behavior management procedures can be *substantially* reduced without affecting their overall effectiveness. The extent to which this goal can be achieved will make such procedures much more palatable to classroom teachers.

The crucial element in the application of behavioral procedures is that a child's performance be rated on a regular basis and that such ratings be tied to a reinforcement system. That is, if the child's behavior is judged to be appropriate, a reinforcer is delivered (e.g., point, star, token, checkmark, etc.), if it is not appropriate, then the reinforcer is withheld. In terms of recording, a simple rating and reinforcement delivery system is *all* that is required to implement a system that will be effective.

A simple point card placed either on the child's desk or kept on the teacher's desk can be used for this purpose. A number of variations of such cards are available. An example of a very simple one is presented below using pluses both as a rating and as a unit of reinforcement.

	Classroom Behavior	*Academic Work*
9:00– 9:30	+	+
9:30–10:00	+	–
10:00–10:30	–	+
10:30–11:00	+	+

In this variation each plus counts as a reinforcer, e.g., one minute of free time or as one point toward the cost of some event, activity, or privilege. Minuses mean that the child's behavior was not up to standard, and they do not count toward earning an activity.

A second variation, somewhat simpler, is presented below:

Classroom Behavior	*Academic Work*
× × × × ×	× × ×

Checkmarks also serve both as ratings and as units of reinforcement in this variation. More flexibility is available with this system since it is not tied to time, and a variable number of points can be awarded to differentially reinforce high quality performance.

The important point to remember is that the minimal recording involved in these two systems is *all* the recording that is necessary to make them work effectively. The points, pluses, or checkmarks earned daily become a permanent record of the child's performance. However, it is not necessary to either observe or record child behavior independently of the ratings to determine whether the system is working. If you as the teacher can see changes in the child's behavior and the child's behavior is meeting your standards as indicated in your ratings of his/her performance, then that is all the documentation that is required. It is also not necessary to graph the child's daily point, plus, or checkmark totals unless you as the teacher are interested in seeing the child's performance visibly displayed over days for your inspection.

If a response cost system is used in conjunction with the reinforcement system, then another recording/rating component is added. However, this component can be very simple to administer also. For example, the reverse sides of the point cards presented above can be used to deliver response cost to child behavior. A sample variation is presented below.

Response Cost

Behavior	*Cost*	*Rating*
1. Out of Seat	– 2	. .
2. Talk outs	– 2	.
3. Teacher Defiance	– 3	.
4. Disturbing Others	– 3	
5. Off Task	– 1	: . .
6. Hitting	– 5	

Whenever the teacher has to use response cost he/she simply turns the point card over and places a dot, using a felt-tipped pen, in the appropriate column opposite the behavior displayed by the child. Each day, the dots are multiplied times their corresponding point losses, and the appropriate number of points is subtracted from the point total earned for that day. The child gets to keep the difference.

If the teacher wants the system being used to appear less obtrusive, then the point card can be kept at her/his desk and operated from there. It is desirable, but not essential, for the child to be aware each time that a point is earned or lost. The teacher can rate the child's performance and both award and subtract points as indicated at his/her desk. At certain times during the day, depending on the teacher's preference, the child can be called up to her/his desk and given feedback. A system such as this will work quite well for most children, but there are children who would probably require more immediate feedback and monitoring for the program to impact on their behavior. For such children it may be necessary to leave the card on their desks for awhile and then gradually change until the teacher keeps exclusive control of the card and the child receives feedback at certain times during the day.

Another reason teachers have rejected the use of behavior management procedures is that they tend to see them as an add on–that is, as involving extra work for them. If applied correctly, the systematic use of behavior management procedures can significantly *reduce* the amount of time the teacher has to devote to the management and consequation of child behavior. Simultaneously, the classroom would become a much more pleasant environment for both pupils and teachers. It is also possible that if classroom behavior problems were reduced, the rate of learning and achievement per child would show a corresponding increase. It is sometimes difficult to get teachers past the point of viewing behavior management procedures as an added burden and to recognize the potential benefits their effective application can yield.

It is truly amazing how much time and energy some teachers invest in the process of managing child behavior via the use of reprimands, warnings, threats, and occasionally yelling. These techniques, at best, produce a temporary suppression in the inappropriate child behavior to which they are applied. Sometimes, they have no effect whatever in suppressing behavior. As has already been noted, these techniques are instrumental in actually strengthening inappropriate behavior for some children over the long term.

If teachers would simply count the number of times they reprimand, warn, threat, criticize, or yell in response to child behavior, they would often be amazed at the totals for a one-week period. This is not only the weakest and most ineffectual form of behavior management, it is extremely frustrating as well. A systematic behavior management program can eliminate the need for such control techniques and allow the teacher to focus upon appropriate child behavior and the process of teaching.

A third reason teachers reject the use of behavior management procedures has to do with their expectations concerning an effective treatment and how much time it should take to produce the desired effects. It appears that many educators are still waiting for the ultimate miracle treatment for human behavior. Such a treatment would be extremely easy and simple to implement and would *permanently* change behavior regardless of settings or conditions. Unfortunately, such a treatment is not likely to be developed in the foreseeable future.

At present, the closest thing we have to such a treatment is drug therapy for hyperactive children. Once the correct dosage is found, the treatment is very simple to implement, e.g., the child takes a pill one or more times per day. In those cases where drug therapy is successful, the resulting changes in child behavior can be very reinforcing to adults, e.g., the aversive features of the child's behavior are greatly suppressed or totally eliminated. There is little wonder that drug therapy is such a popular treatment for children who are judged to be hyperactive.

However, as noted in Chapter 1, drug therapy for hyperactivity can have some undesirable side effects. In addition, such a treatment teaches the child nothing about his/her behavior or how to control it. When the drug therapy program is terminated, the child's behavior pattern usually shows an instant reversal to predrug therapy levels.

Drug therapy does not appear to be a desirable treatment procedure for the great majority of children experiencing behavioral and learning problems in the school setting. Even if it were, it does not appear feasible to keep children on such programs throughout their school careers.

When one considers the problem of changing child behavior in its total perspective, it is apparent that there are no easy answers and no shortcuts to producing significant and socially desirable changes in child behavior. Most children with learning and behavior problems in school have developed them over a number of years. Given this length of time and the complex nature of such problems, one should expect that considerable effort will have to be invested in order to reverse this process and to teach a new behavior pattern. This is precisely what is required.

It should be noted that powerful behavior management procedures can produce dramatic and sometimes immediate changes in child behavior. Unfortunately, their abrupt termination tends to produce equally dramatic and generally immediate reversals of the behavioral gains achieved. What is needed are intensive and maximally powerful intervention procedures, implemented on a short term basis, followed by a shift to a low cost variation of the original intervention that maintains behavior, but that is significantly easier for teachers to implement and manage. The low cost maintenance program should be implemented on a permanent basis or until it is clear that it is no longer required to maintain the child's changed behavior. If necessary, such programs should be continued across school years, with each new teacher being trained to operate the program. This may appear to be a great deal of work, but if significant and permanent changes are to be produced in child behavior, this level of effort is usually required.

Systematic behavior management procedures are highly cost-effective. The potential benefits to both teachers and children more than offset the effort and energy required in their implementation.

Behavior Management Procedures Do Not Produce Enduring Changes That Are Internalized and Displayed Throughout All Aspects of the Child's Functioning

As in the medical treatment of various physical pathologies, the goal of traditional psychotherapies and educational interventions has been to produce comprehensive and enduring changes in human behavior.

In fact, the usual standard for judging the efficacy of such treatments has been whether one's behavior shows evidence of generalized and enduring changes over time and across settings. Unlike medical practitioners, however, psychologists and educators have been greatly disappointed in their ability to produce such changes.

The failure to achieve such therapeutic effects is often attributed to the failure of human behavior to generalize across settings (Mischel, 1968). The research literature in psychology and education provides overwhelming evidence as to the situational specificity of human behavior (Herman & Tramontana, 1971; Johnson, Boldstad, & Lobitz, 1976; O'Leary & Drabman, 1971; Wahler, 1969, 1975). Human behavior, in large part, appears to be a function of the situation in which it occurs, and it is highly responsive to the stimuli setting events and contingencies that exist within such situations (Mischel, 1968). To the extent that there is a close "match" of these variables across settings, behavioral consistency within and across them can be expected.

Given that child behavior is highly situation-specific, one would not logically expect behavior changes produced in one setting, through alteration of existing contingencies in that setting via a behavior management program, to generalize to nonintervention settings in which deviant behavior had occurred at equivalent or even higher levels. With a few exceptions (Hauserman, Walen, & Behling, 1973; Kazdin, 1973; Walker, Mattson, & Buckley, 1971) this is precisely what the research literature is showing (Herman & Tramontana, 1971; Johnson, et al. 1976; Meichenbaum, Bowers, & Ross, 1968; O'Leary & Drabman, 1971; Wahler, 1969, 1975; Walker & Buckley, 1972).

This is a particular problem in situations where psychological/educational treatments are administered within artificial or special settings and generalization of changed behavior to natural settings is expected. Treatments administered within the psychologist's office or clinic and within special or resource classrooms have been very popular within the last two or three decades. However, the effectiveness of such treatments in impacting upon child behavior in natural settings, where treatment procedures are not implemented, is being increasingly questioned by psychologists and educators (Stuart, 1972; Tramontana, 1971).

Tramontana (1971) suggests that even if such generalization effects were in evidence, one must wonder about the effects the unmodified natural environment would eventually have on the changed behavior. Under such circumstances it would be expected that the deviant behavior would be restrengthened and that the experimentally produced behavior changes would eventually extinguish. The limited information available on this question seems to bear out Tramontana (Herman & Tramontana, 1971; O'Leary & O'Leary, 1976; Walker & Buckley, 1972, 1974).

Given this information, what can one expect concerning the long term durability and generalizability (across settings) of behavior changes produced through the systematic application of behavior management techniques? One should expect that (1) behavior changes will not endure permanently following the abrupt termination of an intervention program, and (2) that behavior changes produced in one setting will not as a rule generalize to other settings where the intervention program has not been implemented. In a sense, these are depressing expectations, since we are trained to think in terms of "cures" that are pervasive in their effects across settings and throughout all facets of a child's life. This just does not seem to be the case with human behavior.

Basically, behavior tends to show change in whichever settings treatment is implemented, and it tends to remain unchanged in those settings in which treatment is not implemented. Similarly, when treatment is introduced, behavior tends to change, and when it is withdrawn it tends to revert back to pretreatment levels. There are limited exceptions to each of these assumptions, but as a general rule, they are representative of what one can expect, particularly in the educational setting.

These effects are not just specific to one type of behavior change procedure or theory. They are characteristic of human behavior in general and apply equally to all procedures capable of producing changes in behavior. The treatment procedure has not been invented as yet that reliably produces *enduring* changes in behavior or that produces generalization of changed behavior to nontreatment settings.

What are the implications of these findings for teachers faced with the task of modifying child behavior? To begin with, they suggest that "what you teach is what you get." That is, one should plan on implementing the intervention program, or a variation of it, in all settings in which child behavior is problematic and in which behavior change is expected. Second, one should initially implement an intensive and comprehensive intervention program that is designed to have a powerful impact upon child behavior. After the child has adjusted well to the program and the goals of treatment have been initially achieved, a fading program should be introduced to gradually reduce the more obvious features of the program and to make it more manageable for the teacher. However, *a low cost variation of the intervention should remain in effect for the foreseeable future or until the child's behavior no longer requires this support.* Several variations of this procedure are discussed in the case studies presented in Chapter 5.

There is considerable reluctance on the part of some teachers to accept such a depressing, but realistic, view of the process of changing child behavior. This is certainly understandable, but given what we know about human behavior and procedures for changing it, this view appears to be most accurate and valid. The sooner we accept reality, the sooner we as educators will be able to respond effectively to the learning and behavior problems presented by children we are responsible for educating. It is extremely unlikely that any intervention procedure will ever be developed that will automatically produce either generalization of behavior changes to nontreatment settings or enduring and permanent changes in child behavior.

The Issue of Powerful Behavior Management Techniques Represents an Undesirable Form of Behavioral Control

Powerful behavior management procedures in general, and behavior modification procedures in particular, have generated a great deal of controversy in the last ten years. They have been associated with the spectre of mind control and with the corruption of basic human values. In addition, both lobotomies and drug programs to control hyperactivity have been mistakenly associated with and labelled as behavior modification. Neither of these procedures has anything to do with the practice of behavior modification as it has come to be known in the professional literature, and in the fields of education and psychology.

It is unfortunate that behavior modification's controversial status is in part a result of incorrect information surrounding what it represents. Behavior modification does represent a powerful form of behavioral control—the power of this technology in changing human behavior has been demonstrated literally hundreds of times in studies reported in the professional literature. It is easily the most powerful and effective system for changing human behavior ever developed.

As such, it is obvious that it could be abused in the process of changing behavior. In fact, some abuses in prison and institutional settings with captive populations have been documented (Martin, 1974; Wexler, 1973). There have been a number of legal challenges to the use of behavior modification in such settings. The courts have increasingly become involved in the regulation and supervision of behavior modification in institutional settings. For example, it is no longer possible to deny patients access to basic comforts, such as bed and food, in order to motivate them to change their behavior. This appears to be a highly appropriate prohibition.

Behavior modification has also been criticized on the grounds that it restricts the freedom of choice of individuals to whom it is applied by motivating them to behave in carefully prescribed ways. Clearly, this would be theoretically possible, but the author knows of no instance in which this has occurred. In fact, in classroom applications, it appears that behavior management techniques based upon principles of behavior modification actually broaden a child's freedom of choice by increasing basic competence levels and by teaching a pattern of adaptive behavior. It appears that the method of application, rather than the procedures themselves, could potentially restrict one's freedom.

Concern has also been expressed, particularly by teachers, that the use of systematic behavior management procedures will teach children an artificial set of values. That is, children will learn to expect rewards for everything they do, as a result of being exposed to a program in which reinforcement procedures are used. There is no evidence that this is true. However, it would certainly be possible to give children this expectancy depending upon how the program was represented to them.

It is difficult to abuse the use of behavior management procedures in the educational setting. However, they do represent powerful and highly effective teaching procedures; consequently, one should attend very carefully to what is communicated and taught via their implementation in the classroom setting. In the author's opinion, most teachers would be quite sensitive to such issues.

APPENDIX A, CHAPTER 4 SAMPLE PRAISE STATEMENTS FOR CLASSROOM TEACHERS *

1. "Allin, your math paper was 100 percent correct."
2. "Your math is improving every day."

* Reprinted from CORBEH's CLASS Program.

3. "It took you less time to finish the assignment today and you did two more problems."
4. "You're exactly right."
5. "Allin is really paying attention."
6. "Allin is sitting quietly and doing his work very nicely! Good job!"
7. "That's good thinking, Allin!"
8. "Wow, look at Allin study!"
9. "Everyone in here stop and look at Allin. He's really working hard!"
10. "Good job!"
11. "I can really tell Allin is thinking by what he just said. Good!"
12. "I really like the way Allin is working on his math book; keep up the good work!"
13. "I really like the way Allin has listened today. That's very polite, Allin, thank you."
14. "Fantastic!"
15. "Excellent!"
16. "You're doing just great!"
17. "Far out!"
18. "You look nice today."
19. "Allin is thoughtful."
20. "I really appreciate the way you sit quietly and listen to me when I'm giving a lesson."
21. "Thank you for your attention."
22. "Allin just earned another point by sitting and listening to me when I was reading. Good job, Allin!"
23. "Allin's a hard worker today."
24. "Right on!"
25. "Right!"
26. "Good!"
27. "That's the best job I've seen you do."
28. "Nice!"
29. "That makes me very happy to see you working so well."
30. "Allin walked to his seat very quietly. Thank you, Allin."

31. "When Allin got up to get his materials, he returned to his desk and started right to work; good job!"
32. "I like the way Allin raised his hand when he wanted to share something with the class."
33. "The whole class is really being polite in listening to one another."
34. "That was a courteous thing to do for Ann, Allin."
35. "I'm glad you sharpened your pencil before class; now you're all set to go. Good!"
36. "Allin has all of the supplies on his desk and is sitting quietly waiting for instructions. Good!"
37. "Allin and his whole row are sitting with their materials ready."
38. "It's been a long time since I had to take any objects away from the people in this class. You really know how to show me you're responsible people."
39. Pat on the back when sitting quietly and studying.
40. "Allin knows how to follow instructions."

APPENDIX B, CHAPTER 4 REWARDS LIST: IN SCHOOL, OUTSIDE SCHOOL, AND AT HOME

I. School Rewards

a. Activities

1. Presenting at "Show and Tell"
2. Helping teacher
3. Being in a play
4. Playing teacher
5. Singing
6. Reading with a friend
7. Holding the flag
8. Being captain
9. Reading a new book
10. Cleaning the blackboard
11. Time to play a game on rug with friend
12. Time to draw on blackboard

13. Teacher "Surprise" (Teacher-selected reward)
14. Stamping papers for teacher
15. Chance to change partners on swimming bus
16. Teacher "Surprise" for boys
17. Teacher "Surprise" for girls
18. Teacher "Surprise" for whole class
19. A poster to take home
20. Eating in the room with teacher
21. All boys eating in room with teacher
22. Whole class eat in room with teacher
23. Eat in room with a friend
24. Girls, five minutes free time
25. Working film projector
26. Being score keeper for "Spelling Baseball"
27. Surprise for teacher
28. Game during P.E.
29. Read a book on the rug with a friend
30. Boys, five minutes extra recess
31. Five minutes extra recess
32. Five minutes early dismissal
33. Special story or extra story time
34. Special record or film strip
35. Joke/riddle book
36. Free time for class
37. Special art activity
38. Special game during P.E.
39. Use of special equipment during P.E.

Use of Special Materials (usually for a specified length of time)

1. Language master
2. Special book to look at or read
3. Viewmaster
4. Special game with friend
5. Tape recorder
6. Record
7. Typewriter

8. Special art materials
9. Bring own game or records

Time with a Special Person (Teacher, Aide, Counselor, etc.)

1. To hear or read a story
2. To play a game
3. To talk

Time in a Special Place

1. In the library
2. In the art mobile
3. In the office helping the secretary

Special Classroom Duties

1. Messenger
2. Time leader
3. Attendance taker
4. Scorekeeper

b. Classroom Games

1. Seven-up
2. Musical Chairs
3. Simon Says
4. 'Round the World'
5. Hot/Cold
6. Fruitbasket Upset
7. Twenty Questions
8. Eraser Game
9. Black Magic
10. "It is I"
11. Blanket Cover-up
12. Activity Pantomime

II. Rewards Outside the Classroom

1. A field trip
2. Taking a class pet home

3. Trip to a fair
4. Tutoring younger children
5. A class picnic
6. A bus ride
7. A swimming trip
8. Trip to a museum
9. Trip to the zoo

III. Home Rewards

1. Extra TV time
2. Staying up later than usual
3. Extra play time
4. Having a friend stay over
5. Having a special dish prepared
6. A family picnic
7. Going to a movie
8. Being excused from daily chores/tasks
9. Increased allowance
10. Earning special toys or equipment
11. Participating in special events with Mom or Dad, e.g., shopping or going fishing.

REFERENCES

Anderson, P. S. Teacher expectations and self-conceptions. (Doctoral dissertation, University of California, Irvine, 1971). *Dissertation Abstracts International*, 1971, *32* (3–A), 1619. (University Microfilms No. 71–22, 121).

Ayllon, T. & Azrin, N. *The token economy: A motivational system for therapy and rehabilitation.* New York: Appleton-Century-Crofts, 1968.

Bandura, A. *Principles of behavior modification.* New York: Holt, Rinehart & Winston, 1969.

Barrish, J., Saunders, M., & Wolf, M. Good behavior game: Effects of individual contingencies for group consequences on disruptive behavior in a classroom. *Journal of Applied Behavior Analysis*, 1969, *2*, 119–124.

Beez, W. V. Influence of biased psychological reports on teacher behavior and pupil performance. In M. B. Miles & W. W. Charters, Jr. (Eds.),

Learning and social settings: New readings in the social psychology of education. Boston: Allyn and Bacon, 1970.

Birnbrauer, J. S., Wolf, M. M., Kidder, J. D., & Tague, C. E. Classroom behavior of retarded pupils with token reinforcement. *Journal of Experimental Child Psychology*, 1965, *2*, 219–235.

Blakey, M. L. The relationship between teacher prophecy and teacher verbal behavior and their effect upon adult student achievement. (Doctoral dissertation, Florida State University, 1971). *Dissertation Abstracts International*, 1971, *31* (9–A), 4514–4516 (University Microfilms No. 71–06, 965).

Bostow, D. E. & Bailey, J. B. Modification of severe disruptive and aggressive behavior using brief timeout and reinforcement procedures. *Journal of Applied Behavior Analysis*, 1969, *2* (1), 31–37.

Brophy, J. E. & Good, T. L. Teachers' communications of differential expectations for childrens' classroom performance: Some behavioral data. *Journal of Educational Psychology*, 1970, *61*, 365–374.

Brown, E. R. & Shields, E. Results with systematic suspension: A guidance technique to help children develop self-control in public school classrooms. *Journal of Special Education*, 1967, *1*, 425–437.

Bushell, D., Jr., Wrobel, P. A., & Michaelis, M. L. Applying "group" contingents to the classroom study behavior of preschool children. *Journal of Applied Behavior Analysis*, 1968, *1*, 55–61.

Cossaint, A., Hall, R. V., & Hopkins, B. L. The effects of experimenter's instructions, feedback, and praise on teacher's praise and student attending behavior. *Journal of Applied Behavior Analysis*, 1973, *6*, 89–100.

Drabman, R. & Lahey, B. Feedback in classroom behavior modification: Effects on the target and her classmates. *Journal of Applied Behavior Analysis*, 1974, 7, 591–598.

Elam, D. & Sulzer-Azaroff, B. *Group versus individual reinforcement in modifying problem behaviors in a trainable mentally handicapped classroom.* Unpublished paper. Carbondale, Illinois: Southern Illinois University, 1973.

Elliott, R. & Tighe, T. Breaking the cigarette habit: Effects of a technique involving threatened loss of money. *Psychological Record*, 1968, *18*, 503–513.

Ferster, C. B. & Skinner, B. F. Schedules of reinforcement. New York: Appleton-Century-Crofts, 1957.

Firestone, G. & Brody, N. Longitudinal investigation of teacher-student interactions and their relationship to academic performance. *Journal of Educational Psychology*, 1975, *67*, 544–550.

Greenwood, C. R. & Hops, H. *Generalization of teacher praising skills over time and setting: What you teach is what you get!* Presented at the 54th Annual Convention of the Council for Exceptional Children, Chicago, Ill., 1976.

Greenwood, C. R., Hops, H., Delquadri, J., & Guild, J. Group contingencies for group consequences in classroom management: A further analysis. *Journal of Applied Behavior Analysis*, 1974, 7, 413–425.

Hamblin, R. E., Hathoway, C., & Wodarski, J. Group contingencies, peer tutoring, and accelerating academic achievement. In E. A. Ramp and B. L. Hopkins (Eds.), *A new direction for education: Behavior analysis* (Vol. 1). Follow-Through, University of Kansas, 1971.

Hanley, E. M. Review of research involving applied behavior analysis in the classroom. *Review of Educational Research*, 1970, *40*, 597–625.

Hauserman, N., Walen, S. R., & Behling, M. Reinforced racial integration in the first grade: A study in generalization. *Journal of Applied Behavior Analysis*, 1973, *6*, 193–200.

Herbert, E. W., Pinkston, E., Hayden, M., Sajwaj, T., Pinkston, S., Cordua, G., & Jackson, C. Adverse effects of differential parental attention. *Journal of Applied Behavior Analysis*, 1973, *6*, 15–30.

Herman, S. H., & Tramontana, J. Instructions and group versus individual reinforcement in modifying disruptive group behavior. *Journal of Applied Behavior Analysis*, 1971, *4*, 113–119.

Holz, W. C., Azrin, N., & Ayllon, T. Elimination of behavior of mental patients by response-produced extinction. *Journal of the Experimental Analysis of Behavior*, 1963, *6*, 407–412.

Homme, L. E. *How to use contingency contracting in the classroom.* Champaign: Research Press Co., 1969.

Homme, L. E., de Baca, D. C., Devine, J. V., Steinhorst, R., & Rickert, E. J. Use of the Premack principle in controlling the behavior of nursery school children. *Journal of the Experimental Analysis of Behavior*, 1963, *6*, 544.

Hops, H., Beickel, S., & Walker, H. M. *CLASS* (*Contingencies for Learning Academic and Social Skills*). Eugene, Ore.: Center at Oregon for Research in the Behavioral Education of the Handicapped, University of Oregon, 1976.

Hops, H., Greenwood, C. R., & Guild, J. *Programming generalization of teacher praising skills: How easy is it?* Presented at the Annual Convention of the Association for the Advancement of Behavioral Therapy, San Francisco, California, 1975.

Hops, H., Walker, H. M., & Fleischman, D. *CLASS: A standardized inclass program for acting-out children: II. Field test evaluations.* CORBEH Report #22, Eugene, Ore.: Center at Oregon for Research in the Behavioral Education of the Handicapped, University of Oregon, 1976.

Hundert, J. The effectiveness of reinforcement, response cost, and mixed programs on classroom behaviors. *Journal of Applied Behavior Analysis*, 1976, *9*, 107.

Jacobs, J. *A comparison of group and individual rewards in teaching reading to slow learners.* H.E.W., U.S.O.E. Project #9–0257, 1970.

Johnson, S. M., Boldstad, O., & Lobitz, G. Generalization and contrast phenomena in behavior modification with children. In E. J. Mash, L. A. Hamerlynck, & L. C. Handy (Eds.), *Behavior modification and families.* New York: Brunner/Mazell, 1976.

Jones, F. H. & Miller, W. H. The effective use of negative attention for reducing group disruption in special elementary school classrooms. *The Psychological Record*, 1974, *24*, 435–448.

Kazdin, A. E. Role of instructions and reinforcement in behavior changes in token reinforcement programs. *Journal of Educational Research*, 1973, *64*, 63–71.

Kazdin, A. E. Response cost: The removal of conditioned reinforcers for therapeutic change *Behavior Therapy*, 1972, *3*, 533–546

Madsen, C. H., Becker, W. C., & Thomas, D. Rules, praise, and ignoring: Elements of elementary classroom control. *Journal of Applied Behavior Analysis*, 1968, *1*, 139–150.

Martin, R. *Legal challenges to behavior modification.* Champaign: Research Press Co., 1975.

Meichenbaum, D. H., Bowers, K. S., & Ross, R. R. Modification of classroom behavior of institutionalized female adolescent offenders. *Behavior Research and Therapy*, 1968, *6*, 343–353.

Mischel, W. *Personality and assessment.* New York: John Wiley, 1968.

O'Leary, K. D. & Becker, W. C. Behavior modification of an adjustment class: A token reinforcement program. *Exceptional Children*, 1967, *34*, 637–642.

O'Leary, K. D., Becker, W. C., Evans, M. B., & Saudargas, R. A. A token reinforcement program in a public school: A replication and systematic analysis. *Journal of Applied Behavior Analysis*, 1969, *2*, 3–13.

O'Leary, K. D. & Drabman, R. Token reinforcement programs in the classroom: A review. *Psychological Bulletin*, 1971, *75*, 379–398.

O'Leary, K. D., Kaufman, K., Kass, R. E., & Drabman, R. The effects of loud and soft reprimands on the behavior of disruptive students. *Exceptional Children*, 1970, *37*, 145–155.

O'Leary, K. D. & O'Leary, S. G. Behavior modification in the school. In H. Leitenberg (Ed.), *Handbook of Behavior Modification and Therapy.* Englewood Cliffs, New Jersey: Prentice-Hall, 1976.

Packard, R. G. The control of "classroom attention": A group contingency for complex behavior. *Journal of Applied Behavior Analysis*, 1970, *3*, 13–28.

Patterson, G. R. An application of conditioning techniques to the control of a hyperactive child. In L. P. Ullman and L. Krasner (Eds.), *Case studies in behavior modification.* New York: Holt, Rinehart & Winston, 1965.

Patterson, G. R. & Gullion, E. *Living with children.* Champaign: Research Press Co., 1968.

Phillips, E. L. Achievement place: Token reinforcement procedures in a home style rehabilitation setting for "predelinquent" boys. *Journal of Applied Behavior Analysis*, 1968, *1*, 213–223.

Phillips, E. L., Phillips, E. A., Fixen, D. L., & Wolf, M. M. Achievement place: Modification of the behaviors of pre-delinquent boys within a token economy. *Journal of Applied Behavior Analysis*, 1971, *4*, 45–59.

Pinkston, E. M., Reese, N. M., Le Blanc, J. M., & Baer, D. Independent control of a preschool child's aggression and peer interaction by contingent teacher attention. *Journal of Applied Behavior Analysis*, 1973, *6*, 115–124.

Rothbart, M., Dalfen, S., & Barrett, R. Effects of teacher expectancy on student-teacher interaction. *Journal of Educational Psychology*, 1971, *62*, 49–54.

Rubovits, P. & Maehr, M. Pygmalion analyzed: Toward an explanation of the Rosenthal-Jacobson findings. *Journal of Personality and Social Psychology*, 1971, *19*, 197–203.

Schmidt, G. W. & Ulrich, R. E. Effects of group contingent events upon classroom noise. *Journal of Applied Behavior Analysis*, 1969, *2*, 171–179.

Siegel, G. M., Lenske, J., & Broen, P. Suppression of normal speech disfluencies through response cost. *Journal of Applied Behavior Analysis*, 1969, *2*, 265–276.

Strain, P., Shores, R., & Kerr, M. An experimental analysis of "spillover" effects on the social interaction of behaviorally handicapped preschool children. *Journal of Applied Behavior Analysis*, 1976, *9*, 31–40.

Stuart, R. B. Behavior modification techniques for the educational technologist. In R. C. Sarri & F. F. Maples (Eds.), *The Schools in the Community*. Washington, D.C.: National Association of Social Workers, 1972.

Sulzbacher, S. I. & Houser, J. E. A tactic to eliminate disruptive behaviors in the classroom: Group contingent consequences. *American Journal of Mental Deficiency*, 1968, *73*, 88–90.

Thoresen, C. E. & Mahoney, M. J. *Behavioral self-control.* New York: Holt, Rinehart & Winston, 1974.

Tramontana, J. A review of research on behavior modification in the home and school. *Educational Technology*, February 1971, 61–63.

Upper, D. *A "ticket" system for reducing ward rules violations on a token economy program.* Paper presented at the Association for Advancement of Behavioral Therapy, Washington, D.C., 1971.

Wahler, R. G. Some structural aspects of deviant child behavior. *Journal of Applied Behavior Analysis*, 1975, *8*, 27–42.

Wahler, R. G. Setting generality: Some specific and general effects of child behavior therapy. *Journal of Applied Behavior Analysis*, 1969, *2*, 239–246.

Wahler, R. G. Oppositional children: A quest for parental reinforcement control. *Journal of Applied Behavior Analysis*, 1969, *2* (3), 159–170.

Walker, H. M. & Buckley, N. K. *Token reinforcement techniques: Classroom applications for the hard to teach child.* Eugene, Oregon: E-P Press, Inc., 1974.

Walker, H. M. & Buckley, N. K. Programming generalization and maintenance of treatment effects across time and across settings. *Journal of Applied Behavior Analysis*, 1972, *5*, 209–224.

Walker, H. M. & Buckley, N. K. The use of positive reinforcement in conditioning attending behavior. *Journal of Applied Behavior Analysis*, 1968, *1*, 245–250.

Walker, H. M. & Hops, H. Use of normative peer data as a standard for evaluating classroom treatment effects. *Journal of Applied Behavior Analysis*, 1976, *9*, 159–168.

Walker, H. M. & Hops, H. The use of group and individual reinforcement contingencies in the modification of social withdrawal. In L. A. Hamerlynck, L. C. Handy, & E. J. Mash (Eds.), *Behavior change: Methodology, concepts and practice*, Champaign: Research Press, 1973, 269–307.

Walker, H. M., Hops, H., & Fiegenbaum, E. Deviant classroom behavior as a function of combinations of social and token reinforcement and cost contingency. *Behavior Therapy*, 1976, 7, 76–88.

Walker, H. M., Hops, H., & Greenwood, C. R. *A comparative analysis of home and school components of a treatment package for acting out children.* Proposal submitted to the Division of Innovation and Development, Bureau of the Handicapped, U.S. Office of Education, 1977.

Walker, H. M., Hops, H., Greenwood, C. R., Todd, N., & Garrett, B. *The Comparative effects of teacher praise, token reinforcement, and response cost in reducing negative peer interactions.* CORBEH Report #25. Eugene, Oregon: Center at Oregon for Research in the Behavioral Education of the Handicapped, University of Oregon, 1977.

Walker, H. M., Mattson, R. H., & Buckley, N. K. The functional analysis of behavior within an experimental classroom setting. In W. C. Becker (Ed.) *An empirical basis for change in education.* Chicago: Science Research Associates, 1971.

Walker, H. M., Street, A., Garrett, B., & Crossen, J. *Experiments with response cost in playground and classroom settings.* CORBEH Report #35. Eugene, Oregon: Center at Oregon for Research in the Behavioral Education of the Handicapped, University of Oregon, 1977.

Wasik, B., Senn, K., Welch, R. H., & Cooper, B. R. Behavior modification with culturally deprived school children: Two case studies. *Journal of Applied Behavior Analysis*, 1969, *2*, 171–179.

Weiner, H. Response cost and the aversive control of human operant behavior. *Journal of the Experimental Analysis of Behavior*, 1963, *6* (3), 415–421.

Weiner, H. Some effects of response cost upon human operant behavior. *Journal of the Experimental Analysis of Behavior*, 1962, *5*, 210–218.

Wexler, D. B. Token and taboo: Behavioral modification, token economies and the law. *California Law Review*, (Vol. 61), #1, January 1973.

White, M. A. Natural rates of teacher approval and disapproval in the classroom. *Journal of Applied Behavior Analysis*, 1975, *8*, 367–372.

White, G., Nielsen, G., & Johnson, S. M. Timeout duration and the suppression of deviant behavior in children. *Journal of Applied Behavior Analysis*, 1972, *5*, 111–120.

Winkler, R. C. Management of chronic psychiatric patients by a token reinforcement system. *Journal of Applied Behavior Analysis*, 1970, *3*, 47–55.

Wolf, M. M., Hanley, E. L., King, L. A., Lachowicz, J., & Giles, D. K. The timer-game: A variable interval contingency for the management of out-of-seat behavior. *Exceptional Children*, 1970, *37*, 113–117.

CHAPTER

5

Case Studies

The purpose of this chapter is to illustrate practical applications of the treatment techniques and intervention procedures presented in Chapter 4. A second, and equally important goal, is to illustrate potential implementation problems that may be encountered in such applications. Adaptive responses to such problems are presented for the reader's consideration.

This chapter is divided into two sections. Section One presents four case studies which illustrate the correct application of intervention procedures to behavior problems commonly encountered in the school setting. The case studies are fictional; however, they are composites of actual intervention programs implemented by the author and his colleagues. The studies presented in this section contain (1) a set of behavioral characteristics of the fictional target child, (2) referral problems, (3) intervention procedures used, (4) problems encountered in the implementation process and responses to them, and (5) a set of outcomes resulting from application of the procedures. Each case study deals with a different behavior disorder or problem frequently encountered in the school setting.

Section Two presents background information and child behavioral characteristics *only* for an additional three case studies. Based on the information presented, the reader is asked to: (1) develop an appropriate set of behavior change goals that could be achieved given the correct application of appropriate intervention procedures, (2) develop a set of intervention procedures for achieving the identified behavior change goals, and (3) identify potential problem areas in the implementation process. The reader will be able to compare his/her responses to those furnished by the author. Hopefully, these tasks will provide the reader with some direct experience in developing original responses to behavior management problems.

SECTION ONE: ILLUSTRATIVE CASE STUDIES

Four case studies are presented here to illustrate application of behavior management techniques in the remediation of classroom and playground behavior problems. Case studies are presented respectively for (1) an acting-out child, (2) a socially aggressive child, (3) a minimally disruptive child, and (4) an entire classroom.

Case Study: An Acting-Out Child

Background. Jody was an acting-out boy enrolled in a regular third-grade classroom. Even though he was only in the third grade, he had already acquired a reputation as a "holy terror." Labels that had been used to describe his classroom and playground behavior included "incorrigible," "hyperactive," "unmanageable," "a little monster," "mean," "out of control," "unteachable," "lazy," "a bully," "sneaky," and "just plain ornery!"

Jody had run the full gamut of school psychological services. He experienced difficulty from the first day of school in responding to ordinary classroom demands such as listening to instructions, following directions, working on assigned material(s), and participating in group activities in an acceptable manner. He was constantly in motion, even when in his seat. He had great difficulties in concentrating on any task for more than a minute or two. To make matters worse, he was constantly disturbing others whenever he was not engrossed in a task or activity—which was infrequently! Jody was usually the center of attention, in a negative sense, in his classroom—a role he seemed to enjoy immensely.

As might be expected, his academic skills and achievement were both well below grade level. He had difficulties with both oral and silent reading tasks and was especially weak in number concepts.

Jody was literally the bane of his teacher's existence. She commented a number of times how pleasant her life would be if it were not for having to deal with Jody each day. The thing that was particularly irritating for her was the disruptive effect he had on the classroom and the influence he seemed to have with his classmates. It was as though Jody and his teacher were in a contest for influence and control of the allegiance of other class members.

Everything the teacher tried, from reprimands to timeout, seemed to have no effect or a minimal impact at best upon Jody's overall behavior. Jody's teacher was extremely discouraged about his behavior pattern and felt that he would be a behavior problem and low achiever for the remainder of his school career.

Jody's school record, test results, and the opinion of his previous teachers, the school counselor, and his principal all pointed to the same conclusion—that he would be a school failure and constant adjustment problem. Jody had been referred for psychological testing shortly after entering first grade because of numerous and highly visible behavior problems. The testing confirmed that he was of normal intelligence but suggested that he was both unhappy and had low self-image problems. Unfortunately, the testing provided little in the way of useful information for coping with Jody's behavior.

Jody was assigned to a special classroom for disturbed children for awhile. Although he received specialized attention and an individualized instructional program in this setting, his overall behavior pattern was approximately the same as in the regular classroom.

By the time he had reached the third grade, Jody had been reassigned to the regular classroom as part of a mainstreaming policy adopted by the school district. He was assigned to a teacher who seemed to relate well to children in general and who had experienced considerable success in working with children who had learning and behavioral difficulties. By her own admission, however, Jody was the most difficult and least cooperative child she had ever encountered in her twelve years of teaching.

Jody's behavior became so disruptive and generally aversive that a parent-school conference was called to consider alternatives for coping with his behavior. Jody's school record was reviewed and his future prospects were discussed. His parents were quite defensive about his school behavior, but they felt incompetent to deal with it.

Indications were that Jody's behavior was out of control at home much of the time and that he was a neglected child.

Alternatives that were considered included

(1) referring the family to a mental health clinic for psychological treatment,
(2) placing Jody on a drug program designed to control his school and home behavior,
(3) assigning Jody to a residential mental institution for severely disturbed children and adults,
(4) suspending him from school for a period of time, and
(5) developing a comprehensive intervention program designed to gain control of his school behavior.

After much discussion, it was decided to try the intervention program, and if that didn't work, to consider either a powerful drug program or assignment to a mental institution for a period of time in the hope that a twenty-four-hour a day total program would turn his behavior around. The school psychologist was assigned to work with Jody, his classmates, his teacher, and parents in developing the most powerful intervention program possible for coping with his behavior.

The Intervention Program. Before beginning the task of developing an intervention program for Jody, the school psychologist interviewed Jody, his teacher, and his parents. He had Jody's teacher and parents complete several rating scales that were designed to provide descriptions of Jody's *overt, observable* behavior at school and at home. The parents and teacher were questioned in considerable detail about the following issues: (1) What specific behaviors did Jody engage in that they found particularly irritating and aversive? (2) What situations, if any, seemed to prompt the occurrence of such behaviors? In other words, were there situations that seemed to elicit such behavior from Jody? (3) What activities did Jody seem to enjoy at school and at home? Results of the parent and teacher interviews revealed that Jody had acquired a set of behaviors that were highly irritating to adults. For example, he had a high rate of noncompliance with commands from adults. If told to do something, he would often ignore the command or do it only under duress after numerous prompts. At home, he was constantly arguing and fighting with his brothers and sister.

Usually, parental intervention was required to stop these episodes. Jody was just as irritating at school. His noncompliance rate was equally high with his teacher and his general disruptiveness was a constant source of irritation. Jody also had a habit of interrupting his teacher when she was engaged in tasks, rather than waiting until she was free and able to respond to him.

When Jody was interviewed, it was apparent that he perceived much of his school and home behavior to be inappropriate and as irritating to his parents and teacher. However, he was unable to verbalize why he continued to behave in this fashion in the face of such massive disapproval from his parents and teacher.

Next, the psychologist observed Jody's behavior in the classroom on several occasions. The purpose of these observations was threefold: (1) to obtain a visual picture of Jody's inappropriate behavior, (2) to observe his interactions with the teacher and peers, and (3) to determine whether there were any antecedents of a situational nature that prompted Jody's episodes of inappropriate behavior.

The psychologist then called a second parent-school conference to review his findings and to describe details of a comprehensive intervention program designed to change Jody's behavior. The psychologist revealed that there were marked similarities in Jody's behavior at home and at school, and in the responses of his parents and teacher to his behavior. It was apparent that Jody had learned a very controlling and forceful pattern of behavior in which he usually got his way and by which he received a great deal of attention, albeit negative, in the process. Jody was highly persistent in his efforts to control situations and to get his own way. Usually, his parents and teacher would give in rather than expend the energy required to carry through in a given situation. When this occurred, Jody was rewarded by getting his own way and the parents were rewarded by the termination of Jody's highly disruptive and aversive behavior. If the parent or teacher refused to give in, Jody usually threw a tantrum—which was even more disruptive and irritating.

It was also apparent that the attention Jody received for his *inappropriate* behavior from his parents, teacher, and classmates was very reinforcing for him and was instrumental in maintaining his inappropriate behavior. This was true, even though much of this attention was negative, critical, and disapproving. Jody seemed to thrive on it and he enjoyed his ability to dominate situations, to control the behavior of others toward him, and to be the center of attention. It was ironic that the best efforts of adults to control his behavior actually strengthened the inappropriate behavior they were directed toward.

The school psychologist noted that hostile episodes between Jody and his teacher often followed situations in which Jody appeared to engage in "needling" type behavior. That is, Jody would engage in teacher irritant behaviors such as asking irrelevent questions, dawdling, ignoring teacher instructions, and violating minor classroom rules in the teacher's presence. Often, the teacher would become visibly upset and verbally reprimand Jody for such behavior. Jody usually argued back, which made the teacher even more upset.

Finally, it was noted that Jody's behavior was much more likely to be inappropriate in reading and math periods than it was in other academic periods. This was due, at least in part, to Jody's weak skills in these two academic areas.

The psychologist suggested that an extremely powerful intervention procedure would be necessary to effectively change Jody's behavior in the classroom. He described an intervention plan consisting of three major components. These were (1) teacher praise for appropriate behavior, (2) a point system implemented on a short term basis, and (3) a response cost system backed up by timeout. In addition, he recommended that the teacher develop a set of clear, explicit classroom rules governing appropriate child behavior and that she go over them with all children in the class, including Jody. Finally, it was suggested that a formal written contract be developed which would specify (1) Jody's appropriate and inappropriate classroom behavior, (2) the consequences at school and at home that would be applied to Jody's behavior, and (3) the role of Jody, his classmates, his teacher, and his parents in the program. The plan was discussed and agreed upon and then presented to Jody by the psychologist and his teacher. Jody displayed some initial reluctance and lack of enthusiasm but agreed to go along with it.

A contract was drawn up as a first step and signed by the parents, teacher, and psychologist. The terms and details of the contract were explained carefully to Jody and all efforts were made to insure that he understood them. A listing of Jody's appropriate and inappropriate behavior in the classroom was included in the contract and each behavior was discussed with Jody. Efforts were made to insure that he could clearly discriminate the difference between appropriate and inappropriate classroom behavior.

Next, the consequences that would be applied to his appropriate and inappropriate behavior were carefully reviewed with Jody. It was explained that Jody could earn teacher praise and points once each ten-minute period during the day if his behavior was appropriate and if he was following classroom rules. The teacher would make an overall evaluation of his behavior for each ten-minute period and either award or withhold praise and points, depending upon his behavior. The form on which points would be awarded was described and shown to Jody. The inappropriate classroom behaviors that would result in point losses were also explained to him. The listing of inappropriate behaviors had been ranked by the teacher from least serious to most serious, and point loss values ranging from five to one were assigned accordingly. Each behavior and the corresponding point lost was explained. The form on which point losses were to be recorded was also described and shown to Jody. The use of timeout as a backup consequence whenever point totals approached zero was also explained.

Finally, Jody's pattern of interactive behavior with his teacher was discussed. The teacher irritant behaviors that he engaged in were described, explained, and modelled for Jody. As noted earlier, these included asking irrelevant questions, dawdling, ignoring teacher instructions, and violating minor classroom rules. He was informed that the teacher would be keeping track of these behaviors during the day and that if he did well in controlling them, he would earn a number of bonus points at the end of the day.

The psychologist met with the teacher and explained the intervention procedures in detail, provided the necessary forms, and answered all questions. The teacher had a number of concerns about how much time the program would take. However, the psychologist pointed out the extraordinary amounts of time the teacher had been spending already in attempting to manage the child's behavior and noted that the intervention program would, in all likelihood, not require any more of her time than she had been investing already. Further, the attention given would be directed largely toward Jody's appropriate rather than inappropriate behavior. The psychologist further noted that after the program was over, the teacher would probably have to spend less time in managing Jody's behavior and that her efforts would likely be more effective than at present. After expressing some initial skepticism about these arguments, the teacher agreed to go along with the program.

Before implementing the program, the psychologist collected several days of baseline data on both Jody and his teacher's behavior during daily thirty-minute observation periods. A stopwatch was used to record the amount of time Jody was following classroom rules and behaving appropriately. A simple tally was used to record his teacher's frequency of praising and reprimanding Jody's behavior.

Figure 5.1 below presents these data for a 3 day baseline period.

The data in Figure 5.1 show that Jody had a very low proportion of appropriate classroom behavior, averaging only 27 percent for the three days of observation. There appeared to be an inverse relationship between the teacher's frequency of reprimanding Jody and his proportion of appropriate classroom behavior; that is, the higher the frequency of teacher reprimands, the lower the proportion of Jody's appropriate classroom behavior, and vice versa. The teacher could manage to praise Jody only once in the three-day period in which observations were recorded.

The psychologist and teacher met with Jody the day before the program was to begin and explained how it would work. Jody could earn a school reward for himself and his classmates each day if he

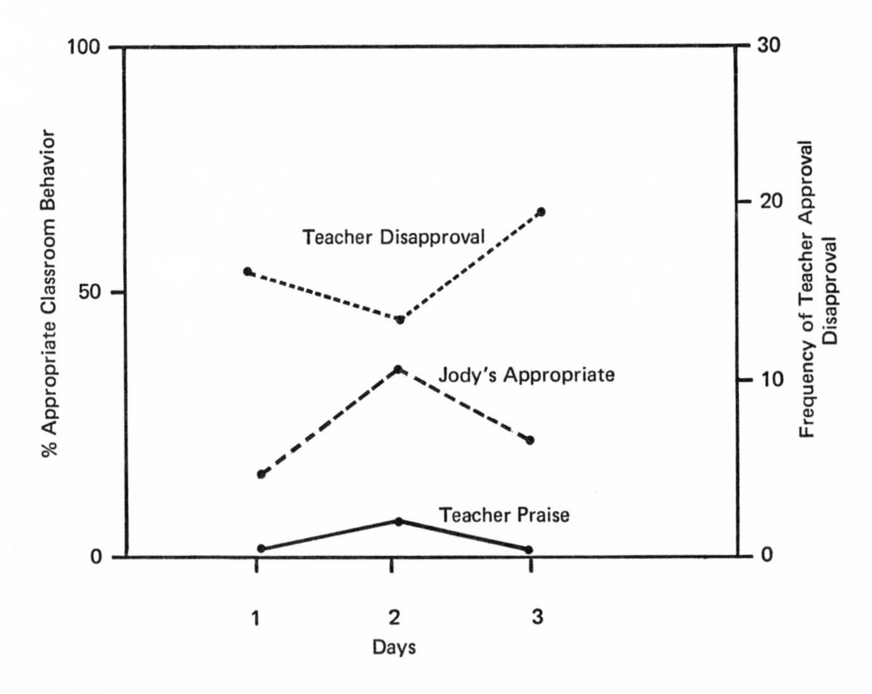

FIGURE 5.1. *Baseline Data for Jody's Classroom Behavior and His Teacher's Responses to It*

earned, and kept, 80 percent or more of the available points each day. He had an opportunity to earn teacher praise and one point during each ten-minute period. At the end of the ten-minute interval, the teacher made an overall judgment as to whether or not Jody's behavior had been *reasonably* appropriate and therefore earned praise and one point. Early in the program, the teacher tended to give Jody the benefit of the doubt and to make it as easy as possible to earn praise and points. Later on, she raised her standards and demanded more of Jody as his behavior improved and he adapted to the program.

Points were subtracted for Jody's inappropriate behavior whenever it occurred. The response cost delivery system described earlier was used to implement this component of the program. Points were subtracted from Jody's earned total of points existing at the time the inappropriate behavior occurred. Whenever Jody's total was at zero or near zero, a ten-minute timeout was used to consequate inappropriate behavior so that he did not "go in the hole" with his points.

Initially, the program operated throughout all classroom periods during the day or for a total of approximately four hours each day. Thus six points could be earned each hour or a total of twenty-four points per day. Point loss values ranged from −5 for fighting or physically aggressive behavior to −1 for persistent off-task behavior, e.g., nonattending. Thus, the ratio of points available to those that could be lost was rather stringent, thereby making the actual loss of earned points a relatively high magnitude form of mild punishment. If Jody lost *any* points during a given ten-minute interval, teacher praise and the points were withheld for that interval. Thus in a sense, inappropriate behavior resulted in a double cost for Jody—the actual subtraction of previously earned points and the withholding of praise and a point for the ten-minute interval in which it occurred.

It was explained to Jody that he could earn a daily group reward at school that would always be shared equally with classmates. Most of these rewards were of an activity nature such as extra recess, classroom games, a film, or a class party. A number of such activities were identified, a card made for each, and the cards placed in a jar with one card to be drawn out (by Jody) each day that he made the group reward (by earning and keeping 80 percent (20 points) or more of the available points).

It was also explained that he could take home the number of points remaining at the end of the day and exchange them for a special privilege there. The psychologist and teacher had met previously with

Jody's parents to work out a reinforcement menu to be used at home. Activities and events were included on the menu that his parents felt Jody really liked. A range of options was provided varying from a family picnic in the park, which cost 125 points, to a movie, which cost 100 points, to fifteen minutes of extra play time, costing ten points. The parents were very cooperative in setting up the home part of the program; this is not always the case. Had Jody's parents been uncooperative in this respect, an individual reward would have been arranged for Jody at school.

The teacher, with Jody present, explained to his classmates how the program would work, and that they would be included in the group reward each time it was earned. The teacher mentioned that Jody had been having some problems and that he was going to work with her in a new program designed to help him learn and behave better. Jody's classroom problems were no secret to his classmates. As a matter of fact, they were quite supportive of the program and realized that they could assist Jody in achieving the daily reward criterion by encouraging his attempts at appropriate behavior and by withholding their attention and approval from his inappropriate behavior.

Results. The first day Jody had some difficulty with the program. He earned a total of eighteen points but lost ten of them because of classroom rule infractions. He ended up with a net total of eight points for the day, thus, he did not earn the group reward because he ended up with only 33 percent of the available points. The teacher explained to the class that while Jody had made some good progress, he was still having difficulties in some areas, but that she was confident he could do better the next day. Jody agreed.

The next day, Jody proved to be as good as his word, earning twenty-two points and losing only one. Thus, he earned the group reward and was able to take home twenty-one points. With his total from the day before (eight) he was able to purchase fifteen minutes of extra TV time, and to have his favorite, hot dogs, for supper.

Jody was quite enthusiastic about the program at this point, but again encountered difficulties on the third day. He lost a number of points in math period, a difficult subject area for him, and displayed visible anger several times when points were subtracted. The teacher did an excellent job of ignoring his expressions of anger and did not argue with him about whether he had or had not broken classroom rule(s). Jody earned only seventeen points and lost five. He was not able to earn the group reward. His classmates were somewhat disappointed, but did not place undue pressure on him because of his failure to earn the reward.

On program day four, Jody's performance was exceptional. He earned a total of twenty-two points and lost only one, thereby earning the group reward. Jody's general status among his classmates had improved dramatically.

For the next seven school days, Jody was a model student. He earned the group reward for seven days in a row. His classmates continued to be extremely supportive of his changed behavior pattern. Both the home and school rewards were meaningful for Jody. Each represented a powerful source of motivation for him. In checking with the parents, the teacher found that Jody saved his points at home and exchanged them regularly for special privileges that he really seemed to like.

The next week was different, however. Jody would earn the group reward one day and not the next. This variability in his performance concerned the teacher, so she sat down and talked with him about it. By this time, Jody and the class had experienced all of the available group rewards at least once. Jody said he was bored with them and would like to choose from some new activities. Coincidentally, he was losing interest in the available backup rewards at home as well. This information told the teacher that the change in Jody's behavior was probably due to his losing interest in the available rewards at school and at home. Therefore, she met with his parents and planned a new menu at home, and she included Jody in the process of selecting privileges he could earn. She also arranged for Jody and the class to select a new list of group rewards that could be earned at school.

The results were immediately apparent in Jody's behavior at school. Over the next two weeks, he failed to earn the group reward only once and missed on that occasion by only one point. This experience taught Jody's teacher to monitor carefully and frequently the effectiveness of backup rewards in maintaining appropriate behavior. She learned the importance of varying available backup rewards often and checking with the child to detect changing preferences as methods of maintaining the reinforcing effectiveness of backup rewards.

During the next month, Jody continued to respond well to the program. Jody's teacher, classmates, and other teachers in the school were frankly amazed at the dramatic change in his behavior.

At this point, Jody's teacher introduced a systematic fading procedure designed to gradually remove the major components of the intervention program. She informed both Jody and his parents of the intent of the fading program, e.g., to teach Jody to maintain his new pattern of behavior with much less reliance upon external rewards. She explained to Jody that instead of being able to earn praise and one point every ten minutes, he would now be able to do so every twenty minutes instead. The exchange ratios for both the school and home rewards were adjusted accordingly, to take into account the reduced number of points that could be earned. Jody seemed to adjust to the changed routine quite well. His behavior pattern showed no effects of the fading procedure. The teacher was careful, however, to program occasional praises in between the twenty-minute periods in which teacher praise and points were usually awarded. This was important since, by doubling the interval from ten to twenty minutes, the teacher had reduced her overall attention to Jody by approximately one-half. After having been consistently paired with the delivery of points, the teacher's praise seemed to have more value for Jody. He appeared to be much more socially responsive to the teacher's praise than he had been previously.

The teacher next doubled the interval, to forty minutes, so that Jody was now earning praise and one point each forty minutes. Exchange ratios were again adjusted to take this change into account. The teacher continued to praise Jody's behavior at random times during the forty-minute period. Jody seemed to adjust to the forty-minute interval reasonably well. The reduced teacher attention seemed to be more of a problem for him than was the smaller number of available points that could be earned each day. Overall, his classroom behavior was quite appropriate.

At this point, Jody's teacher introduced a major change in the program by eliminating the point system. Instead of earning points, it was explained to Jody that he could now earn a plus or a minus for each hour of the school day. If he followed the rules and behaved appropriately he could earn a plus each hour; if not, he earned, a minus. A simple 3 × 5 card, with the day divided into five one-hour periods of classtime was used for this purpose. The card remained on Jody's desk with an evaluation made each hour as to whether he had earned a plus or a minus. If four out of five hourly ratings were pluses, Jody earned the school reward. If not, the reward was not made available for that day. Whenever Jody earned the school reward, the teacher filled out and signed a good day card, indicating that he had earned the school reward and that he qualified for a minor, special privilege at home (such as extra TV time). Thus, the point system was no longer available at home either. The privileges that could now be earned at home were of an activity nature, such as staying up later, watching extra TV, or playing special games with his parents. It was no longer possible to earn tangible items such as hamburgers or athletic equipment via the home reward system.

Jody reacted to this change in the system by showing more variability in his day-to-day performance. However, his overall level of appropriate behavior remained quite high–in the neighborhood of 85 percent.

Next, the teacher changed the reward requirement at school so that Jody had to earn four out of five pluses for two days in a row in order to earn the school reward and thereby the home privilege. After Jody had adapted satisfactorily to this change, the requirement was shifted to three out of four days, and then subsequently to four out of five days so that he was earning one group and home reward each week. As the requirement for earning the reward was gradually increased at school, higher magnitude rewards were made available both at home and at school. An attempt was made to make the rewards special and unusual as well. For example, a popcorn party was made available at the end of the week at school instead of five or ten minutes of extra recess time. Similarly, at home, a movie could now be earned instead of just fifteen minutes of extra TV time.

The higher magnitude rewards were made available at this stage of the program for several reasons. First the amount of time Jody was required to follow classroom rules and to behave appropriately in order to earn the reward was increased dramatically. Therefore, it was appropriate to make valuable rewards available to him as he was able to accommodate these increased demands. Secondly, it was important to motivate Jody to work for longer and longer periods of time in order to achieve the reinforcement criterion. Providing higher magnitude and more valuable rewards for doing so is a very effective means of achieving this goal.

The variability in Jody's day-to-day performance increased still more under these conditions. However, he earned the weekly reward approximately two out of every three weeks. His overall level of appropriate behavior hovered around 80 percent.

At this stage, Jody's teacher met with his parents and reviewed his progress during the program. It was decided to move Jody off the system, except to provide occasional surprise rewards at school and at home for Jody's appropriate school behavior.

The teacher explained that she would give Jody an overall rating each day, e.g., either a plus or minus as to the appropriateness of his behavior. She would inform him of the rating and review his school behavior at the end of each day. When he had accumulated a certain number of pluses, she would make an occasional surprise group reward available. Whenever this happened, she would send a note home with him and the parents were instructed to arrange something special at home. The teacher worked it so that if Jody's behavior were reasonably appropriate at school, a special surprise reward would be made available every three to four weeks. This system was in effect for the remainder of the school year, a period of approximately four and a half months.

Jody's behavior maintained reasonably well during this period. Compared to his pre-intervention behavior pattern, he was truly a changed individual. Both his parents and teacher were pleased with his progress. In addition to his changed classroom behavior, he made noticeable gains in the basic skill areas of reading, language, and math. His gains in math were especially noteworthy since this was a difficult subject area for him. Jody was quite aware of his new behavior pattern and verbalized frequently to the teacher how much easier and more fun school seemed to be.

Jody did encounter difficulties from time to time. If his behavioral episodes were disruptive and out of control, a brief timeout procedure was used (fifteen to twenty minutes). Usually, this worked quite well for Jody. In those cases where it didn't, he was suspended from school for one day and had to make up all his assigned work in order to get back into school the next day. It was rare that suspension had to be used to control Jody's behavior.

Jody's teacher tried to maintain a reasonable frequency of praising his appropriate behavior, e.g., once every thirty minutes or so. However, she was not always able to reach this goal. It seemed that Jody was more inclined to experience difficulties whenever the teacher ignored his appropriate behavior for long periods of time. After several such episodes, Jody's teacher began keeping a tally, on a 3 × 5 card on her desk, of her praises to Jody. Her goal was ten to twelve praises per day, delivered whenever she could "catch Jody being good!" Using this system, she was able to maintain a much more consistent and regular praise rate toward Jody's behavior. His appropriate classroom behavior quickly reflected this change.

In reviewing the intervention program, it seemed to Jody's teacher that she had invested a relatively large amount of time, energy, and effort in the process of changing Jody's classroom behavior. The question she mulled over was: did the change in Jody's behavior justify the effort involved? On balance, she decided that it did.

During pre-intervention baseline observations recorded by the psychologist, it was found that Jody received approximately 14 percent of the teacher's total attention. With a teacher-pupil ratio of 25 to 1, Jody could expect to receive approximately 4 percent of the teacher's overall attention. Thus, he was consuming slightly more than three times as much of the teacher's time as the average student in her class. Further, the great majority of this attention was negative in quality and directed toward Jody's inappropriate classroom behavior.

The teacher actually gave less attention to Jody during and after termination of the intervention program than she did before it was implemented. Implementation of the program required far less than 14 percent of her total time. Further, the attention she did give Jody was almost totally positive—a marked contrast to their interactions prior to the program.

Jody seemed to feel much better about himself and his overall behavior pattern. He was getting along much better with his classmates, and his incidence of rule breaking episodes in the classroom was greatly reduced. His general work rate and the quality of his academic performance were also improved. Jody's teacher saw him as a much more pleasant child and he was far easier to teach than before. For the first time in his school career, Jody's parents had occasion to be pleased with his school performance. As a matter of fact, they asked that the maintenance part of the program be continued into the next school year with Jody's new teacher.

Case Study: A Socially Aggressive Child

Background. From the earliest recollections of his behavior, Nathan had been perceived as a very active child. He always seemed to be on the go, could rarely sit still for any length of time, and was constantly fidgeting. Nathan was large for his age and he had always been able to physically dominate his playmates.

Nathan was an only child and had been more than a little spoiled by his parents. Nathan was accustomed to getting his own way most of the time. His play behavior was no exception. Almost invariably, he dominated the play activities that he engaged in with his friends. He controlled the kinds of games and activities that were selected during play times, he decided who assumed which roles in acting out fantasies of popular television heroes, and he determined when play activities would begin and end. In short, Nathan was a very controlling and dominating individual. He was also extremely powerful in terms of the influence he was able to exert on his peers.

Nathan had acquired a set of tactics that he applied systematically for the purpose of getting his own way. He was very manipulative and quite skilled in the use of influence tactics designed to insure that things went his way in his interactions with peers. If all else failed, he would simply apply intimidating pressures to peers who resisted him until they agreed to do things his way. It was rare that Nathan came out the loser in such confrontations. The early success he encountered in using such tactics increased the chances that he would behave this way as a matter of course. This is precisely what happened.

Nathan entered preschool at the age of four, whereupon he consistently applied the behavior pattern he had acquired earlier. As a general rule, he was successful in dominating play situations and controlling events to his own satisfaction. However, he became increasingly aggressive and forceful in his social interactions with peers. This was because he faced some stiff competition from several other children in his preschool class who were equally forceful and dominating. In order to maintain his effectiveness in controlling situations, he had to increase both the magnitude and intensity of the coercive pressures he applied to the behavior of other children. Because the preschool he attended was largely play-oriented and had only a limited academic focus, Nathan's behavior was not perceived as a serious problem. His teachers felt that while Nathan was definitely assertive and dominating in his social interactions with peers, his overall behavior pattern was well within normal limits and could be tolerated within the preschool setting.

It was a different story when Nathan entered first grade. He was an exceptionally intelligent child, was easy to teach, and had no difficulty with the academic demands that were placed upon him by his teachers. Although he could not be called a model student, his classroom behavior was clearly acceptable and within normal limits.

However, almost from the first day of school, Nathan was labelled as a behavior problem on the playground. The relatively unconstrained nature of recess periods seemed to bring out the worst aspects of his socially aggressive pattern of behavior. Over the course of his two-year preschool experience, Nathan had become increasingly negative, aggressive, and coercive in his social interactions with peers. The severity of his playground behavior was quickly brought to the attention of his classroom teacher and the school counselor.

The playground supervisors blamed Nathan's inappropriate playground behavior upon Nathan's classroom teacher and demanded that she do something to control it or they would deny Nathan access to recess. Nathan's teacher felt helpless to do anything about his playground behavior and was quite surprised at the intense reaction of the playground supervisors to it, especially since he was a relatively well behaved and capable student during class times. His teacher felt that Nathan's problems on the playground were probably the result of his basic personality and of his parents' failure to properly socialize him. However, she did agree to talk with him about his playground behavior and to try and persuade him to be less aggressive and more positive and cooperative with his peers.

Nathan and his teacher had quite an involved talk about his problems on the playground. Nathan realized that some of his behavior was inappropriate, e.g., fighting and arguing, but he did not see that there was anything wrong or inappropriate with the vast majority of his playground behavior. There was no discernible change in Nathan's overall behavior pattern as a result of his talk with the teacher. The playground supervisors continued to complain loudly and frequently about Nathan's behavior. Further, Nathan's peers began to complain both to the playground supervisors and to their own teachers about his intimidating tactics and generally aggressive behavior. Nathan was quickly becoming a school-wide problem and it was clear that steps would have to be taken to get some control over his playground behavior. This was necessary both from the standpoint of Nathan's social development and from the school's position that certain behavioral standards must be met, even on the playground.

Nathan's teacher and the playground supervisors held a joint conference with the school counselor and principal to discuss his behavior. It was decided to contact Nathan's parents as a first step to see what their perspective was on Nathan's overall behavior pattern and whether they could do anything at home to control his school behavior.

Nathan's parents were shocked at the news that he was perceived as a behavior problem at school. They had always seen Nathan as an active, but clearly normal child. They were angry and defensive at the suggestion that they were in any way responsible for Nathan's playground problems. In fact, they insisted that Nathan was no more aggressive than most children and that since his behavior was appropriate at home, it must be the school's fault that he was perceived as having difficulties on the playground.

The school, of course, disagreed with this view of Nathan's behavior and insisted that something would have to be done to improve his playground behavior. Nathan's parents were informed that a parent-school conference would be set up in the near future to discuss the nature of Nathan's playground problems and to consider steps that might be taken to deal with it.

The counselor decided to collect some information on Nathan's playground behavior that would help document the exact nature of the problems he was experiencing. The playground supervisors were instructed to keep a running log or tally of the inappropriate behaviors Nathan displayed over a four-day period. A partial listing of Nathan's inappropriate behavioral episodes is provided below.

Nathan's Playground Tally

10–4

1. Took the kickball away from Pamela.
2. Hit Fred for no apparent reason and knocked him down.
3. Called Jimmy a dirty name.
4. Told Jamie he was going to beat him up after school.
5. Insulted the playground supervisor.

10–5

1. Shoved Billy when he refused to play exclusively with him.
2. Told Carol she was a stupid bitch.
3. Grabbed the softball and bat and ran away with them (to the gym) so the game could not be played.
4. Threw a rock at Jason and barely missed his head.

10–6

1. Refused to take his turn on the sliding board–shoved smaller children out of the way.

2. Kicked a child from another class in the shins for no apparent reason.
3. Humiliated a smaller child who refused to play with him.

10–7

1. Continued to play on top of the swing set despite repeated attempts by the supervisor to get him to come down. Suspended from recess for remainder of the day.
2. Kicked a ball directly at Jenny in an obvious attempt to hurt her.
3. Got in an argument with Susan and taunted her until she cried.
4. Teased Mary until she left the playground in tears.

The playground supervisors emphasized that they had not recorded *all* of Nathan's inappropriate social behavior or violations of playground rules—only the more obvious ones. The playground supervisors in all three recesses were quite consistent in their tallies of Nathan's behavior. He seemed to be no better or worse in one recess period than in any other.

The counselor felt she needed some estimate of the frequency with which Nathan broke playground rules and displayed socially aggressive and negative behavior toward peers. She designed a simple tally sheet for collecting this information.

Tally Sheet for Coding Nathan's Playground Behavior

Date 10–12

Recess Period (morning, noon, afternoon)

Playground Behavior Categories

Physically Negative/ Aggressive Behavior	*Verbally Negative/ Aggressive Behavior*	*Rule Violations*
~~IIII~~ II	~~IIII~~ ~~IIII~~ I	IIII

The counselor began by coding Nathan's behavior in a fifteen-minute morning recess on October 12. His rate of physically negative/aggressive behavior in this recess was .47—a very high rate when compared to that of his peers. His verbal rate of negative/aggressive behavior was .73, which is also a very high rate. He averaged one playground rule violation about every three and a half minutes.

During the next week, the counselor continued to observe and record Nathan's playground behavior, choosing a different recess period each day. As the playground supervisors had reported, Nathan's behavior was highly consistent and predictable across each of the three recess periods. He displayed a very high rate of both verbal and physically negative/aggressive behavior during each of the periods in which his playground behavior was recorded.

The counselor next met with Nathan's teacher and the three recess supervisors to plan an intervention program designed to get control of Nathan's inappropriate playground behavior and to teach him a new pattern of prosocial, interactive behavior.

The Intervention Program. Because each of the playground supervisors was responsible for approximately ninety to one hundred students in the recess periods they supervised, the counselor tried to design a program that would be as simple as possible to implement, yet would be effective enough to have a significant impact upon Nathan's inappropriate playground behavior. She decided upon an intervention program with the following major components: (1) adult praise, (2) a response cost point system, (3) a group activity reward at school and an individual reward at home, and (4) timeout as an alternative backup procedure.

The counselor met with the recess supervisors and Nathan's teacher to explain how the program would work. First, the counselor would meet with Nathan and go over the playground rules with him. In addition, she would insure that Nathan clearly understood the difference between positive and negative interactive behavior. As part of this process, the counselor would review his playground behavior using the running log kept by the playground supervisors and the frequency data recorded by her.

Nathan would be awarded one point for each minute of recess in the three recess periods. The morning and afternoon recesses were fifteen minutes in length and the noon recess was twenty minutes in length. Thus a total of fifty points were available each day. The points were awarded at the start of each recess period on a simple 5 × 8 index card containing the date and space for each of the recess period points. A new card was used each day. The cards provided a permanent record of Nathan's performance in each of the three periods. An example of the point card is provided below.

Nathan's Point Card

Date ________

Morning Recess

Noon Recess

Afternoon Recess

Total Points Retained ________

It would be explained to Nathan that it was his task to keep the points awarded him at the start of each recess. He could keep the points by not breaking playground rules and by avoiding negative or aggressive interactions with his peers. If he did not break any playground rules or have any negative and/or aggressive interactions, he would be able to keep all the points awarded to him at the start of the recess period. However, he would lose two points for each rule violation and five points for each negative/aggressive behavior he engaged in. If he lost all his points in any recess period, he would sit out the remainder of that recess.

If Nathan had zero negative or aggressive behaviors in two out of the three recess periods and no more than one playground rule violation in each, he could earn a group activity reward for himself and his classmates arranged by his teacher. He could take home the points remaining at the end of the day and exchange them for a variety of special privileges to be provided by his parents.

The playground supervisors would be expected to scan the playground regularly, to observe and evaluate Nathan's behavior, and to praise him *at least* once each ten minutes. If he broke a rule or engaged in negative/aggressive social behavior, the supervisor would go over to him, describe the inappropriate behavior or rule violation, and cross out the required number of points on the point card.

Two of the three recess supervisors and Nathan's teacher were enthusiastic about the program. However, the remaining supervisor objected to it, primarily because he felt Nathan was in a sense being rewarded for acting out on the playground. That is, it seemed grossly unfair to make special rewards available to a child like Nathan to help him behave normally. The supervisor saw the program as a form of bribery.

The counselor argued that Nathan had acquired a very deviant pattern of behavior over a number of years, that it was strongly developed, and that a very powerful program would be required to change his behavior. She suggested that a special program, designed to motivate and teach Nathan to behave differently, was necessary to reverse his pattern of deviant behavior. She noted that the total program would be in effect only on a short term basis, and then gradually withdrawn so that only a low cost variation of the original program would remain in effect over the long term.

After arguing the issues of bribery, fairness, and special treatment of individual children, it became apparent that neither the playground supervisor nor the counselor would be able to change one another's positions. However, the supervisor finally agreed, although reluctantly, to try the program since there did not appear to be any other readily available methods for coping with Nathan's playground behavior.

A parent-school conference was scheduled to present the program to Nathan's parents and to obtain their support, cooperation, and willingness to participate in it. Nathan's parents were interested in seeing documentation that he was in fact a behavior problem on the playground. The counselor shared the supervisors' logs with them and presented the tally data she had collected on Nathan's playground behavior. Nathan's parents became defensive and said it was the school's responsibility and not theirs to manage his behavior. They suggested further that Nathan had never been a problem at home or in the neighborhood.

The counselor stated that Nathan's playground behavior was a problem and that all efforts by the school to cope with it had proved to be ineffective. She explained that a program had been developed to teach Nathan a new pattern of appropriate playground behavior and that she would like to explain how it would operate and what their role in it would be. The parents understood the program and agreed to support it. However, they objected to providing home rewards for Nathan's school behavior and refused to carry through with that part of the program. The counselor asked if they objected to his earning individual activity rewards at school such as free time. They did not, so it was agreed that an individual reward system would be established for Nathan at school.

Nathan's teacher and the counselor met with him and explained the program and how it would work. Nathan agreed to participate in the program and to cooperate with it.

The program was then explained to Nathan's classmates with Nathan present, and their role was described. Nathan and the counselor role played various components of the program (praising, subtracting points) for the class. A discussion was then held focusing on how Nathan's classmates could help him follow playground rules and interact more positively with his classmates.

Results. Nathan lost all his points in the first recess period. He lost five points on three separate occasions for displaying socially aggressive behavior toward peers. In the noon recess, he had one negative interaction with a peer, but violated classroom rules on three separate occasions. Thus, he lost a total of eleven points and retained only nine of the twenty points available in the noon recess. In the afternoon recess, he had no negative or aggressive interactions and violated only one classroom rule, thereby losing only two of the fifteen available points. Nathan ended up with a total of twenty-two points at the end of the day out of a possible fifty.

The counselor who operated the program in the three recess periods for the first ten days reviewed Nathan's behavior and discussed the situations in which he had experienced difficulty. It was as though Nathan was testing the program, its limits, and the counselor to see if things would work as they had been represented to him. Nathan was greatly disappointed that he had not earned the group school reward. The counselor told him that he would have to improve considerably in order to meet the school reward criterion–zero negative or aggressive behavior (and only one rule breaking) in two out of the three recess periods. Nathan replied that he felt the counselor was being too strict and was checking his behavior too closely. The counselor told him that her standards were no different for him than for any other children on the playground and that learning a new pattern of behavior was not easy, but she felt sure he would do it. Nathan promised to try harder the next day.

The next day, Nathan had a perfect morning recess—no negative or aggressive behavior and no rule breakings. However, he lapsed into his old behavior pattern in the noon recess, and he got into several arguments and a shoving contest with several peers over the rules of a kickball game. He lost fifteen of the twenty points available in the noon recess and complained loudly to the counselor that the arguments were not his fault and that he shouldn't have lost the points. She ignored his protests and informed him that she was only following the rules they had previously agreed on. In the afternoon recess, Nathan tended to avoid social contact with his peers whenever possible so as not to risk losing points and was very careful about following playground rules. He kept all his points for the afternoon recess thereby earning the group reward and ending up with a total of thirty-five points for the day. Both Nathan and his peers were pleased about the outcome and seemed really excited about playing a seven-up game in class. Nathan exchanged his individual points for some free time to watch some favorite educational cartoon clips. He seemed truly excited about the program, and said that he felt sure he could continue to earn the daily group reward.

However, on the third day of the program, Nathan again experienced difficulties on the playground. He violated several minor, but nevertheless established, playground rules and got into a scuffle with a peer from another class whom he did not like. As a result he did not earn the group reward and was greatly disappointed.

On the fourth program day, he tried really hard and lost only two points during the whole day, thereby easily earning the group reward. He received a great deal of support, encouragement, and appreciation from his peers for doing so. In contrast to day two, he did not avoid social contact with peers for the purpose of reducing his risk of losing points. He simply tried harder. The program seemed to be teaching Nathan to be much more sensitive to and aware of his own behavior and its effects upon others. The playground supervisors had also observed and commented on this.

Nathan earned the group reward for the next three days. There was a marked difference in his overall playground behavior and in the quality of his social behavior. He was a much more pleasant child to be around. The program was having a significant impact upon both his verbal and nonverbal behavior. He was much less verbally punishing with peers, less inclined to argue as a matter of course, and was also less physically aggressive in his peer interactions.

On the eighth day of the program, the counselor began training the playground supervisors to operate the program. As a first step, she had each supervisor praise Nathan's appropriate playground behavior at least once every five minutes. Next she had the supervisors operate the card and subtract points, whenever necessary, in addition to praising Nathan an average of once every five minutes. Initially, the counselor prompted the supervisors when to praise and when to subtract points. However, as the supervisors' skills in praising and operating the card improved, the counselor gradually faded out her prompts. By the eleventh day of the program, the supervisors had assumed complete responsibility for the program, with only occasional resource support and monitoring provided by the counselor.

Nathan earned the group reward every day except one during this transition period. Because the playground supervisors were responsible for so many students at any one time, they were not able to monitor Nathan's behavior as closely as the counselor who had remained close to Nathan (within twenty to thirty feet) throughout the recess period. As a result, Nathan was able to "get away" with subtle instances of negative and/or aggressive behavior and not lose points, since the supervisors often did not see them. However, the program continued to control effectively the more obvious instances of Nathan's socially negative and aggressive playground behavior. The supervisors, Nathan's teacher, and other school personnel were most pleased with the overall results of the program.

Nathan's peers, however, began to complain that he was being verbally negative with them and that he was using abusive language on the playground. The playground supervisors had not observed this because as a rule they were not able to hear and monitor Nathan's verbal behavior. Nathan had come to realize that he could engage in subtle negatives without penalty. The supervisors talked with the counselor about this problem. She suggested that because of the sheer numbers of children involved, it would be impossible for them to monitor all or even a major part of Nathan's verbal behavior. She said that it was probably too much to expect that Nathan's subtle verbal negatives could ever be controlled completely in a playground situation. However, she did suggest some procedures that could be tried that might have an impact upon the problem.

As a first step, she agreed to meet with Nathan and discuss the problem with him. By communicating to him that everyone was aware of what was going on, it was possible that he would reduce the frequency of such behavior. Next, the counselor suggested that the supervisors scan the playground more frequently, at least once every three to four minutes, if possible, in an attempt to monitor Nathan's behavior more closely. Finally, the counselor recommended that the supervisors occasionally try to stand within earshot of Nathan so that his verbal behavior could be monitored. In such situations, the supervisors should always subtract the required points if there were any doubt as to whether Nathan's verbal behavior was negative or inappropriate.

This change in the program was introduced and it seemed to have a moderate impact on Nathan's behavior. His peers stopped complaining about his negative/abusive language and the supervisors felt they could see a change in his behavior.

The overall program proceeded without incident for the next several weeks. Nathan missed the group reward three times during this period; however, he was very close to making it each time. At this point, the counselor suggested that the point system and the individual reward should be discontinued. She met with Nathan and discussed this change with him. He did not object to the change, indicating that the individual reward was not that important, but that he really liked the group reward. It seemed that Nathan enjoyed the new status his earning of the school reward had given him with peers. His interactions with his peers appeared to be much more cordial as well as genuine, and the approval of peers had taken on a new meaning for him.

It was explained to Nathan that the playground supervisor would award him a plus or a minus for each recess period. If his behavior was appropriate, he would earn a plus; if not, he would earn a minus. He would need two out of three recesses rated plus in order to earn the group reward. If his behavior were out of control or grossly negative and/or aggressive, he would have to sit out the remainder of the recess period and also forfeit the chance to earn a plus for that recess.

Nathan responded to this program change reasonably well. However, he tested the program change to see if it would work as described. He had to sit out three recesses within the first two days of the program change. However, he earned the group reward for four out of the next six days.

It was decided to introduce a fading procedure wherein Nathan would be required to work for longer and longer periods in order to earn the group reward. The counselor explained this change to Nathan, answered his questions, and told him that as he learned to control his playground behavior for longer and longer periods of time, the group rewards would become more special.

As a first step, Nathan was required to earn two out of three recess periods as plus for two consecutive days in order to earn the group reward. After learning to perform satisfactorily at this level, the criterion was raised to three out of four days, and finally to four out of five days. Nathan had some initial difficulty with each transition, however, he eventually adjusted quite well to a schedule where a group reward could be earned approximately once each week.

Because Nathan had had such a long history of negative and aggressive interactions with other children, it was decided to leave the program in effect for the remainder of the school year, rather than trying to fade it further or eliminate it altogether. Nathan's teacher, the playground supervisors and the counselor all agreed that Nathan needed the program and that it was relatively easy to manage as it was presently set up.

The counselor cautioned the playground supervisors and Nathan's teacher concerning certain aspects of the maintenance program. She emphasized how important it was to achieve the following goals on a continuing basis. These were (1) that Nathan's appropriate playground behavior be described, praised, and actively approved of whenever possible—preferably once every ten to fifteen minutes at a minimum; (2) that the recess supervisors be consistent (both among themselves and on a daily basis) in the standards they used to judge Nathan's playground behavior as either appropriate or inappropriate; (3) that Nathan be required to sit out the remainder of recess periods whenever his playground behavior was out of control or unusually negative and/or aggressive; and that (4) the array of group rewards that could be earned be varied frequently so that their reinforcing effectivenees could be maintained. The counselor stressed that the extent to which Nathan's changed behavior maintained during the rest of the school year would depend to a great extent upon how well these goals were achieved.

A final parent-school conference was arranged to review Nathan's progress with his parents. They were pleased with the overall outcome, but it was clear they still saw Nathan's playground behavior problems as the school's responsibility. They had no objections to the program remaining in effect for the remainder of the school year and agreed to support it.

Case Study: A Minimally Disruptive Child

Background. Frank could hardly be called a disruptive or deviant child; yet, he engaged in a number of classroom behaviors that were of concern to his fifth-grade teacher, Ms. Brown. For example, he seemed to be an unmotivated child who was not especially interested in school, in spite of ample academic ability. He was easily distractible, was frequently off task, did not listen carefully to instructions, and was somewhat careless about following directions. In addition, he had a habit of asking the teacher irrelevant questions and of interrupting her when she was busily engaged in a task or talking to another student.

Ms. Brown was concerned about Frank's classroom behavior for several reasons. First, he was performing far below his academic potential. He was approximately one year below grade level in the basic skills areas of reading, language, and math. Second, his classroom behavior, though not disruptive, was a constant source of irritation to her. He required far more of her attention than was necessary, and she had to repeat instructions and directions for him constantly. Finally, Frank was a very powerful child in a social-personal sense and was very popular with his classmates. It appeared that several of his classmates were starting, whether consciously or unconsciously, to imitate his pattern of classroom behavior.

The teacher was sufficiently concerned about Frank's behavior pattern that she contacted his parents and asked them to come in for a conference. Frank's parents had never seen him as a behavior problem either at home or school. They were not especially concerned about the problems described to them by Frank's teacher, but they did agree to work with the teacher in carrying out a program designed to motivate Frank to do better in school.

The Intervention Program. The teacher and parents met to work out a list of favorite activities that Frank enjoyed at home. The activities were ranked from highest to lowest according to Frank's preference for each. The final list is presented below:

List of Home Reward Activities for Frank

1. Going to a favorite matinee movie.
2. Having a friend over to spend the night.
3. Having a family picnic.
4. Shooting pool at a friend's house.
5. Not having to carry out the garbage at night.
6. Playing chess with Dad.
7. Staying up one-half hour later.
8. Extra TV time.
9. Having hot dogs for supper.
10. Playing "Battleship" with the family.

Frank's parents agreed to make these activities available to him only when he had earned them by improving his school performance. The teacher said she would develop a contract between herself and Frank that would specify tasks at school he needed to work on and the consequences that would be available to him at home for doing so.

The teacher developed several trial versions of a contract and finally settled on the one below.

Performance Contract for Frank

Frank agrees:

1. to pay attention and concentrate on assignments,
2. to listen carefully to teacher instructions,
3. to follow directions,
4. to work hard on assignments,
5. to avoid asking unnecessary questions,
6. to not interrupt the teacher when she is busy or talking with some one else.

Ms. Brown agrees:

1. to check Frank's classroom behavior and schoolwork regularly during the day,
2. to review his overall performance at the end of the day and

award tickets based on how well he has done on each of the above tasks.

Frank's parents agree:

1. to make special privileges available at home which Frank can exchange for the tickets earned at school.

Signatures

Frank ____________

Ms. Brown ____________

Frank's Parents ____________

Ms. Brown met with Frank and presented the program to him. She went over each of the classroom behaviors included in the contract and discussed them with Frank. She also told him he was capable of doing much better in school and that she expected his academic performance to improve.

Frank responded well to the discussion with Ms. Brown. However, he seemed upset about the home privileges part of the program. Ms. Brown asked him what was the matter and he said that many of the privileges on the home reward list were already available to him and that now he would have to earn them. Ms. Brown agreed that this was true, but she explained that she was quite concerned about his performance at school and the program was a way of motivating him to do better. She said his parents had agreed to cooperate with the program and that they would also like to see him do better. These arguments did not seem to assuage Frank's objections, but he finally agreed to sign the contract and to give the program a try.

The intervention program was a private arrangement between Frank, the teacher, and his parents. His classmates were not informed about either the presence or nature of the program.

The program operated unobtrusively throughout the school day when Frank was in Ms. Brown's classroom—a total of three and a half hours. At regular intervals, usually once each twenty minutes, Ms. Brown would quietly give Frank feedback on his classroom behavior and when appropriate, on his academic performance. The feedback she gave him was realistic. That is, if his behavior or performance had been unacceptable or not up to standard, she would tell him so. However, she made a point of finding at least one thing specifically to praise him for as part of this feedback process. If his behavior had been totally unacceptable and inappropriate during a given twenty-minute period, she *did not* praise him. However, these instances were relatively rare.

At the end of the school day, Ms. Brown had a review session with Frank concerning his classroom behavior and academic performance. She would go over the six target behaviors listed in the contract and give Frank a rating of good, fair, minimally acceptable, or unsatisfactory on each behavior, based on his performance for that day. The teacher purchased a role of standard theater tickets and awarded Frank three tickets for a "good" rating, two tickets for a "fair" rating, one ticket for a "minimally acceptable" rating, and no tickets for an "unsatisfactory" rating. Frank really liked the idea of earning tickets which he could exchange for special privileges at home. He asked Ms. Brown if they would be good for entrance into movies at the local theatres. She answered, only if he had earned enough tickets to exchange for a movie, which was one of the options on the reward list.

The exchange ratios were arranged so that Frank had to have a nearly perfect day in order to exchange for the least expensive privilege on the reward list. For example, a total of eighteen tickets could he earned for a perfect day. The least preferred privilege on the list was playing "battleship," which cost fifteen tickets. The most preferred privilege, going to a favorite movie, cost eighty tickets. The costs for the remaining privileges were spread out between these two extremes.

After answering all Frank's questions about the program, the home rewards, and the delivery system, Ms. Brown indicated that the program would begin the next day.

Results. There was a dramatic change in Frank's behavior on the first day of the program. He earned fifteen of the eighteen available tickets. It appeared that it was quite easy for him to meet the behavioral requirements of the situation. Clearly, he was capable of behaving appropriately and of meeting the teacher's expectations.

During the next five days of the program, Frank's daily totals ranged from ten to eighteen tickets. He made noticeable improvement in each of the six target behaviors included in the contract, but he had the greatest difficulty and slowest rate of progress with his school work.

Everyone seemed to be pleased with the way the program was working. Ms. Brown was much more optimistic about Frank's classroom behavior and felt that he would finally begin to live up to his academic potential. Frank's parents were very supportive of the program and followed through in implementing the home reward portion of it.

In conversing with Frank's other teachers about the program she had designed, Ms. Brown discovered that there had been no change in his behavior in other classes. If anything, according to his other teachers, Frank's behavior was slightly worse in their classes. It was apparent that his changed behavior was not generalizing to other classrooms in which the program had not been implemented.

Ms. Brown indicated that it was a fairly simple task to extend the program to their classrooms. Each of the teachers expressed interest in such a possibility. Ms. Brown explained how the program worked and what would be involved in extending it to their classrooms.

Ms. Brown indicated that she would give Frank a card each day with their subject areas noted on it. These were social studies, language, and health. Each day they were to rate Frank's overall performance in their classes as good, fair, minimally acceptable, or unsatisfactory. Frank would then exchange the daily ratings for either three, two, one, or zero tickets in Ms. Brown's room. Thus, Frank would be able to earn a maximum of nine additional tickets each day in classes other than Ms. Brown's. The prices of the home privileges were raised accordingly to take these extra tickets into account.

Ms. Brown explained the program change to Frank and answered his questions about it. She indicated the program extension would begin the next day and that she expected him to improve his performance in those classes. Frank realized he would have to work harder and longer for the home privileges. However, he seemed to accept the change without any difficulty.

There was an immediate change for the better in Frank's classroom performance in the extension classrooms. None of his teachers had any difficulty in running the program, and all reported seeing significant improvements in Frank's classroom behavior.

The program ran without incident for the next month. A major change in Frank's overall behavior pattern was his work output. The amount of work he completed nearly doubled, with a corresponding increase in quality as well. All of his teachers were greatly pleased with the results.

At this point, Ms. Brown began to consider ways of getting Frank off the system while maintaining the gains and new behavior pattern that he had acquired. The options ranged from terminating the program abruptly and completely, to gradually fading the number of tickets that could be earned each day to zero. Neither of these alternatives appealed to Ms. Brown.

Ms. Brown called a parent-teacher conference to discuss a program for moving Frank off the system. Frank's parents and all of his teachers attended. Both his parents and Frank's teachers were concerned that he did not lose the gains he had made. After discussing a number of alternatives, it was decided to implement a system wherein major components of the program would be eliminated a step at a time, while simultaneously reducing the frequency with which home rewards would become available.

As a first step, the ticket system was eliminated. Instead of receiving a rating each day and exchanging them for tickets, a plus or minus system was used to reinforce Frank's appropriate behavior. During the day, his behavior was rated as plus or minus approximately once each hour. Ms. Brown had Frank in her class for three of the six rating periods and the other teachers had him in their classes for the remaining three.

Frank could now earn home privileges with pluses and minuses instead of tickets. The exchange ratios were adjusted downward to take into account the reduced number of pluses, compared to tickets, that were now available.

Frank responded well to this program change. He adjusted easily to having his overall performance rated each hour as plus or minus. His rate of earning home privileges remained about the same as it had been under the ticket system. Frank's other teachers had no trouble with the program and reported no change in his classroom performance.

Next, it was decided to make a single, high magnitude reward available to Frank approximately once each week. These included such things as a movie, family outing, a picnic, or a trip to the bowling alley. There were thirty pluses available during a five-day week. In order to earn the weekly reward, Frank had to receive twenty-five of the thirty ratings as plus. If not, it was withheld.

Frank also had no difficulty with this program change. His behavior was no different from what it had been in the previous phase.

After approximately three weeks, Frank was simply given an overall satisfactory or unsatisfactory daily rating by Ms. Brown. If his behavior was satisfactory in all classes, he got a satisfactory rating. If it was unsatisfactory in one or more classes, he received an unsatisfactory rating. Now, in order to earn the home reward, Frank's behavior had to be rated as satisfactory four of the five days in the week.

Frank had some initial difficulty with this program change. He complained that it was more difficult to earn the weekly reward. His behavior reflected this by becoming increasingly variable from day to day. After approximately three weeks, Frank's performance began to stabilize as he responded better to this program change.

After approximately a month of satisfactory performance on Frank's part, it was decided to shift to an occasional home reward for good school performance. Frank was told by Ms. Brown that starting now, he would receive an occasional special reward for doing well at school. When his performance warranted it, she would send a good day card home with him. Whenever this happened, he could exchange the card for a special home reward.

Under this system, Frank's daily performance showed even more variability than before. After approximately a month of such fluctuations, he began to adapt reasonably well to the change. It was decided to leave this final variation of the program in effect for the remainder of the school year. In this form, the program was no trouble to operate and it continued to have a significant impact upon Frank's overall behavior pattern for the remainder of the school year.

Case Study: An Entire Classroom

Background. Mr. Endicott was a first year teacher in a regular, self-contained second-grade classroom. He was assigned a total of thirty-one children, more than any other teacher in the school. To make matters worse, there were five children in the class who were quite disruptive, underachieving, and very difficult to manage.

Mr. Endicott had the usual adjustment problems common to first year teachers. These problems were further accelerated by having such a large class, by having a group of disruptive children in the class, and by being overloaded with extra curricula duties such as supervising production of the school newspaper.

Mr. Endicott was engaged in a constant struggle to maintain only a minimal level of control in the classroom. The average rate of talk outs, out of seat, yelling, and class disruptions was quite high when compared to most regular classrooms. The rate of compliance with his commands and directives was below fifty percent. Mr. Endicott felt the children had little respect for his teaching skills–and he was right.

He had had no formal or systematic training in behavior management techniques in his undergraduate education and preservice teacher training. He felt unprepared to manage such a difficult group of children. He was extremely frustrated; he began to question his competence and was wondering whether teaching was the profession for him.

He continued to rely upon verbal reprimands, warnings, and sending children to the office as methods of controlling the classroom. These techniques were only minimally effective at best, and in some cases, seemed to actually make the children act out more.

The school counselor became aware of the difficulties Mr. Endicott was having with his class. She and the principal were both concerned with the large numbers of children that were being sent to the office each week from Mr. Endicott's class. She met with him to discuss the situation.

By this time, Mr. Endicott was past the point of being defensive about his inability to control his classroom. The counselor communicated to him that she was aware of the difficulty of his situation, e.g., that he had a large number of pupils and that many of them were behavior problem children that other teachers had also experienced difficulty in managing. She indicated that it was common for first year teachers to have difficulty in the area of behavior management, given their lack of experience and lack of preparation in techniques for managing child behavior in the classroom.

She asked Mr. Endicott if he would be willing to work with her in implementing some behavior management procedures designed to get some control over the classroom. Mr. Endicott enthusiastically agreed to this proposal.

The Intervention Program. As a first step, the counselor said she would like to schedule some times when she could observe in Mr. Endicott's room. He said anytime would be fine. She asked if there were times when the children seemed to be better than at others. Mr. Endicott wasn't sure, but he said the class seemed easier for him to manage during individual seatwork times than during activity periods, teacher-led discussions, or instructional activities that involved the whole group. The counselor scheduled class observations in all these periods.

After completing her observations, she scheduled a meeting with Mr. Endicott to discuss what she had learned. She began by saying that he was not nearly so bad a teacher as he was representing himself to be. However, until he could get control over the class in a behavioral sense, his teaching would continue to be less effective than he would like. Mr. Endicott couldn't have agreed more.

The counselor noted that in all the periods in which she observed, the children did not seem to have a clear idea of his behavioral expectations for them, nor did they seem to be aware of the rules governing appropriate and inappropriate classroom behavior. She observed further that he had a habit of giving out instructions and directions for assignments, especially during group activities, while the class was not paying attention and sometimes were even out of control. This was in effect an admission that he could not control the classroom and insured that only a portion of the pupils would hear and comprehend the instructions/directions for any given assignment. As a result, Mr. Endicott was spending a great deal of his time repeating instructions for children who did not hear them the first time. He was becoming increasingly frustrated as a result.

The counselor also observed that the children were giving each other a great deal of attention and approval for "getting under Mr. Endicott's skin." A number of children were very skilled at needling Mr. Endicott and irritating him by doing such things as dawdling, breaking minor classroom rules in his presence, requiring multiple repetitions of the same instructions, and asking unnecessary questions that they already knew the answers to. Mr. Endicott usually responded in a very predictable fashion in such situations—he would become very irritated and reprimand the children involved. Mr. Endicott's reaction only strengthened the children's "needling" behavior and increased the chances that they would do it again.

The counselor suggested that it would be impractical to try and solve the behavior management problems in his class on a case-by-case basis (by designing individual intervention programs for all children who needed them). She recommended they design and implement a group behavior management program for the entire class. Mr. Endicott agreed to give it a try.

The counselor recommended a program that consisted of the

following components: (1) developing a set of explicit classroom rules governing appropriate behavior in Mr. Endicott's classroom, (2) a rating system in which the behavior of the entire class would be rated as either plus or minus by Mr. Endicott according to whether the children had followed classroom rules and behaved appropriately, (3) a systematic praising procedure wherein the class as a whole and individual children would be praised intermittently for following classroom rules, and (4) a daily activity reward made available to all class members when the reinforcement criterion had been achieved. The counselor explained how the program would operate.

First, Mr. Endicott and the counselor would meet with the class and develop a set of classroom rules, couched in overt, observable terms, that would govern appropriate child behavior in the classroom. Mr. Endicott said that he could easily come up with thirty or forty such rules. The counselor suggested that that would probably defeat the purpose of this part of the program, since children have difficulty keeping track of more than seven to ten rules at a time. She said it would be much better to develop a list of ten major rules that Mr. Endicott felt comfortable with and that clearly communicated his behavioral expectations for the class.

Next Mr. Endicott would mark off a space approximately ten to twelve inches wide on one end of the blackboard. The school day would then be divided into ten-minute segments and the segments listed vertically from the top to bottom of the blackboard within this space. Every ten minutes, Mr. Endicott would award the class either a plus or a minus in the appropriate ten-minute segment. A plus rating meant that the behavior of all children in the class was reasonably appropriate and consistent with Mr. Endicott's expectations for the class. If a minus was awarded, that meant that the behavior of one or more children in the class had been inappropriate for part or all of the ten-minute period. An example of the rating system is presented below:

Rating System for Mr. Endicott's Class

Time	*Rating*
9:00– 9:10	+
9:10– 9:20	+
9:20– 9:30	–

9:30– 9:40	+
9:40– 9:50	–
9:50–10:00	–
10:00–10:10	+
10:10–10:20	+
10:20–10:30	+
10:30–10:40	–
10:40–10:50	–
10:50–11:00	+
11:00–11:10	–
11:10–11:20	+
11:20–11:30	+
11:30–11:40	+
11:40–11:50	–
11:50–12:00	+

Of the eighteen ten-minute intervals between 9 A.M. and 12 noon, the behavior of the class, in this hypothetical case, was rated as plus in eleven and as minus in seven. Thus, in the morning session, the behavior of the entire class was rated as appropriate in 61 percent of the intervals.

Mr. Endicott felt he would have no difficulty in managing this part of the program. However, he was a little concerned, that in the process of teaching he might forget to rate the class every ten minutes. The counselor said this occasionally happened, but that there was no problem with awarding the rating a little later. Besides, she indicated that in operating such systems, teachers become very skilled in estimating time. Further, she said she was sure that if he forgot to rate a given interval one of the children would almost certainly remind him to do so.

Next, the counselor discussed the praising component of the program with Mr. Endicott. She emphasized how important it was for him to praise the class and individual children regularly for following class rules and behaving appropriately. She gave him a list of sample praise statements to help him vary his praises. The counselor and Mr. Endicott had a role playing session in which they practiced both call out praises to the entire class and specific praises to individual children. Mr. Endicott felt some awkwardness initially in praising, but was able to demonstrate behavioral mastery of correct praising skills. The counselor said this feeling of awkwardness would probably disappear as he began to praise on a regular basis.

The counselor discussed another use of praise with Mr. Endicott as a behavior management technique. That is, instead of reprimanding an individual student for breaking a classroom rule or for behaving inappropriately, he could praise an adjacent child who was behaving appropriately. In this instance, the adjacent student becomes a behavioral model for the student who is behaving inappropriately. In addition, the procedure communicates that teacher attention will be given for appropriate classroom behavior and not for rule breaking episodes in the form of warnings or verbal reprimands. The counselor indicated that if used appropriately, this procedure could be highly effective in teaching children new patterns of appropriate behavior.

Finally, the counselor and Mr. Endicott discussed the group reward system that would be used to backup the rating system. She said that during the first part of the program, a daily group reward of an activity nature should be available for meeting the reinforcement criterion. Activity rewards would include games, activities, or events the children enjoyed. Examples would include such things as five minutes of extra recess, free time in the classroom, and classroom games such as seven-up, Simon Says, and Flying Dutchman. She said he was free to make available whatever rewards of this nature that he felt were appropriate.

However, she cautioned that the children should be included in the selection process and should be free to contribute and vote on potential backup rewards. The counselor recommended that initially, ten to twelve activity reward options should be selected, a card made for each with the cards placed in a jar or box, and that a different student should be selected each day the criterion was met to draw out a card from the jar or box. The activity on the card would then be available for that day and would not be replaced until all the cards had been drawn out. At that time, the cards would be placed back in the jar or box or a new set of cards and backup rewards developed.

Mr. Endicott asked the counselor how he would know whether to give or withhold the daily reward. She said that a good rule of thumb is that the class's behavior would have to be eighty percent appropriate in order to earn the daily reward. If less than this, the reward should be withheld. The procedure for calculating the percent of time in which the class' behavior was appropriate was explained to Mr. Endicott. That is, the total number of intervals during the day in which pluses were awarded is divided by the total number of intervals in which ratings were given. For example, in a five-hour school day in which the class' behavior was rated every ten minutes, there would be a total of thirty intervals in which a rating would be given. Thus, the class would have to have a minimum of twenty-four of these intervals (80 percent) rated as plus in order to earn the group reward. If fewer than twenty-four intervals were rated plus, the reward would be withheld for that day, but the class would start fresh the next day with the opportunity to earn one of the backup rewards.

The counselor and Mr. Endicott met once more to plan how the program would be presented to the class and the roles that each would play in explaining it and in developing classroom rules and a list of backup rewards. It was decided to present the program at the beginning of classtime the next day and to implement it immediately following the presentation—after the class rules had been developed and the backup rewards had been selected. The presentation went without incident and a list of classroom rules was prepared in block letters on construction paper and posted on the bulletin board. It took a long time for the class to decide on which ten backup rewards they would like to work for. They voted on a series of potential rewards, finally selected ten, and made a card for each. The counselor remained in the classroom for the first hour of the program and came back several times during the remainder of the day to see how things were going.

The counselor told Mr. Endicott that in the early stages of the program it was a good idea to give the class the benefit of the doubt in awarding ratings so as to increase their chances of earning the group reward and experiencing it. He could then gradually become more strict as the children adjusted to the program and the changed behavioral requirements. However, she cautioned against being *too* lenient in his ratings, since this would teach the children that only a very minimal effort would be necessary to earn the daily group reward and the goals of the program would, in all likelihood, not be achieved. Mr. Endicott understood what the counselor was telling him, but said he would like some feedback from her whenever possible on the appropriateness of his ratings of the class' behavior. The counselor agreed to visit his classroom once each day for the first week of the program to rate the class simultaneously, but independently with Mr. Endicott, and to compare ratings at the end of the session. Mr. Endicott said he felt this feedback would be of assistance to him in learning to accurately rate the behavior of the class when using the class rules as a standard for making such judgments.

Result. The class did not earn the group reward the first day of the program. There were thirty-three ten-minute segments during the day. The class received plus ratings in twenty-one of the thirty-three intervals, for an overall percentage of appropriate behavior of 63 percent, well below the 80 percent level required for the reward. The class was greatly disappointed in their failure to earn the reward. At the end of the day, Mr. Endicott reviewed their performance with them and told the children that they had shown some good improvement in their overall performance, but that they would have to work harder to earn the group reward. He said he felt sure they could do it and that they would have a new opportunity to try again tomorrow.

The counselor and Mr. Endicott reviewed the first day of the program and decided that overall it had gone fairly well. The counselor had observed and rated the class for a one-hour period during the day or for a total of six ten-minute intervals. They rated the class the same on four of the six intervals. They discussed their differences and the specific reasons for the ratings they had given.

The next day, the class earned the group reward, but just barely. They received twenty-six of the thirty-three intervals as plus ratings which is the minimum number required to earn the group reward. Mr. Endicott told the class how proud he was that they had earned the group reward. The card drawn out of the jar had five minutes of extra recess written on it, which was one of the more desirable of the reward options. At this point, the class seemed quite excited about the program.

On the third day of the program, the class again earned the group reward—this time by a comfortable margin. The class received thirty-one out of the thirty-three intervals as pluses. Mr. Endicott found the change in the class hard to believe. The class drew a card which was exchanged for a game of seven-up. Mr. Endicott and the counselor again compared notes and found they agreed on all six of the ten-minute intervals in which they simultaneously rated the overall performance of the class. The counselor complimented Mr. Endicott on the accuracy of his ratings and on how well he was running the program. However, she indicated he was not praising either the class as a whole or individual children frequently enough. She suggested he set a goal of praising the class at least twice each hour when their behavior was appropriate and of praising individual children a total of five to ten times each day. He decided to keep a simple tally on his desk to help him keep track of praises and said that he would try to do better.

The class earned the group reward for the next three days in a row. Mr. Endicott improved both his praise rate and his praising skills. His accuracy in rating the class' performance continued to be high. Everyone concerned—the counselor, Mr. Endicott, and the children—felt very good about the program.

The class failed to earn the group reward on the seventh and eighth days of the program. The failure to earn the reward was due almost exclusively to the behavior of two children. They were both boys and were members of the group of five children who had a history of behavior problems prior to their entry into Mr. Endicott's class.

The class as a whole was quite disappointed in this failure to earn the reward. They communicated a fair amount of disapproval to the two boys over this issue. However, this seemed to have little or no impact upon their behavior. Mr. Endicott decided to have a chat with them to see if he could get to the bottom of the matter. The two boys said they were no longer interested in the program, didn't care about it, and weren't going to cooperate any more. Mr. Endicott talked with the counselor about it and she suggested they give the program another try to see if the boys would change their minds. They didn't. The class failed to earn the group reward a third day primarily because of the uncooperativeness of the two boys. Mr. Endicott and the counselor decided something would have to be done since the two boys were spoiling the program for everyone else.

They decided to place the boys on a separate system from the class wherein they could earn some free time at the end of the day if, in Mr. Endicott's judgment, their behavior had been appropriate 80 percent of the time during the day. Their system was designed to be (and was perceived as being) of much lower value than that for the class. The two boys were thus no longer able to deny the rest of the class access to the group reward by their behavior. They were not allowed to participate in the group reward activities earned by the rest of the class.

The class proceeded to earn the group reward for the next five days in a row. The two boys seemed to be in a power struggle with Mr. Endicott. They earned access to free time only once during the five-day period and had to be sent to the office several times because of their disruptive behavior. Mr. Endicott noted that other children tended to ignore the two boys, especially when they were behaving inappropriately. This was a marked change compared to the situation existing prior to the program when the children subtly approved of each other's inappropriate behavior.

The class earned the group reward on four out of the next five days, and the two boys earned free time on two of these days; however, the separate system was starting to have an impact upon them. After approximately two weeks, they asked Mr. Endicott if they could be put back on the program for the whole class. He asked if they were now willing to cooperate and they said yes. He agreed to place them back on the program.

The program ran relatively smoothly over the next month. The class earned the group reward for two weeks in a row and then failed to meet the criterion on two consecutive days. It was apparent that some of the children were beginning to lose interest in the program, especially in the available backup rewards. This was a cue for Mr. Endicott to work with the class in developing a new list of backup rewards. In so doing, it was apparent that this was the source of the problem. The class earned the group reward for the next eight days in a row.

The counselor suggested that they should consider a fading program that would both reduce Mr. Endicott's time and effort required to run the program, and would teach the children to be less reliant on the program. As a first step, she recommended that the rating interval be expanded. Over the next month, the rating interval was expanded from ten to twenty to thirty to sixty minutes. The criterion for the group reward remained the same, that is 80 percent of the rated intervals had to be pluses. There was no change in the behavior of the class as a result of these changes.

Next, Mr. Endicott changed the rating to only once per day. The class was now given a plus or minus rating covering the entire day. A plus was awarded if, in Mr. Endicott's judgment, the class had been 80 percent appropriate for the entire day. The class had some difficulty with this change, but adjusted to it reasonably well.

The system was next changed by requiring that two consecutive days be rated as plus in order for the group reward to be earned. Later, the requirement was raised to three out of four days, and finally to four out of five days so that a reward was available approximately once each week. More valuable rewards were made available to motivate the children to work for longer periods of time in order to earn them.

The overall level of appropriate behavior increased in daily variability following this change. However, there was still a marked difference in Mr. Endicott's classroom compared to the pre-program situation.

Mr. Endicott and the counselor decided to leave the system, in its present form, in effect for the remainder of the school year. Mr. Endicott continued to have difficulty in achieving his daily praising goals. The counselor reminded him of the importance of frequent praising in maintaining the gains that had been achieved.

The program operated quite well for the remainder of the school year. Both Mr. Endicott and the children were changed by the program. He greatly improved his skills in behavior management, and the behavior of the class as a whole increased and maintained for the remainder of the year.

SECTION TWO: APPLYING BEHAVIOR MANAGEMENT PROCEDURES TO HYPOTHETICAL CLASSROOM/PLAYGROUND SITUATIONS

Case Study: The Noncompliant Child

Fred was a fourth-grade boy who had established a reputation as being very difficult to manage. He gave his kindergarten teacher a very hard time, right from the first day of school. His primary-grade teachers were no exception. Each teacher dreaded to have him and was greatly relieved when he passed on to the next grade. Ms. Lumsden, his fourth-grade teacher, was extremely frustrated with his behavior, and was considering trying to have him assigned to a special class setting where she felt more specialized techniques could be used to manage him and cope with the more aversive aspects of his behavior. In short, she was nearing the end of her rope with Fred.

Fred was a highly intelligent child and a good student. His reading skills were well developed and he achieved at or above grade level in all subjects.

However, he was a very powerful child who had been over-indulged by his parents. He managed to "get his way" most of the time. He was often persistent to the point of stubbornness. His most exasperating traits were his noncompliance with adult commands and his tendency to argue over every little point.

Adults were usually no match for him. He could usually get his way by either wearing them down or waiting them out. As a result, Fred developed a pattern of typically resistive behavior that created severe problems for his teachers, his peers, and ultimately himself.

Task One: Behavior Change Goals

(Develop a list of appropriate behavior change goals for the teacher to consider in this situation. Compare your list with that provided by the author on the next page. No set number of goals is required.)

1.

2.

3.

4.

5.

6.

7.

8.

Author's List of Behavior Goals:

1. Insure that Fred is *consciously aware* of those specific aspects of his behavior that are considered aversive and/or inappropriate.
2. Teach him to comply promptly with adult commands, directives, and/or instructions.
3. Teach him to suppress his argumentative behavior with adults.
4. Teach a more cooperative pattern of interaction with adults.

Task Two: Intervention Procedures

(Describe a specific intervention procedure that would be appropriate for achieving *each* behavior change goal that *you* have listed). Compare your intervention procedures with those presented by the author on the next page for the four goals listed above.

1.

2.

3.

4.

5.

Author's Intervention Procedures:

Goal #1: Children are sometimes not aware that certain features of their behavior are considered inappropriate. In other cases, adult expectations with respect to classroom and playground rules are not clearly communicated. Thus, as a first step, the teacher should develop a list of specific behavioral pinpoints that are considered inappropriate and review them with the child, being careful to define each one. This could be handled via an individual conference with the child.

Goal #2: There are several options for achieving this goal. Option #1: praise the child for each compliance on the first trial. Option #2: award one minute of free time (which accumulates during the day) for each compliance on the first trial. Option #3: award one point for each compliance on the first trial. If 80 percent or more of adult commands/directives are complied with, sign a good day card which can be exchanged at home for a special privilege.

Goal #3: As a first step, a series of situations should be identified in which Fred is likely to argue. Then a private role playing session should be scheduled where these situations are reviewed and Fred is allowed to rehearse nonargumentative responses to these situations. Fred could then be awarded a bonus point, which could accumulate toward a special individual reward, for handling such situations in a nonargumentative fashion. Another option would be to subtract one point (earned for complying with adult commands) for each episode of argumentative behavior. Thirdly, the teacher could simply ignore instances of argumentativeness and refuse to interact until Fred can converse without arguing. A backup consequence such as a brief timeout would probably be necessary to make this third option effective.

Goal #4: The role playing sessions described above would no doubt assist Fred in acquiring a more cooperative pattern of social behavior. However, they would probably not be sufficient by themselves.

It would be important to systematically define for Fred what constitutes a cooperative pattern of behavior and that which does not. The two respective behavior patterns could be contrasted in general terms for Fred and then specific instances of cooperative and noncooperative behavior discussed and/or role played for him. Fred should be able to consistently discriminate such instances at a 90 percent accuracy level or better.

It would be especially helpful to inform Fred's parents of this procedure and if possible to involve them at home in supporting Fred's attempts at acquiring a more cooperative behavior pattern. Fred should be given positive feedback and praised regularly, both at school and at home, for making progress in this area. He should also be informed when he doesn't handle situations well. An occasional special privilege should be made available either at home or school when Fred makes significant progress in this area.

Task Three: Implementation Problems

(List potential implementation problems with the intervention procedures *you* have selected and compare your list with those provided by the author on the next page.)

1.

2.

3.

4.

5.

6.

7.

Author's list of potential implementation problems:

1. Fred chooses to be uncooperative when the teacher attempts to explain classroom rules to him and to identify aversive/inappropriate features of his behavior.
2. Fred deliberately noncomplies, after the intervention program is in effect, to test the program and to see how consistent the teacher can be.
3. Fred doesn't appear to be especially motivated by the home and other special rewards made available to him as part of the program.
4. The teacher often forgets to reinforce Fred for handling difficult situations well without arguing.
5. Both Fred's parents and his teacher "expect" him to become more cooperative with them as a matter of course and are not willing to invest the necessary effort to make it happen.
6. Fred refuses to cooperate in the role playing sessions.

Note: Any or all of these problems are *possible, not necessarily probable*, in an intervention program of this type. The reader should consider how she/he would respond to them should they be encountered.

Case Study: The Socially Withdrawn Child

Maria was an extremely withdrawn child. She was a second grader who had a history of nonresponsiveness to and avoidance of social contact with peers. She was less withdrawn from adult social contact than peer contact, but interactions with teachers and other school personnel were still quite difficult for her.

Maria's parents indicated that she showed signs of social withdrawal from her earliest contacts with other children. Maria has an older sister who also exhibited social withdrawal tendencies in the first two years of school. However, at present her social relationships with other children appear to be quite normal. Both Maria's parents and teachers agreed that Maria's sister had not been nearly as withdrawn as was Maria.

Maria's second-grade teacher expressed growing concern to the school counselor about her social relationships with other children. Basically, her teacher felt that her limited social skills repertoire and her persistent avoidance of social contact with peers would have a detrimental impact upon her social and possibly her academic development. She communicated these concerns to the counselor who decided to observe Maria's playground behavior before proceeding further.

The counselor observed Maria on the playground on three separate occasions and recorded the amount of time she was engaged in social contact of any kind with peers. The results confirmed the extent of Maria's social withdrawal. She engaged in social contact less than 10 percent of the time in which she was observed. As a rule, children are involved in social interactions 40 to 50 percent of the time on the playground. Thus, Maria was significantly below average in the amount of available time she engaged in social interactions with peers.

Further, it was rare for Maria to initiate social contact with peers. Most of the social interactions she was engaged in were a result of peers initiating to her. Both the counselor and teacher felt that a major problem for Maria was her lack of prerequisite social skills which should allow her to initiate and maintain positive social relationships with others.

Maria's parents were contacted and a conference scheduled to discuss Maria's problems and the counselor's findings. Based on this conference, it was agreed that an intervention program should be developed and implemented to improve Maria's social relationships with peers.

Task One: Behavior Change Goals

(Develop a list of appropriate behavior change goals for the teacher to consider in this situation. Compare your list with that provided by the author on the next page. No set number of goals is required.)

1.

2.

3.

4.

5.

6.

Author's List of Behavior Change Goals:

1. Maria should receive direct instruction in social skills training for the purpose of insuring that she develops the competence necessary for participating in social interactions.
2. Maria should be given opportunities to rehearse and apply these skills in social interactions with selected peers.
3. Steps should be taken to insure that Maria is not unnecessarily traumatized by social contact with peers.
4. Both Maria and her peers should be motivated to engage in social exchanges with each other.
5. The interactions between Maria and her peers should be of acceptable quality, e.g., positive, should be reciprocal, and should have some verbal content.

Task Two: Intervention Procedures

(Describe a specific intervention procedure that would be appropriate for achieving *each* behavior change goal that *you* have listed). Compare your procedures with those provided by the author on the next page.

1.

2.

3.

4.

5.

Author's Intervention Procedures:

Goal #1: Many withdrawn children appear to have low rates of social contact with peers due to deficient social skills. That is, such children have not learned to initiate to others, to respond to initiations by others, and to continue social interactions over time.

The author and his colleagues have developed a set of social tutoring procedures to teach withdrawn children key components of social interaction. Direct instruction and role playing techniques are used to teach mastery of three key components of the social interaction process. These are (1) starting, (2) answering, and (3) continuing.

Before implementing a program designed to motivate a socially withdrawn child to interact with peers, it is imperative that steps be taken to teach essential social skills. Thus, in Maria's case, it would be important to make sure that she possessed these skills prior to implementing the intervention program.

Goal #2: Maria should be taught key social skills in a one-to-one teaching situation. As a next step, she should be given opportunities to try out these skills in limited, carefully supervised social interactions with selected peers. It is recommended that several socially skilled and responsive peers be selected to give the child practice in initiating, responding to, and continuing social interactions over time. These interactive exchanges should be supervised by an adult, e.g., teacher or counselor, and the children should be given feedback on the quality and appropriateness of their social interactions. These children could then assume the role of special helpers on the playground once the intervention program begins, e.g., they would facilitate social interactions between the target child and other peers.

Goal #3: Some withdrawn children actively avoid social contact with peers because they are fearful of or are traumatized by social exchanges with others. It is difficult to know why such children develop fears of social contact.

However, if this situation should occur, steps should be taken to desensitize the child to social contact in a series of gradual steps. This procedure can be incorporated into the intervention program as a first step. The withdrawn child should be largely desensitized to such fears before he/she is expected to interact with peers for the purpose of earning rewards.

A suggested procedure would be to begin by having the withdrawn child practice interacting with a friend in a series of private interactions supervised by an adult. As the child can accommodate this type of social contact, more children who are less well known to the withdrawn child can be scheduled to participate in such sessions. These approximations should continue until the withdrawn child can approach social situations without signs of fear or anxiety. If the child needs instruction in social skills as well, it should be scheduled after such desensitization has been achieved.

Goal #4: A contingency should be set up where Maria can earn a daily group activity reward for herself and her classmates by achieving a reward criterion based upon her interactive behavior. It is recommended that the program be implemented during recess periods where social interactions are free to occur. Peers should be actively encouraged to facilitate Maria's interactive behavior. It is in their interest to do so, since they will share equally in whatever activity rewards are earned by the target child.

Reinforcement can be delivered through two primary methods—by reinforcing Maria with praise and points for each social interaction with peers, or by interacting for a certain proportion of the time available in recess periods. The amount of time or the number of interactions required to achieve the daily reinforcement criterion can be gradually increased over time as the child's skills and competence develop.

Goal #5: It is important that Maria (1) learn to initiate to peers as well as respond to initiations by others, (2) learn to interact positively, and (3) have a certain proportion of interactions involving verbal exchanges. The author and his colleagues have found that as the child engages in greater and greater amounts of social interaction, it is important to inspect her/his interactive behavior for quality, verbal content, and reciprocity. For example, some withdrawn children will allow peers to do all the initiating. Others become negative in their social behavior as they interact more. And still others interact nonverbally, but not verbally. When these situations occur, the contingency should be adjusted to produce desired changes in such parameters.

Task Three: Implementation Problems

(List potential implementation problems with your intervention procedures and compare your list with those provided on the next page.)

1.

2.

3.

4.

5.

6.

Author's List of Potential Implementation Problems:

1. Maria's parents do not see why she should be reinforced during recess for her interactive behavior.
2. Maria continues to be fearful about social contact with peers even after extensive desensitization training.
3. Maria does not seem to be sufficiently responsive to the intervention program.
4. Maria's special helpers appear to lose interest in performing their facilitative roles in the intervention program.
5. Maria's rate of verbal interactions continues to be extremely low, even after the contingency has been adjusted to increase them.

Case Study: The Tantruming Child

Bobby was a normal, relatively well adjusted first grader except in one respect. He would throw screaming tantrums that had the effect of bringing everything around him to a standstill.

His parents reported that he started having them around the age of two. They were unsure as to how this behavior pattern became established. His rate of tantrums continued at a high rate until he started kindergarten. During the first two months of kindergarten he had only one tantrum. However, his rate began to gradually increase until he was up to approximately one tantrum per day.

Mr. Unruh, his first-grade teacher, reported that his rate seemed to be slightly above one tantrum per day. Mr. Unruh, the counselor, the principal, and Bobby's parents all agreed that something must be done to get his tantruming under control. Bobby's outbursts had an extremely disruptive effect on the entire class, and it was felt that this behavior pattern would have a deleterious impact upon both his social and academic adjustment.

A conference was scheduled to discuss strategy. Both Mr. Unruh and Bobby's parents observed that his tantrums seemed to be set off by two events: (1) not getting sufficient attention, and (2) not getting his way. His tantrums usually had the effect of providing him with massive amounts of attention and frequently resulted in his getting his own way.

Task One: Behavior Change Goals

(Develop a list of appropriate behavior change goals for the teacher to consider in this situation. Compare your list with that provided by the author. No set number of goals is required.)

1.

2.

3.

4.

5.

6.

7.

Author's List of Behavior Change Goals:

1. Bobby should be interviewed by the teacher or counselor to determine whether he is aware of the situations that precipitate his tantrums.
2. Bobby should be taught that his tantrums will (a) no longer have any functional effect in producing desirable consequences

as in the past, and (b) that tantrums will result in a mildly aversive consequence.

3. Bobby should be taught more adaptive strategies for producing reinforcing consequences from the environment and for coping with situations he finds frustrating or is unable to control in a way that he would like.

Task Two: Intervention Procedures

(Describe a specific intervention procedure that would be appropriate for achieving *each* behavior change goal that *you* have listed.)

1.

2.

3.

4.

Author's Intervention Procedures:

Goal #1: The teacher or counselor should interview Bobby to determine whether he has an awareness of those situations and events which set off his tantrums. In rare cases, a conscious awareness of such factors will make it possible for the child to control tantruming.

Bobby should be informed of each situation or event that seems to precipitate tantrums. It is unlikely that he would be aware of why he has tantrums, e.g., that they allow him to control his environment and produce desirable consequences in many instances. The functional value of tantrums in this regard should be reviewed and discussed with him. Finally, he should be informed that in the future, tantrums at school will no longer have such functional value and that he will be taught new ways of responding to these situations.

Goal #2: It is very important for Bobby to learn that his tantrums will no longer be effective in dealing with his environment. The most effective means for achieving this goal is to use a brief timeout each time a tantrum occurs. A ten- to fifteen-minute timeout is recommended. However, Bobby should not be allowed to return to the classroom until his tantruming has subsided.

The timeout should be implemented as soon as the tantruming behavior begins. A good rule to consider implementing is that Bobby be sent home if more than three timeouts are accumulated in any school day. Sometimes going into timeout becomes a game wherein the child deliberately engages in behavior that warrants timeout. When this occurs, the child rather than the teacher is in control of the situation. A suspension procedure is usually an effective response to this situation *provided that* the child is not allowed access to such things as play activities or TV privileges during the remainder of the school day.

The timeout procedure for tantruming offers a number of advantages. For example, it prevents the tantrum from disrupting the classroom and the child from controlling the classroom situation in this way. It prevents the child from obtaining excessive peer and teacher attention via the tantrum. Timeout is usually an aversive consequence for children and may therefore suppress the frequency of tantrums. The prompt and correct application of timeout for tantrums makes it impossible for them to have functional value in producing immediate reinforcing consequences from the natural environment. In applying timeout, it is recommended that the guidelines presented in Chapter 4 governing its usage be followed closely.

Goal #3: The timeout procedure described above would probably be effective in controlling Bobby's frequency of tantruming. However, it is extremely important that he be taught alternative, adaptive methods for coping with his environment to replace his previous reliance on tantrums. It is likely that tantrums actually prevent the acquisition of such positive coping methods because tantrums are usually so effective in producing immediate and desirable (to the child) consequences.

It is recommended that each situation which precipitates Bobby's tantrums be analyzed and a series of alternative, acceptable responses be developed. These should be reviewed with Bobby in a one-to-one teaching session and behaviorally rehearsed if possible. Bobby should then be given feedback, praise, and/or bonus points for handling such situations adaptively and without tantrums. This procedure should be continued until there is clear evidence that Bobby's coping skills in this area are well developed.

Task Three: Implementation Problems

(List potential implementation problems with the intervention procedures you have selected and compare your list with those provided below.)

1.

2.

3.

4.

5.

Author's List of Potential Implementation Problems:

1. Bobby refuses to cooperate and defies the teacher (or counselor) in the initial review situation where his tantruming is discussed.
2. Bobby's parents refuse to follow through at home with procedures that would make the school portion of the program

more effective. Thus, Bobby learns that he is free to continue his tantruming behavior pattern at home.

3. Bobby sometimes refuses to go into timeout voluntarily, and also refuses occasionally to return to the classroom from timeout.
4. Bobby shows no interest whatever in learning alternative adaptive responses to tantruming.
5. Bobby suppresses his rate of tantruming. However, he develops more covert, but equally inappropriate, methods of controlling his environment, obtaining peer and teacher attention, and getting his own way.

CHAPTER

6

Involving Parents in the Intervention Program

As professionals in the areas of mental health and education have come to recognize the value of behavior management procedures in remediating child behavior problems, there has been a movement to extend the impact of these procedures into natural settings, such as the home and school, via parents and teachers. A number of studies have been carried out in which parents have been trained as behavior therapists for their own children (Johnson & Katz, 1973). The results of such studies have been highly encouraging and have stimulated parent training efforts on a widespread basis.

There are a number of positive reasons for involving parents in behavior change programs for their children as either direct behavior therapists or as auxiliary, supportive social agents in the behavior change process. For example, educators have traditionally expressed considerable pessimism about the futility of trying to change child behavior at school when the home environment consistently maintains or actually strengthens the inappropriate child behavior that is of concern to the school. It is argued that what is achieved at school is essentially undone at home. Therefore, programs implemented at school without active parent involvement are viewed as essentially fruitless.

The author does not share this pessimistic view of the efficacy of school only based procedures for changing child behavior. Study after study has shown that intervention procedures implemented only at school without parent involvement can have a dramatic impact upon child behavior. However, it is highly unlikely that such behavior changes would show evidence of generalization to the home setting unless parents were involved also in actively reinforcing them. Nevertheless, a child experiencing behavior problems at school should not, in the author's opinion, be denied access to a potentially effective intervention program at school simply because his/her parents are perceived as nonsupportive, uncooperative, or even as undoing the program at home through their normal interactions with the child.

It should be noted that there is a broad consensus among educators that parent training is essential if a significant impact on child behavior is to be achieved. A number of school districts are now employing parent educators for the purpose of working with the parents of children experiencing learning and behavioral problems at school.

If parent involvement can be obtained in either directly changing or supporting a behavior change program at school, the chances for the program's overall success are probably increased. On a logical basis, this would certainly seem to be the case; however, to date there has been almost no research carried out on the impact of parent involvement in school based intervention programs.

Herbert and Baer (1972) have noted that there is a growing concern with the generality and durability of behavioral gains, especially from treatment to nontreatment settings, e.g., school to home. This concern has led to an increasing emphasis on reprogramming the social environments of young children involved in formal intervention programs for the purpose of maximizing the impact of such interventions. As Herbert and Baer (1972) note, a critically important part of a child's social environment is the behavioral consequences provided by parents at home. Studies carried out by Bijou and Sloane (1966); Patterson (1969); and Patterson, McNeal, Hawkins, and Phelps (1967) have dealt directly with the issue of reprogramming the social environments of young children via parent training.

In Chapter 1, it was noted that children in general and deviant children in particular are highly sensitive to the contingencies and conditions that exist in different settings, with resulting effects upon their behavior. If, for example, the consequences for a child's noncompliance are radically different at school and home, the child's behavior with respect to compliance with adult commands is also likely to differ in the two settings. If the child's teacher and parents are trained to change the way they respond to noncompliance, and they are both internally consistent and consistent with each other in their responses to it, the child's behavior is likely to show changes in both settings. If the teacher applies the procedures correctly and the parents do not, or vice versa, the child's behavior is likely to show change only in the setting where the procedures are correctly implemented. Thus, in terms of achieving a maximum impact upon child behavior, it is highly desirable to implement behavior change programs in both home and school settings.

Johnson and Katz (1973) note that parents, as change agents, represent an inexpensive, continuous treatment resource that can augment existing therapeutic capabilities. If parents are trained systematically to change the way they respond to child behavior, this treatment procedure is, in a sense, permanently installed, since the parents remain with the child across school years. This is not true with classroom teachers. It would be a massive task to change the way *all* a child's teachers interact with her/him across school years and to build in an effective level of consistency. It would be far easier to achieve this task with parents.

Because parents do have a much more powerful impact upon child behavior than the school, and because the child spends so much more time in the home as opposed to the school, it could be that the same intervention procedures implemented at home would produce a relatively greater impact upon the child's life than if implemented at school. Ideally, it would be desirable to implement such procedures in both settings simultaneously in order to maximize their effect.

On a strictly humanitarian basis, it is desirable to involve parents in school-based intervention programs and to attempt to teach them rudimentary behavior management skills they can apply at home. Research by Johnson, Bolstad, and Lobitz (1976) and Patterson (1974) shows that approximately 50 percent of children who display deviant behavior at school are also deviant in the home setting when compared to normal families. Thus, one half of the children having behavior problems at school are probably also experiencing them at home. Many parents would probably welcome being exposed to simple tactics or procedures for managing child behavior at home. A number of researchers have reported that parents of children having behavior problems at school communicate a feeling of incompetence in managing the child's home behavior as well (Wahler, 1969(b)). Presumably, such parents would be motivated to improve their skills in managing their child's behavior at home, especially if the behavior is aversive to them. However, there is no guarantee that this would always be the case.

Finally, an excellent reason for involving parents in a school-based intervention program is the array of backup rewards that can be provided via parents at home. Though a variety of appealing reward activities can be arranged at school (free time, classroom games, extra recess), some children are simply not responsive to them. A much larger variety of rewards as well as higher magnitude rewards (movies, picnics) can be arranged through the home.

In fact, Ayllon, Garber, and Pisor (1975) carried out a study in which an intervention program was initially based upon a set of school rewards only, and later it was based upon a combined school and home reward system, wherein the children earned a "good behavior letter" at school that was exchanged at home for a special privilege. This system proved to be highly effective for the children involved and was more effective than the school reward system had been.

The author, on numerous occasions, has used a combined home and school reward system where target children earn a group reward at school and an individual reward at home, delivered and monitored by parents (Hops, Beickel, & Walker, 1976; Walker, Street, Garrett, & Crossen, 1977). This combination appears to maximize the effectiveness of the intervention program since some children are quite responsive to the home reward only, others to the school reward only, and still others to both rewards equally.

Thus, it appears that potentially parents are in a position to greatly increase the effectiveness of an intervention program and also to facilitate the cross setting transfer of changed child behavior. There are a number of critical issues that must be addressed in the major areas relative to parent involvement. These are: (1) the nature of parent involvement in intervention programs, (2) the types of training procedures used to teach parents behavior management skills, and (3) techniques that have been used to motivate parents to acquire such skills and to apply them effectively. These issues are discussed below.

THE NATURE OF PARENT INVOLVEMENT IN CHILD INTERVENTION PROGRAMS

Increasingly, parents have been involved in the implementation of both school-based and nonschool-based intervention programs designed to change child behavior. Parent involvement has ranged from the simple dispensing of school-earned rewards at home (Ayllon, Garber, & Pisor, 1975; McKenzie, Clark, Wolf, Kothera, & Benson, 1968), to teaching parents of target children to apply systematic behavior management procedures at home (Christophersen, Arnold, Hill, & Quilitch, 1972; Herbert & Baer, 1972; Zeilberger, Sampen, & Sloane, 1968), to involving parents directly in efforts to produce changes in behavior at home that may facilitate appropriate school behavior (Wahler, 1969(a), (b)).

In the great majority of studies reported in the literature involving parents in child behavior management programs, the parents have been under some form of guidance and either direct or indirect supervision from a more skilled professional. This involvement has ranged from simple office conferences, to telephone contacts, to home visits, to requiring parents to present data on assigned home projects in order to continue participating in the intervention program (Johnson & Katz, 1973).

As a rule, parents have implemented intervention programs designed for them by highly trained behavior management professionals. An exception to this rule occurred in a study reported by Hall, et al., (1972). Four parents enrolled in a three-hour credit course called Responsive Teaching. The course was concerned with successfully implementing projects designed to modify aspects of their children's behavior in the home. The skills and knowledge the parents had acquired in the course no doubt accounted for their ability to carry out this task successfully.

Other researchers have implemented programs for children directly in the clinic, laboratory, or classroom, strengthened the target behavior to an appropriate level, and then trained the children's parents to run the program at home. For example, Hewett (1965) and Risley and Wolf (1968) used fading and reinforcement procedures to develop functional speech in speech deficient children. After the children were responding appropriately to the program, their parents were trained successfully to continue the program at home.

Patterson (1966) involved parents concurrently in a program to remediate a case of school phobia. Systematic desensitization procedures were implemented by the investigator in a structured doll play situation, while the child's parents were instructed to reinforce instances of independent behavior at home.

Parents have been trained to implement a variety of behavior management techniques at home. These include: *self recording of attention to appropriate child behavior* (Herbert & Baer, 1972); *feedback and a point system with response cost* (Christophersen et al., 1972); *differential attention and timeout* (Wahler, 1969(b)); *contracting procedures* (Patterson, 1971); and *extinction and reinforcement of incompatible behavior* (Wahler, Winkel, Peterson, & Morrison, 1965). The above procedures are relatively complex. The fact that parents can be trained to implement them successfully is an indication of the extent to which effective behavior management procedures can be extended into natural settings via social agents within them.

A truly remarkable variety of child behaviors has been modified successfully, using parents either as primary or as secondary behavior change agents. These include *tantrums and crying behavior* (Williams, 1959); *firesetting* (Holland, 1969); *aggression* (Patterson, 1974; Bernal, 1968); *social and academic skills* (Mathis, 1971); *encopresis* (Conger, 1970); *enuresis* (Lovibond, 1964); *self-injurious behavior* (Allen & Harris, 1966); *noncompliance* (Engeln, Knutson, Laughly, & Garlington, 1968); and *following instructions* (Zeilberger et al., 1968). The range of successfully modified behaviors listed above attests to the power of parents as auxiliary therapists in producing socially significant changes in child behavior.

Thus, the available literature indicates that parents have been involved in a variety of roles in modifying child behavior. The techniques that have been used to train parents and the amount of time invested in such training are critically important issues in the delivery of behavior management services to children in home settings. These are reviewed below.

TRAINING PROCEDURES USED TO TEACH PARENTS BEHAVIOR MANAGEMENT SKILLS

Training procedures used to teach parents systematic behavior management skills have ranged from simply giving parents instructions (Herbert & Baer, 1972) to the use of a systematic cuing, feedback, and reinforcement system in a clinic setting during mother-child interactions (Wahler et al., 1965). As a rule, the more complex the behavior management task(s) involved, the greater the training required and the more professional time that must be invested.

A number of investigators have used didactic instruction in behavior management principles and procedures to teach parents the skills required to change child behavior (Hall et al., 1972; Holland, 1969; Conger, 1970). In these studies, training was usually delivered via individual counseling sessions with the parents, and with the professional parent trainers having only limited contact, if any, with the target children during implementation.

Other investigators have developed comprehensive parent training procedures built around a group instructional format (Patterson, Shaw, & Ebner, 1969; Salzinger, Feldman & Portnoy, 1970; Walder, Cohen, Breiter, Daston, Hirsch, & Leibowitz, 1967). A combination of training procedures has been used in such formats including (1) lectures, (2) assigned reading, (3) instruction in how to pinpoint, observe, and record child behavior, and (4) direct instruction and role playing in the application of behavioral procedures. The common experiences and mutual support that parents in such training groups share with each other no doubt contribute significantly to the success of such training. Usually, such training takes place over a series of meetings and can involve considerable time and effort.

Christophersen et al., (1972) reported a study in which parents were trained to apply behavior management procedures successfully within approximately ten hours of training time. The parents were taught to use the following procedures successfully: (1) extinction, (2) positive token reinforcement, e.g., a point system, and (3) response cost. Training was individualized and included didactic instruction in the above procedures, role playing, home visits, and telephone contacts. The results of the parents' use of the procedures were quite impressive.

Herbert and Baer (1972) reported a highly cost-effective study in which parents were required to self-record the instances in which they gave attention to their children's appropriate behavior. Training consisted of a one-hour home visit, instructions in how to record their own behavior using a golf counter, and definitions of appropriate child behavior. The parents proved to be accurate in their self-recordings, and the self-recording procedures were instrumental in dramatically increasing their attention to appropriate child behavior. The appropriate behavior of the children involved showed increases in the desired direction as a result of the intervention procedures. This study provides an important demonstration that significant changes in both parent and child behavior can be achieved with only a minimal amount of external training and supervision.

A number of investigators have brought parents into the clinic or laboratory and trained them in systematic behavior management procedures (Wagner & Ora, 1970; Bernal et al., 1968; and Wahler et al., 1965). The children usually accompany their parents and their interactions are observed and analyzed in this setting. In these studies, a combination of instructions, modelling, shaping, cuing, and prompting procedures are used to teach parents appropriate child management skills. Although such training can be highly effective, it can also be quite expensive and time consuming, and the extent to which such skills generalize to the home setting is variable.

The training procedures described above proved to be effective generally in the process of teaching parents behavior management skills. However, the relative cost-effectiveness of such procedures has been largely ignored to date. As schools become increasingly involved in parent training efforts, this issue will assume greater importance.

TECHNIQUES USED TO MOTIVATE PARENTS TO ACQUIRE AND IMPLEMENT BEHAVIOR MANAGEMENT SKILLS

Parent motivation to acquire and use effective behavior management skills has been a persistent problem for investigators in the parent training area. If a child is a behavior problem at home and his/her behavior is aversive to the parents, presumably, they would be quite receptive to training in procedures for coping effectively with it. Unfortunately, this does not always seem to be the case.

As mentioned earlier, only about half of the children identified as behavior problems at school are also deviant at home. Given that this is the case, parents of such children may feel no pressures from their children's home behavior to seek training in behavior management.

A number of parents have been referred for psychological services to mental health clinics because of their child's behavior problems at school. The clear implication in such a referral is that the locus of the child's school problems is in the family and that the parents are responsible for its solution. Such parents have a high rate of terminating their participation in such services. Under these conditions, their relative lack of motivation is understandable.

Finally, some parents whose children may be behavior problems only at school, see their child's behavior at school as being totally the school's responsibility. Such parents may not be supportive of or cooperative with a school-based program designed to change their child's behavior.

Investigators have developed a number of procedures for motivating parents to acquire and implement systematic behavior management skills. These include such things as *fee reductions* (Mira, 1970; Patterson, McNeal, Hawkins & Phelps, 1967), *praise* (Johnson & Brown, 1969; Toepfer, 1972), and *monetary rewards* (Peine & Munro, 1970). The relative effectiveness of these procedures in facilitating the acquisition and long term maintenance of parent's use of behavior management skills is not clear at present. It is apparent that schools have only a limited capacity to motivate parents to acquire behavior management skills or to encourage them to cooperate with a school intervention program. However, to the extent that this goal can be achieved, child behavior effects at school and at home may be enhanced.

GUIDELINES FOR INVOLVING PARENTS IN A SCHOOL-BASED INTERVENTION PROGRAM

As a general rule, it is desirable to involve parents in school-based intervention programs. This involvement can range from simply informing parents of the program and its goals, to involving parents directly in the process of strengthening at home the child behavior that facilitates school performance, e.g., listening to instructions, following directions, complying with adult requests, and academic skills. The extent of parent involvement will depend upon several factors such as (1) their general receptiveness to the use of behavior management procedures, (2) their level of motivation, (3) their educational level, and (4) the type of program being implemented and the goals for it.

As a minimum goal, the parents should be informed of the program, the reasons for its development and implementation provided, and an attempt made to obtain their active support and cooperation. The more deviant and/or disruptive the target child, the more necessary it is to have as much parent involvement as possible. This is because parents can provide at home a powerful source of special privileges and rewards that are contingent on school performance, and because the more deviant and well established the behavior pattern, the more likely it is that involvement of multiple social agents across settings will be required to significantly impact upon the child's behavior.

Four levels of parent involvement are presented below for the reader's consideration. Each level involves greater demands on the parents and requires larger amounts of time, effort, training, and monitoring/supervision on the part of the teacher or other school personnel assigned responsibility for this part of the intervention program.

INFORMING PARENTS OF THE PROGRAM AND EXPLAINING AND DISCUSSING IT WITH THEM

For the school personnel involved, this is the least costly and probably least cost-effective of the four options. It can be handled via a parent conference, a letter, or a telephone call if necessary. These three methods are presented in their order of desirability. It is important that parents thoroughly understand the program, its goals, and the procedures that will be used. All questions should be answered thoroughly and in detail.

If a more active involvement is desired, various options can be presented to them and discussed. Their receptivity to such involvement can be gauged in addition to their ability to master and carry through the necessary home procedures.

Some parents object to the use of reinforcement procedures with their children on religious, moral, or philosophical grounds. Objections of this type will usually arise as a result of a parent conference, letter, or telephone call designed to acquaint parents with the program. Other parents have no objection to the use of such procedures, but do not wish to implement or become involved in them at home. The wishes of parents in this area should be respected unless there are compelling reasons for not doing so.

If the parents are receptive to the program and are willing to be involved to the extent of supporting and cooperating with it, they should be urged to discuss it with their child. The teacher should present the program to the child first at school in an individual conference and this should be followed by a discussion of it with the parents at home. It is important that they clearly communicate their acceptance of the program, its importance to the child's school performance, and their expectation that she/he will respond positively to it. Such parental support may increase the chances of the program's success, particularly if the child is hostile toward school.

PARENTAL PRAISE OF SPECIFIC CHILD PERFORMANCE AT SCHOOL

Parental approval and praise of the child's school performance vis à vis the school program can be a powerful auxiliary component and may enhance its overall effectiveness. If parents are receptive to this level of involvement, it should be preceded by a parent conference in which the program is thoroughly explained and discussed. It is *extremely* important that parents be taught proper techniques of reviewing the child's school performance and of correctly praising positive appropriate performance.

Praise should be defined and examples should be given. Its potential effectiveness as a behavior change technique should also be described. Simple parental approval is one of the most powerful techniques at their disposal for improving their child's behavior.

A sample list of praise statements should be given to the parents and discussed with them. They should be informed that praise must be (1) behavior specific, that is, the behavior being approved of must be clearly described to the child as part of the praising procedure, (2) praise statements should be varied as often as possible so they do not lose their spontaneity, (3) praise should be delivered immediately after the child has described some aspect of appropriate or exemplary school performance, and (4) parents should be genuinely enthusiastic and excited in the communication of their approval of the child's performance.

It is recommended that both conceptual and behavioral mastery of reviewing and praising skills be insured before the program is implemented. For example, on a conceptual basis, the teacher should be certain that the parents *understand* how to review the child's school performance systematically and communicate their approval of it.

It is recommended that for each day of the program, the parent(s) sit down with the child for ten to fifteen minutes as soon as possible after arriving home and query him/her about what was done at school, how the program went, if the school reward was earned, what the teacher said, what she/he thinks about how the day went, and so on. Both good and bad features of the child's performance should be discussed. Praise should be given for the good things and encouragement given that performance will improve in the difficult areas.

If possible, it is desirable to have parents role play a session where the child's school behavior is reviewed and praised to build in behavioral mastery. The teacher can play the role of the parent and one of the parents can play the child's role initially. The roles can then be switched and the parent(s) given feedback on their performance.

Some parents will feel awkward in such role playing situations. If they appear embarrassed, reluctant, or especially uncomfortable, role playing should probably not be pursued further. If this occurs, be sure to determine that both parents, on a conceptual level, understand how to implement these procedures. One way to do this is to ask them to describe the procedures to you in their own words. Thus, you will be able to gauge their grasp of the procedures and how to implement them.

At some point, an early home visit may be desirable to discuss the child's progress in the program. If possible, the teacher should try to observe a daily review session as part of this visit and to give the parent feedback on her/his performance. Should this occur, *always* be sure to single out aspects of the parents' performance that can be praised and do so. Be very gentle in giving feedback on aspects of performance that are not up to standard.

Some parents may not have the necessary educational level, creativity, or skills to review and praise the child's school performance on a daily basis. If so, the teacher can send home a daily card listing one or two things the child did well in school that day. Parents can then be instructed to praise these things specifically.

Parents should be monitored to make sure they are following through on the home part of the program. Occasional telephone calls can be used for this purpose. These contacts can also be used to discuss the child's overall progress through the program. Such contacts should be initiated more frequently early in the program when the parents may need support or have questions.

INVOLVING PARENTS IN A HOME REWARD SYSTEM

A home reward system can be set up to either supplement the school reward or to serve as the only reward for a child's school performance.

If parents are willing to become so involved, there are several options that can be selected.

A simple variation of a home reward system that is relatively easy to manage is one wherein a home reward is available on a daily basis if the child meets the school criterion. This is a yes/no judgment, where the teacher makes a decision as to whether the child's behavior was sufficiently appropriate to earn the reward. If so, a card is sent home, with the teacher's signature, indicating the reward was earned. The child then exchanges the card for a home privilege. If the reward was not earned, then no card is sent home or it is indicated on the card via the teacher's signature.

A more complicated variation, but a highly effective one, uses a point system where a child earns points at school and then exchanges them at home for special privileges or rewards. In this system, it is possible for the child to earn X amount of points each day at school which can be exchanged for an array of backup rewards at home. The backup rewards are of varying costs in terms of point values. A variation of this type was presented in one of the case studies in Chapter 5.

In both these variations, it is important that a menu of special privileges or rewards be worked out in advance with the parents. They should be things the child enjoys and sees as desirable. It is a good idea to work out a list of privileges and/or rewards and have the parents post it at home. In the first variation described, the privileges should all be of the same relative value and magnitude. A list of seven to ten or more should be developed to insure sufficient variety from day to day. Only one privilege should be allowed each day.

In the second variation, a list of privileges and rewards should be developed ranging from a very special high magnitude level to a less special level, e.g., a movie or family picnic versus fifteen minutes of extra TV time. In this system, the child can exchange for less expensive privileges/rewards or save his/her points for more costly but valuable options. As a rule, it should be arranged so that the least expensive item can be purchased with the points earned from a good day at school, e.g., 80 percent appropriate behavior or better. The teacher should work with the parents in assigning point values to privileges and rewards so that it is neither too difficult nor too easy to earn them.

As a rule, parents have no difficulty in implementing such systems. However, they do require frequent monitoring to insure that rewards are only dispensed when the child actually earns them. Some parents allow themselves to be talked into privileges or rewards that have not been earned. When this occurs, the reinforcing effectiveness of the system is greatly reduced.

The author and others have had a great deal of success in developing and implementing home-based reinforcement systems of this type. It may be that for most children, a home reward system is more powerful than a school-based system. As such, it represents a valuable resource for motivating children to perform well at school.

INVOLVING PARENTS IN CHANGING CHILD BEHAVIOR AT HOME TO FACILITATE SCHOOL PERFORMANCE

If the child's behavior warrants it, and the parents are both willing and capable of acquiring the skills to change child behavior at home, a highly effective dual intervention program can be established at school and at home. If, for example, a child has low academic skills and has difficulty listening to instructions, following directions, and complying with adult commands, parents can be trained to work on these skills at home.

Although this can be an effective procedure, it requires a fair amount of parent training and joint planning by the teacher and parents. It is recommended that the teacher assume responsibility for designing a home program for the child that will supplement the school program. The teacher should provide instructions in how to operate it, point cards, materials, and so forth. The parent should be thoroughly briefed in the program and trained to run it under the teacher's direct supervision. Several role playing sessions can be planned, with the parent and child involved, either at home or at school. The teacher should assume a very directive role in designing the program, training the parent(s) in its operation, and in monitoring it until it is working smoothly.

The home and school reward systems can either operate independently of each other or be tied together. As a general rule, it is desirable that home and school child performance be tied together in the process of earning the available rewards.

These home-based procedures can be highly effective in enhancing the school performance of children experiencing learning and/or behavioral problems at school. Their success will depend upon the thoroughness with which parents are trained in their effective application and their implementation of them as supervised and monitored by the teacher. As a general rule, it is not recommended that parents use systematic punishment procedures, e.g., response cost, at home unless they are *thoroughly* trained in their correct application.

Five excellent parent training texts are listed below. They have proven to be highly effective in training parents in the systematic application of behavior management procedures.

Miller, W. H. *Systematic parent training procedures: Cases and issues.* Champaign: Research Press Co., 1975.

Zifferblatt, S. M. *You can help your child improve study and homework behaviors.* Champaign: Research Press Co., 1970.

Becker, W. C. *Parents and teachers.* Champaign: Research Press Co., 1971.

Patterson, G. R. & Gullion, E. *Living with children.* Champaign: Research Press Co., 1968.

Madsen, C. & Madsen, C. *Teaching/Discipline: A positive approach for educational development.* Boston: Allyn & Bacon, 1972.

REFERENCES

Allen, K. & Harris, F. Elimination of a child's excessive scratching by training the mother in reinforcement procedures. *Behavior Research Therapy*, 1966, *4*, 79–84.

Ayllon, T., Garber, S., & Pisor, K. The elimination of discipline problems through a combined school-home motivational system. *Behavior Therapy*, 1975, *6*, 616–626.

Bernal, M., Duryee, J., Pruett, H., & Burns, B. Behavior modification and the brat syndrome. *Journal of Consulting Psychology*, 1968, *32*, 447–455.

Bijou, S. W. & Sloane, H. Therapeutic techniques with children. In I. A. Berg and L. A. Pennington (Eds.), *An introduction to clinical psychology.* (Third edition). New York: Ronald Press, 1966, pp. 605–684.

Christophersen, E. R., Arnold, C. M., Hill, D. W., & Quilitch, R. H. The home point system: Token reinforcement procedures for application by parents of children with behavior problems. *Journal of Applied Behavior Analysis*, 1972, *5*, 485–497.

Conger, J. The treatment of encopresis by the management of social consequences. *Behavior Therapy*, 1970, *1*, 386–390.

Engeln, R., Knutson, J., Laughly, L., & Garlington, W. Behavior modification techniques applied to a family unit: A case study. *Journal of Child Psychology and Psychiatry*, 1968, *10*, 245–252.

Hall, R. V., Axelrod, S., Tyler, L., Frief, E., Jones, F., & Robertson, R. Modification of behavior problems in the home with a parent as observer and experimenter. *Journal of Applied Behavior Analysis*, 1972, *5*, 53–64.

Herbert, E. & Baer, D. Training parents as behavior modifiers: Self-recording of contingent attention. *Journal of Applied Behavior Analysis*, 1972, *5*, 139–149.

Hewett, F. Teaching speech to an autistic child through operant conditioning. *American Journal of Orthopsychology*, 1965, *34*, 927–936.

Holland, C. Elimination by the parents of fire-setting behavior in a seven-year-old boy. *Behavior Research Therapy*, 1969, 7, 135–137.

Hops, H., Beickel, S., & Walker, H. M. *CLASS* (*Contingencies for Learning Academic and Social Skills*) *Manual for consultants.* Eugene, Ore.: Center at Oregon for Research in the Behavioral Education of the Handicapped, University of Oregon, 1976.

Johnson, C. A., & Katz, R. C. Using parents as change agents for their children: A review. *Journal of Child Psychology and Psychiatry*, 1973, *14*, 181–200.

Johnson, S. M., Bolstad, O. D., & Lobitz, G. K. Generalization and contrast phenomena in behavior modification with children. In E. J. Mash, L. A. Hamerlynck, & L. C. Handy (Eds.), *Behavior Modification and Families.* New York: Brunner/Mazell, 1976.

Johnson, S. & Brown, R. Producing behavior change in parents of disturbed children. *Journal of Child Psychology and Psychiatry*, 1969, *10*, 107–121.

Lovibond, S. *Conditioning and Enuresis.* New York: Macmillan, 1964.

Mathis, H. Training a "disturbed" boy using the mother as therapist: A case study. *Behavior Therapy*, 1971, *2*, 233–239.

McKenzie, H. S., Clark, M., Wolf, M. M., Kothera, R., & Bensen, C. Behavior modification of children with learning disabilities using grades as tokens and allowances as backup reinforcers. *Exceptional Children*, 1968, *34*, 745–752.

Mira, M. Results of a behavior modification training program for parents and teachers. *Behavior Research Therapy*, 1970, *8*, 309–311.

Patterson, G. R. Intervention for boys with conduct problems: Multiple settings, treatments, and criteria. *Journal of Consulting and Clinical Psychology*, 1974, *42*, 471–481.

Patterson, G. *Families: Applications of social learning to family life.* Champaign: Research Press, 1971.

Patterson, G. A community mental health program for children. In L. A. Hamerlynck, P. O. Davidson, & L. E. Acker, (Eds.), *Behavior modification and ideal mental health services.* Calgary: The University of Calgary, 1969.

Patterson, G. A learning theory approach to the treatment of the school phobic child. In L. P. Ullman & L. Krasner (Eds.), *Case studies in behavior modifications*, New York: Holt, Rinehart & Winston, 1966.

Patterson, G., McNeal, S., Hawkins, N., & Phelps, R. Reprogramming the social environment. *Journal of Child Psychology and Psychiatry*, 1967, *8*, 181–195.

Patterson, G., Shaw, D., & Ebner, M. Teachers, peers, and parents as agents of change in the classroom. In F. A. M. Benson (Ed.), *Modifying deviant social behaviors in various classroom settings*, Eugene, Ore.: Monograph No. 1, University of Oregon, 1969.

Peine, H., & Munro, B. *Training parents using lecture demonstration procedures and a contingency managed program.* Salt Lake City: Unpublished manuscript, University of Utah, 1970.

Risley, T. The effects and side effects of punishing the autistic behaviors of a deviant child. *Journal of Applied Behavior Analysis,* 1968, *1,* 21–34.

Salzinger, K., Feldman, R., & Portnoy, S. Training parents of brain injured children in the use of operant conditioning procedures. *Behavior Therapy,* 1970, *1,* 4–32.

Toepfer, C. The design and evaluation of an obedience training program for mothers of preschool children. *Journal of Consulting and Clinical Psychology,* in press.

Wagner, L. & Ora, J. Parental control of the very young severely oppositional child. Paper presented at the 1970 meeting of the Southeastern Psychological Association, Louisville, Kentucky.

Wahler, R. G. Oppositional children: A quest for parental reinforcement control. *Journal of Applied Behavior Analysis,* 1969(a), *2,* 159–170.

Wahler, R. G. Setting generality: Some specific and general effects of child behavior therapy. *Journal of Applied Behavior Analysis,* 1969(b), *2,* 239–246.

Wahler, R. G., Winkel, G. W., Peterson, R. F., & Morrison, D. C. Mothers as behavior therapists for their own children. *Behavior Research and Therapy,* 165, *3,* 113–134.

Walder, L., Cohen, S., Breiter, D., Datson, P., Hirsch, I., Leibowitz, M. *Teaching behavioral principles to parents of distrubed children.* Paper presented at the 1967 Eastern Psychological Association.

Walker, H. M., Street, A., Garrett, B., & Crossen, J. Experiments with response cost in playground and classroom settings. Eugene, Ore.: CORBEH Report #35, Center at Oregon for Research in the Behavioral Education of the Handicapped, University of Oregon, 1977.

Williams, C. The elimination of tantrum behavior by extinction procedures. *Journal of Abnormal Social Psychology,* 1959, *59,* 269.

Zeilberger, J., Sampen, S. E., & Sloane, H. N. Modification of a child's problem behaviors in the home with the mother as therapist. *Journal of Applied Behavior Analysis,* 1968, *1,* 47–53.

CHAPTER

7

Techniques for Facilitating the Maintenance and Generalization of Changes in Child Behavior

Systematic behavior management procedures, based upon principles of behavior modification, date from approximately 1958. From 1958 to 1968, the focus of research in this area was primarily upon demonstrating the power and efficacy of behavioral procedures in changing behavior in such varied settings as the clinic, home, institution, and classroom. The diversity of human behavior that was successfully modified and the efficacy of the procedures used in these studies were truly impressive (Ullman & Krasner, 1965; Krasner & Ullman, 1965).

Starting around 1968, researchers in this area began to look at the maintenance and generalization of behavior changes beyond the setting or situation in which the treatment procedures were implemented (Wahler, 1969; O'Leary, Becker, Evans, & Saudargas, 1969). Kazdin and Bootzin (1972) define maintenance as the persistence or durability of treatment effects within the treatment setting following withdrawal or termination of the formal intervention procedures. Generalization, on the other hand, refers to the transfer or extension of the treatment effects to settings in which the intervention procedures have not been implemented.

Results of these studies showed that treatment effects tended to be specific to the settings in which treatment occurred, and further that changed behavior tended to revert back to pretreatment levels once the treatment procedures were withdrawn or terminated. Thus, a highly effective technology for changing behavior was developed that did not produce enduring or generalizable effects.

In discussing the current state of applied behavior analysis procedures, Baer, Wolf, and Risley (1968) suggested that the generalization of behavior changes should . . . "be programmed, rather than expected or lamented." In other words, we should not expect treatment procedures to produce enduring and generalizable behavior changes as a matter of course. Instead, procedures should be built into intervention programs to facilitate the maintenance and generalization of such effects. Further, post intervention and nontreatment settings should be programmed to actively support and maintain the changed behavior.

Additional research carried out on this question generally corroborates the original findings noted by Wahler (1969) and O'Leary et al., (1969). The available evidence to date suggests that the generalization and maintenance of changed behavior does not automatically occur when treatment procedures are abruptly withdrawn (Birnbrauer, Wolf, Kidder, & Tague, 1965; Walker, Mattson, & Buckley, 1971). Unless systematic fading procedures are used (O'Leary, Becker, Evans, & Saudargas, 1969), or attempts are made to transfer control of the changed behavior to readily available reinforcers such as teacher praise (Greenwood, Hops, Delquadri, & Guild, 1974), or efforts are made to reprogram the social environments in which maintenance is expected (Patterson, McNeal, Hawkins, & Phelps, 1967; Walker & Buckley, 1972; Walker, Hops, & Johnson, 1975), it is unlikely that the changed behavior will either maintain or generalize satisfactorily. This appears to be especially true of maintenance effects following treatment in special settings where tangible reinforcers (points, poker chips, toys, edibles) have been used extensively (Walker, Mattson, & Buckley, 1971; Walker & Buckley, 1974; Herman & Tramontana, 1971). O'Leary & Drabman (1971) and O'Leary & O'Leary (1976) have noted similar effects occurring in child behavior as a result of the systematic application of behavioral procedures.

Thus, taken together, this research provides very strong evidence that behavior change is a two stage process. In stage one, pro-

TABLE 7.1. *The Relationship between Treatment, Maintenance, and Generalization Effects*

Treatment Classification	*Treatment Effects Achieved*	*Maintenance Effects Achieved*	*Generalization Effects Achieved*
Type One	Yes	Yes	Yes
Type Two	Yes	No	No
Type Three	No	No	No

cedures in behavior must be implemented to produce changes in behavior. In stage two, a second set of procedures must be implemented to insure that such changes endure over the long term and generalize to other settings. Only recently have we begun to systematically pay attention to the second stage of the behavior change process.

Given these findings, we need to reevaluate our criteria as to what constitutes an effective intervention procedure or program. Traditionally, we have assumed that an effective treatment procedure is one that *permanently* changes behavior and that shows evidence of impacting upon one's functioning across settings. This now appears to be a most inappropriate standard for separating effective from noneffective treatments. Table 7.1 can be used to summarize our traditional expectancies concerning effective treatments.

We now know that Type One treatment outcomes are extremely rare and tend to occur only when specific procedures are implemented to produce maintenance and generalization effects. Type Two treatment outcomes are far more common, e.g., treatment effects are produced that are specific to the treatment procedures themselves and show no evidence of generalization beyond the treatment setting. Type Three would be considered an ineffective treatment. Further the questions of maintenance and generalization of treatment effects become somewhat academic unless treatment effects are produced by the intervention procedures.

In the author's opinion, a Type Two treatment outcome would *not* indicate an ineffective or inadequate treatment procedure. A procedure that produces powerful changes in behavior within the treatment setting is a successful one. The maintenance and generalization of those treatment effects is a separate question entirely, and one that requires the development of an entirely new technology—a technology that is currently in its infancy. Thus, it is inappropriate to use lack of maintenance and/or generalization effects as standards for judging the efficacy of treatment procedures. Only behavior changes occurring in the treatment setting should be used for this purpose.

This chapter addresses the issues of treatment maintenance and generalization and presents tactics for facilitating these processes after behavior changes have been successfully achieved via implementation of effective treatment procedures. This is an especially critical problem in the school setting where a child, even in the elementary grades, can have as many as six or seven different teachers each day. A treatment procedure implemented in one teacher's classroom is unlikely to produce changes in child behavior in other classrooms with different teachers *unless* (a) a variation of the original treatment procedure is also implemented in those classrooms, or (b) those classrooms are reprogrammed, e.g., changed to actively support and maintain the gains that have been achieved in the target child's behavior. The remainder of this chapter is devoted to a discussion of procedures for facilitating the maintenance and generalization of treatment effects.

PROCEDURES FOR ACHIEVING MAINTENANCE OF TREATMENT EFFECTS FOLLOWING WITHDRAWAL OR TERMINATION OF FORMAL INTERVENTION PROCEDURES

As noted earlier, systematic behavior management procedures, based on principles of behavior modification, have produced dramatic and powerful changes in child behavior, especially in classroom settings. However, considerable effort has been invested by researchers, and classroom teachers working under their supervision, in producing such changes. For example, teachers are frequently asked to praise a child's performance and/or award points once each three to five minutes, and sometimes more often than this in studies reported in the literature (Hanley, 1970; Lipe & Jung, 1971). If teachers are cooperative, they are willing to invest this level of effort for a short period of time, e.g., a month or two, while under an investigator's supervision and direction. Understandably, however, they are not willing to invest this much effort in one child for the foreseeable future. Thus, as a general rule, when the intervention program is terminated and the teacher's behavior is no longer under the investigator's supervision, the teacher's behavior tends to return to normal–and consequently, so does the child's behavior. Thus, what has been demonstrated is that *temporary* changes can be produced in the way teachers interact with target children, which in turn produces changes in child behavior. The functional impact of such procedures upon both teacher and child behavior has usually been highly ephemeral.

In the author's opinion, the primary reason changes in child behavior do not maintain within treatment settings is that the teacher behavior that produced them does not maintain either. Thus, after formal intervention procedures are terminated or withdrawn, there is usually a simultaneous decay in both teacher and child behavior (Cooper, Thompson, & Baer, 1970; Cossaint, Hall, & Hopkins, 1973). In those rare cases where *short term* followup data show that teacher and child behavior did maintain (Parsonson, Baer, & Baer, 1974), no explanation is given as to what specific features of the intervention procedure accounted for the maintenance effects. Thus, at this point, no one knows for sure why some treatment procedures produce maintenance effects, while the great majority do not. If the specific features of the treatment procedure accounting for the maintenance effects were known, they could be built into treatment procedures of future studies. Given what is currently known about this problem, its solution does not appear likely in the near future.

It is difficut to blame busy classroom teachers for failing to maintain, over the long term, the level of effort required to maintain changed child behavior. Teachers simply do not see such procedures as cost-effective in the classroom setting given the level of effort required to produce *enduring, permanent changes* in child behavior. In contrast, when the procedures are terminated, their level of effort is reduced and the teacher's preintervention style or pattern of interaction with the child is usually resumed with a corresponding decay in child behavior. When this occurs, teachers tend to see the intervention procedures as ineffective.

A number of responses to this general problem are possible. However, what seems to be needed is a strategy wherein (a) treatment procedures are implemented that produce the desired changes in child behavior and that teach the teacher a new style or pattern of interacting with the child, (b) the treatment procedures are gradually changed over time until they are manageable as a part of the teacher's *normal* instructional/management routines, and (c) a low cost variation of the treatment procedure remains in effect over the long term or until the child's behavior no longer requires it. Some strategies for achieving these goals are presented below for the reader's consideration. These include (1) establishing teacher attention, approval, and/or praise as reinforcing events for the target child, (2) learning to respond to appropriate child behavior and to discontinue use of warnings, threats, reprimands, and criticism as methods of controlling inappropriate behavior, (3) reducing the number of times the child's behavior must be attended to and reinforced, (4) eliminating major components of the intervention program, and (5) implementing a low cost variation of the intervention program over the long term.

ESTABLISHING TEACHER ATTENTION, APPROVAL, AND PRAISE AS REINFORCING EVENTS

For most children, the teacher's general attention is a very powerful reinforcer. Many children will work extremely hard for simple teacher approval of their performance. However, for behavior problem children, this is much less likely to be the case. Such children tend to be less responsive to teacher approval; thus, increased teacher praise alone is often not sufficient to produce changes in their behavior (Thomas, Becker, & Armstrong, 1968).

For some children, as noted earlier, systematic teacher or parent attention to their appropriate behavior makes them worse! The point was made earlier that the more deviant/disruptive the child, the more likely this was to be the case. Ironically, the children who are least responsive to adult praise and approval are those whose behavior requires the application of systematic behavior management procedures. Thus, it is of critical importance that teacher praise and approval be established as reinforcing events for these children and that they learn to respond to them. After the formal intervention procedures are phased out, teacher praise/approval is the primary management tool at the teacher's disposal for maintaining the child's changed behavior. Unless the target child is responsive to teacher attention, the propects for achieving long term maintenance effects are dim.

The most effective method of increasing the reinforcing effectiveness of teacher praise/approval is *systematically* to pair them with the delivery of rewards. In this way, teacher praise/approval may take on some of the reinforcing effectiveness and incentive value of the rewards. When this occurs, praise/approval may be more effective when applied to appropriate child behavior. That is, children may be more responsive to it than before.

There are some guidelines to follow in carrying out this task. For example, teacher praise/approval should be presented immediately *prior* to the delivery of the reward. It is best to use a point system, with backup rewards, for this pairing process. The child's appropriate behavior that is being reinforced should be described in specific terms, the teacher should clearly communicate approval of it, and the point(s) delivery should follow immediately. *Never* give the point first followed by praise! The training process will be much more effective if the praise/approval is given first and then followed by the delivery of points. An example of this procedure is as follows: "Frank, you worked hard on your math assignment. You got twelve out of the fourteen problems right. That's really good! I'm very proud of you! You earned three points for your accuracy, and a bonus point for doing better than yesterday. Keep up the good work!"

A second rule is to pair praise and points in this fashion *every time* points are awarded. This pairing should simply become an automatic part of the point awarding process. As the frequency of giving points is gradually reduced (see fading procedures below), occasional unpaired praises should be given in between the times praise and points are awarded. This will help to maintain the child's appropriate behavior in between the delivery of points, and will also help the child adapt to the fading procedure.

A third rule is that once the point system has been faded out (provided this is the teacher's goal), teacher praise should be systematically paired with the delivery of occasional surprise rewards. This will serve as a "booster shot" in a sense and will increase chances that teacher praise will be effective in maintaining appropriate child behavior. The systematic use of powerful teacher praise/approval is probably the most important and significant single thing the teacher can do to build in the long term maintenance of changed child behavior.

LEARNING TO RESPOND TO APPROPRIATE CHILD BEHAVIOR AND TO DISCONTINUE USE OF REPRIMANDS AS A MEANS OF CONTROLLING CHILD BEHAVIOR

In order to change inappropriate child behavior effectively, it is absolutely essential that the teacher change his/her method of interaction with the child. In the great majority of cases, appropriate child behavior tends to be ignored, but noxious, inappropriate child behavior is responded to in the form of threats, reprimands, warnings, etc. In other words, children are usually ignored unless they do something wrong—and then they are yelled at. This is clearly an oversimplification of what actually happens; however, the basic principle involved is both accurate and valid. Both teachers and parents tend to respond to child behavior in this way. It appears to be a very natural, but inappropriate, way of coping with child behavior.

If one observed and recorded the behavior of parents and teachers in a series of homes and classrooms, the use of reprimands would probably exceed that of praise in the majority of cases. White (1975) found that in *every* school grade after second grade, the rate of teacher verbal disapproval exceeded the rate of teacher verbal approval. In one classroom, the author found that the teacher gave her attention to the inappropriate behavior of three deviant children *nine* times as often as she attended to their appropriate behavior (Walker & Buckley, 1973). In another study involving five acting-out children enrolled in five different regular classrooms, Walker, Hops, and Fiegenbaum (1976) found that their teachers actively disapproved of their inappropriate behavior a total of *forty-five* times in a two-week period. In contrast, they approved of their appropriate behavior a total of three times in this same period. This is a ratio of fifteen to one in favor of reprimands!

It is likely that this imbalance would not be nearly so marked with teacher and parent interactions involving nondeviant normal children (Walker & Buckley, 1973). However, the point seems well made that there is a much higher probability of teachers and parents reprimanding inappropriate child behavior than praising appropriate behavior.

Most behavior management intervention programs control teacher attention to appropriate versus inappropriate child behavior. That is, in implementing the procedures, the teacher is *required* to attend to the child's appropriate behavior in order to praise it and award points. Simultaneously, the use of reprimands is greatly reduced or totally eliminated for one or more of the following reasons: (a) the child's behavior changes dramatically so there is a much lower rate of the inappropriate behavior that was previously consequated using reprimands, (b) the teacher is trained to ignore and withhold praise and reinforcement from inappropriate child behavior, (c) mild punishment procedures in the form of response cost or timeout are used to control inappropriate behavior as part of the treatment procedure, thus making reprimands relatively unnecessary.

Thus, a well designed intervention program builds in an appropriate pattern of teacher interaction with the target child. That is, the child's appropriate behavior is attended to and positively reinforced on a regular basis, and inappropriate behavior is either ignored or consequated using mild punishment procedures. Unfortunately, teachers generally do not internalize this pattern of interaction and learn to use it in the absence of the intervention program. Generally, teachers quickly revert to their previous pattern of interaction with problem children in their classes soon after the intervention program is terminated. In the author's opinion, this is one of the major reasons that child treatment effects do not prove durable over the long term. Ironically, we usually blame the child or the intervention program when treatment gains prove to be short lived.

It is essential that the teacher continue to systematically attend to and positively reinforce (praise) a child's appropriate behavior in the postintervention phase. It is equally important that he/she *not* resume the use of reprimands as a means of controlling the child's inappropriate behavior. If this happens, the child will quickly sense the change in teacher behavior and revert to her/his previous behavior pattern.

REDUCING THE NUMBER OF TIMES THE CHILD'S BEHAVIOR MUST BE ATTENDED TO AND REINFORCED

After a child has been exposed to an effective intervention program, has adapted to it, and her/his behavior has stabilized, the number of times the child has to be reinforced in order to maintain the achieved behavioral gains can be greatly reduced. Walker, Hops, Greenwood, Todd, and Garrett (1977) conducted a study with six socially aggressive children assigned to a special classroom. A combination of teacher praise, points, and response cost was implemented to change their social behavior from negative/aggressive to positive. After a month of such treatment, a systematic fading procedure was introduced to reduce the number of times the children had to be reinforced with praise and points each day. Over a four-week period, the number of available points was reduced by 80 percent! There were no deleterious effects whatever upon the children's behavior as a result of the fading procedure.

In this study, the total number of points available on a daily basis during the initial month of the intervention program was reduced by 20 percent each week of a four-week fading period. The children were not told that points were being faded. The exchange ratios of points to backup rewards was not changed. Thus, as fading progressed, the children had to work for longer and longer periods of time in order to earn the available backup rewards.

This study demonstrates that once child behavior is well developed and stable, the number of times it must be reinforced to maintain its newly acquired levels can be markedly reduced without a loss of the behavioral gains achieved. It should be noted, however, that had the children in the above study been informed that a fading program was going to be introduced and that it would take longer to earn the backup rewards and privileges, the results might have been different. However, Bailey, Wolf, and Phillips (1970) reported a study in which both daily reinforcement and feedback were successfully faded with the child's awareness that fading procedures were in effect.

The implications of these findings for the classroom teacher who is responsible for the implementation of a behavior management program are obvious. They suggest that the major features of such programs, e.g., praise and points, can be reduced to levels that are feasible for the teacher to manage on a daily basis as part of his/her ordinary teaching routines. If done correctly, decay in child behavioral gains can be reduced to a minimum.

Several fading procedures were presented in the case study section in Chapter 5. The author recommends that the reader study those fading procedures carefully before implementing a fading program.

There are some general guidelines that, if followed, will increase the chances for success of any fading program. For example, do not attempt a fading program if the child's behavior is showing considerable variability. This means that the program is not entirely successful in controlling the child's behavior and that her/his behavior is partially under the control of variables *other* than the treatment program. This kind of variability should be a cue for the teacher to adjust the program, e.g., check to see if the backup rewards are effective for the child, reexamine the appropriateness of the reinforcement criterion, and so forth, in order to make it more effective. Introducing a fading program in the midst of this kind of variability would be an exercise in futility.

As a rule, the child's behavior should show evidence of stability for three weeks to a month before a fading program is introduced. However, each case should be evaluated individually with respect to this issue and a decision made based on information available within the situation.

Second, as a general rule, the child or children involved should be informed that a fading program is going to be introduced. A good way to introduce the fading program is to say that the child has been doing so well with the intervention program that you would like to see if he/she can learn to work more independently and with less reliance on the teacher. Children will usually accept instructions to this effect without difficulty. However, it is extremely important that a child not be penalized for responding well to the fading program. That is, if a teacher has been awarding praise and points every ten minutes during the day and the child is able to earn a daily reward for achieving the 80 percent criterion, the same daily reward(s) should be available when the teacher shifts to awarding praise and points once every twenty minutes. If a child perceives that fading is essentially a losing game in terms of the backup rewards available, she/he may react negatively in a behavioral sense. This in turn defeats the purpose of fading.

Third, incentives should be provided to the child for learning to significantly reduce reliance or dependence upon the program for maintaining the behavioral gains achieved. If a child is receiving praise/points once every ten minutes, the goal would be to fade the system to the point where the daily reward is dependent upon an overall rating for the entire day, e.g., a plus or a minus rating given at the end of the day. This should be achieved in increments from once each ten minutes to twenty minutes to thirty minutes to each hour to once per day. Once a daily rating is achieved, the goal is to have the child meet the reward criterion for successive days, e.g., two days in a row, in order to earn the reward. At this stage, the ultimate goal is to move to a weekly reward for say meeting the criterion on four of the five days. However, it is essential that the child be motivated to respond positively to these program changes. This can be done by providing more special, higher magnitude rewards for working for longer and longer periods without rewards. Thus, a two day reward should be of relatively greater value than the one day rewards. Similarly, a three day reward should be of greater value than a two day reward, and so on. This will significantly reduce the chances of the child's behavior breaking down and of the achieved behavioral gains being lost as a result of the fading program.

Fourth, teacher praise should be used frequently during the fading period. It is extremely important, in fact essential, that a high frequency of teacher praise and approval to the child's appropriate behavior be maintained during the fading period. After being systematically paired with points during the intervention program, teacher praise should be more effective as a reinforcer of the child's appropriate behavior. Therefore, its use as an auxiliary tool to support appropriate behavior during the fading period may contribute significantly to an enduring treatment effect. Praise should also be used systematically during the fading period to compensate for the reduced teacher attention that occurs as a result of the reduction in the number of points (and consequently teacher attention) available to the child.

If the above guidelines are followed carefully, the chances for a fading program's success will be significantly increased. Whether the program is to be faded beyond a weekly reward depends upon the teacher's preference and perhaps the child's behavior. If it is faded beyond this point, the teacher should remember to provide higher magnitude and more special rewards to encourage the child to work independently for longer and longer periods of time.

ELIMINATING MAJOR COMPONENTS OF THE INTERVENTION PROGRAM

The goal of any fading program is to end up with the child's behavior maintaining over the long term with no external support or with only minimal support required, such as an occasional rating and surprise reward. Thus, ideally, only the rating and reward components of an intervention program should remain in effect. Over the long term, the remaining components such as response cost, timeout, prompting, cuing, etc., should be removed once they are no longer necessary to support the child's behavior. If a dual school reward and home reward system is in effect, one or the other should be terminated since both are probably not required to maintain the behavior gains of most children.

Generally, a gradual fading procedure should *not* be used to withdraw such components of the intervention program. When it appears that a given component is no longer required, it should simply be dropped from the program. It would be very unwise, for example, to attempt to gradually fade out response cost. If response cost operated at some times and not at others, or was only applied to some inappropriate child behavior(s) and not others, the overall effects on child behavior would probably be most undesirable. The intermittent application of punishment procedures could produce some very strange avoidance and risk taking behavior vis à vis classroom rules on the part of children to whom it was applied. It would be much better to leave response cost in effect until the formal point system was eliminated and replaced with a plus or minus rating system (see case studies in Chapter 5). Once the point system is eliminated, response cost no longer operates since it is based upon the subtraction of points.

It doesn't really matter whether the home reward or school reward is eliminated from the program. However, one or the other should be eliminated since both, except in rare cases, would not be required to maintain behavioral gains in the fading period. At this point in the program, the teacher should have a good idea of which reward, school or home, is more meaningful for the child. As a general rule, the less meaningful reward should be eliminated and the more meaningful one retained to support child behavior during the fading period.

If timeout has been used as part of the intervention program, it should probably not be formally withdrawn. Instead it should be left in effect as an option for controlling disruptive child behavior whenever it occurs. Further, for disruptive/deviant children, once response cost is eliminated, it may be very necessary to have a procedure such as timeout available in order to cope with disruptive behavioral episodes.

As is apparent from the foregoing discussion, the decision rules for eliminating major components of the intervention program are fairly arbitrary. A decision needs to be made at some point that a particular component is no longer required in order to maintain child appropriate behavior. Careful observation of the child's response to the intervention program can facilitate this decision process. For example, if either timeout or response cost is being used at a relatively high frequency to control the child's behavior, then withdrawing it would be obviously inadvisable. The rate of usage for such techniques should be quite low before their withdrawal or termination is considered.

As a final note, the correct and frequent use of teacher praise/approval for appropriate child behavior *should never be withdrawn or terminated!* The greater the frequency the teacher can praise appropriate child behavior, the better.

IMPLEMENTING A LOW COST VARIATION OF THE INTERVENTION PROGRAM OVER THE LONG TERM

It has been recommended numerous times throughout this book that a low cost, easy to manage variation of the original intervention program should be implemented to maintain child behavior over the long term. The nature of this variation depends upon what the teacher is willing to accept and feels comfortable with.

For example, one variation is to fade the program to a point where one reward can be earned each week. If a lower cost variation is desired, a reward can be made available on a bi-weekly, monthly, or even bi-monthly basis. If variations such as this are used, the rewards provided should be very special and highly appealing to the child or children involved.

Still another variation is to tell the child that from time to time (she/he won't know exactly when) the teacher will systematically evaluate the child's behavior and if it is appropriate a surprise reward will be awarded. This is an extremely low cost procedure and one that can have a very positive effect in maintaining child behavior over the long term.

In conclusion, low cost variations of this type, implemented across school years if necessary, are extremely important in building in enduring changes in child behavior. Most children will require their implementation in order for such effects to be produced. They should only be terminated when it is absolutely clear they are not required in order to maintain the child's appropriate behavior.

TECHNIQUES FOR FACILITATING GENERALIZATION OF TREATMENT EFFECTS TO NONTREATMENT SETTINGS

In systematic applications of behavior management procedures, it is extremely unlikely that treatment effects will generalize, by themselves, to settings in which the procedures or variations of them have not been implemented. Although there are occasional exceptions to this rule (Walker, Mattson, & Buckley, 1971; Kazdin, 1973), one should not expect such effects to occur in the absence of systematic efforts to produce or program them. The rule to remember is *what you teach is what you get,* and *where you teach it is where you get it!*

Therefore if a program is implemented in the regular classroom for a specific child, one should expect changes *only* in that setting and not on the playground, hallways, lunchroom, or in other classrooms. There is also no reason to expect generalization the other way, e.g., from the playground, lunchroom, or hallways to the regular classroom. Changed child behavior will usually occur only when the intervention program or variations of it are extended to those settings where child behavior is also problematic.

The failure to achieve such generalization has created a great deal of frustration among professionals charged with either the instruction or management of child behavior. It has been an especially crucial problem for special and regular educators vis à vis assignment of handicapped children to special and resource classrooms. Children assigned to such settings tend to show changes in their behavior which then *do not* generalize to other settings of primary interest, such as the regular classroom (Herman & Tramontana; Walker, Mattson, & Buckley, 1971; Walker & Buckley, 1972, 1974).

When a target child is reintegrated into a regular classroom from a special setting, regular classroom teachers usually expect her/him to be "cured," and that the referral problem(s) will have been ameliorated. Almost invariably, regular teachers are disappointed in this respect. Given the specificity of human behavior (Mischel, 1968) and the fact that the contingencies in the referring regular classroom have not really changed (unless they have been systematically reprogrammed), it is not surprising that the treatment gains achieved in the special setting gradually extinguish and vanish within a relatively short time. It should be noted that when the posttreatment setting *is* reprogrammed to support the changed behavior, e.g., the receiving regular classroom teachers are trained in contingency management procedures (Walker, Hops, & Fiegenbaum, 1976), such decay of treatment gains tends not to occur.

There are two primary methods of facilitating generalization of treatment effects to nontreatment settings. These are (1) extending the treatment program or a variation of it to such settings, and (2) reprogramming the social contingencies within these settings to support the changed behavior. These two methods are discussed below.

EXTENDING THE TREATMENT PROGRAM TO NONTREATMENT SETTINGS

Once the intervention program has been implemented, is operating smoothly, and the child's behavior has stabilized, it is appropriate to extend it to other classrooms or areas of the school in which the child is also experiencing difficulties. If a child is experiencing difficulties and behavior problems in all areas of the school, e.g., classrooms, playground, hallways, lunchroom, and so on, it is better to implement the intervention program in one setting such as in a homeroom period initially and extend it later, rather than to implement in all these settings at once.

A simple card system can be used to extend the program to other school areas. The teacher or supervisor in charge of the area gives the child an overall rating on her/his performance and the rating then is exchanged in the treatment setting for X units or credits toward earning available backup reinforcers. Several rating systems are possible. For example, a simple overall plus or minus rating can be awarded on a card for each classroom or other area of the school to which the program is extended. A sample card is presented below:

Program Extension Card

Math	⊕	−
Reading	+	⊖
P.E.	⊕	−
Lunchroom	⊕	−
Recess	⊕	−

At the end of the period, the teacher or supervisor circles either a plus or minus, indicating her/his judgment of the child's behavior. As a rule, the rating is made in terms of whether the rater feels the child's behavior has been reasonably appropriate in that period, using his/her own standards. Each plus earned can count toward earning a reward in the treatment setting, while each minus counts nothing.

Another option is to allow more flexibility in ratings, such as 3, 2, or 1, indicating excellent, acceptable, or unacceptable child behavior. An unacceptable rating would be redeemable in the treatment setting for *zero* units, credits, or points toward a backup reward; an acceptable rating could be exchanged for one; and an excellent rating for two. This allows the teacher or supervisor more discretion in evaluating the child's performance, and makes it possible to differentially reinforce higher quality performance. A program extension procedure using this variation was presented in the case studies section in Chapter 5.

If the treatment program occurs in either a special class or resource room, and the desired goal is to reintegrate the child into a regular classroom(s) while maintaining gains achieved in the special setting, a variation of the treatment program can be extended to the regular classroom setting using either of the above program extension options. In this procedure, the teacher(s) in the regular classroom rates the child's overall performance on a card, which the child carries from class to class. Ratings are then exchanged for units of reinforcement in the special setting where the intervention program operates.

In any of these program extension variations, it would be most desirable if teachers/supervisors in the extension settings would praise the child's performance on a regular basis in addition to awarding ratings. However, it is no easy task to make this happen. One method is to prompt these individuals to praise regularly. Another is to have them circle on the child's point card the number of times they praised her/his performance in their classes. A goal of one praise each fifteen to twenty minutes should be established for them. The importance of praise in facilitating the successful classroom adjustment of children should be emphasized to teachers/supervisors in all program extension areas.

REPROGRAMMING NONTREATMENT SETTINGS TO SUPPORT CHANGED CHILD BEHAVIOR

Instead of formally extending the program to nontreatment settings, it is possible to work with social agents within them to reinforce and support the child's changed behavior. Social agents in this case include the child's peers as well as the classroom teacher.

The author has carried out studies in which both peers and teachers in regular classroom settings have been trained to reinforce and support the child's changed behavior—behavior that was successfully changed in another special setting (Walker & Buckley, 1972; Walker, Fiegenbaum, & Hops, 1976). Results of these studies show that when such reprogramming efforts are made, children maintain gains achieved in a special classroom significantly better than when no such reprogramming efforts are made. The key in both instances, however, is to train and then motivate the peers and/or teachers to actively support the child's changed behavior.

Walker and Buckley (1972) evaluated both a peer reprogramming and a teacher training strategy in facilitating maintenance of appropriate child behavior following the child's reintegration from a special to a regular classroom setting. In the peer reprogramming strategy, the target children involved had an opportunity to earn a group reward activity twice weekly, based upon their appropriate behavior. During these twice weekly occasions, the child's behavior was evaluated for a thirty-minute period by a resource consultant during ongoing classroom activities. A total of ten points could be earned by the child during each thirty-minute period. One hundred points were required to earn a backup activity reward preselected by the child and his/her classmates.

As mentioned, the target child had to *earn* the right to earn points that counted toward a backup group reward for himself and his classmates. The child earned this right if her/his behavior was acceptable, on the average, to the teacher in between the weekly scheduled thirty-minute periods (which usually occurred on Tuesday and Friday). Acceptable behavior included such things as exhibiting appropriate study behavior, completing assignments on time, not disrupting the class, and so forth. It was left up to each target child's teacher to determine what was acceptable and what was not acceptable child behavior. If the child produced a lengthy or unusually disruptive period of inappropriate behavior between the two sessions, the teacher was instructed to notify the project staff, and the next scheduled visit by the resource consultant would be cancelled. Thus the points that might have been earned during the session were not available for that session.

A thermometer type wall chart was posted in the room to record the child's points. The chart ranged from zero to 100 points, and progress toward the backup reward activity could be observed as it occurred. When the 100 point total was reached, it was exchanged for a special group activity reward.

Each target child's teacher was given a set of written instructions for explaining the strategy, its purpose, and how it would operate in maintaining the child's appropriate classroom behavior. Basically, the instructions made the following points: (1) that the target child had been in a special class for awhile, (2) that while there, she/he had made some excellent gains in academic and classroom behavior, and (3) that the teacher wanted to present a program that would help insure that the target child continued those gains in the regular classroom. The peer's role in the program was explained. It was suggested that as a group they could be of great assistance to the target child in his/her attempts at appropriate social and academic behavior by (a) encouraging the child to study and work hard on assignments, and (b) by ignoring her/him whenever the child was engaged in inappropriate classroom behavior.

The child and peers were generally both quite receptive to the program as it was presented. Peers proved to be highly supportive of the target child's attempts at appropriate behavior and were most cooperative with the program. The program, as implemented, motivated the children to support the target child's appropriate behavior rather than to subtly approve of and covertly reinforce inappropriate behavior, as is often the case. Their sharing equally in the backup reward that was being earned no doubt contributed to this effect. Target children who were exposed to this reprogramming maintenance strategy produced significantly higher levels of appropriate behavior in the regular classroom than did those who received no followup services in the regular classroom after their reintegration.

In the followup teacher training reprogramming strategy, the target children's regular classroom teachers were trained in systematic behavior management procedures in an attempt to transfer treatment effects from the special classroom. The purpose of this strategy was to train the classroom teacher to reinforce and support the target child's changed behavior.

Each teacher was enrolled in a division of continuing education class on contingency management (with their tuition paid for them). The participating teachers attended no formal classes, but were required to read and master a semiprogrammed text on applications of behavior modification techniques in the regular classroom setting (Buckley & Walker, 1970). The teacher met with a supervising resource consultant and discussed classroom applications of the principles contained in the text. This individual provided the teacher with direct training in behavior modification techniques and served as a resource consultant in the application of behavioral principles to the task of maintaining the target child's achieved behavorial gains. After a series of initial training sessions, the resource consultant visited the class on a weekly basis and supported the teacher's attempts at maintaining the target child's appropriate behavior.

Children in this strategy did not do as well as those exposed to the peer reprogramming strategy. Some teachers responded quite well to the training and supervision procedures, while others did not. The skill(s) with which teachers applied systematic behavior management techniques and principles to the task of maintaining appropriate child behavior varied considerably from teacher to teacher. Children in the classes of teachers who applied the procedures correctly and consistently tended to maintain higher levels of appropriate behavior than children in the classes of teachers who were less skilled and/or consistent in such applications.

The author felt the teacher training procedures in the above study were deficient in the following areas: (a) careful specification of required tasks to be achieved by the teacher, (b) insuring conceptual mastery of behavior management principles/techniques, (c) providing the teacher with regular feedback as to how well the target child's behavior is maintaining, and (d) making the teacher's grade in the division of continuing education course contingent on how well the target child's behavior maintained (relative to his/her performance in the special classroom). Walker, Hops, and Johnson (1975) designed a teacher training followup study, also for reintegrating behavior problem children into regular classrooms, that was similar to the Walker and Buckley study (1972). However, the four features described above were included in the 1975 study.

The addition of these features produced some extremely powerful effects in teacher and child behavior. For example, the five acting-out children involved in the study averaged 34 percent appropriate behavior in their respective regular classrooms during pretreatment observations. During the last two weeks in the special classroom, the children averaged 94 percent appropriate behavior. The followup strategy spanned a period of approximately four months in each child's regular classroom. During this period, the five children averaged 87 percent appropriate behavior, or a gain of 53 percent over their pretreatment levels in the regular classroom. This strategy produced extremely powerful maintenance effects. However, there was considerable effort in training, supervising, and monitoring involved in producing these effects. While this study demonstrates what *can* be achieved in the way of training regular classroom teachers to maintain behavioral gains produced in other settings, the feasibility and practicality of such procedures for use on a widespread basis are not clear. It is likely that these procedures would have to be adapted considerably for use in most school settings.

It is possible to implement both program extension procedures and reprogramming of the classroom setting(s) simultaneously in order to facilitate generalization of behavioral gains produced in treatment settings. However, as a rule, it is much easier to extend the program than it is to reprogram receiving settings. If extending the program or a variation of it does not produce the desired effects, then reprogramming efforts should be considered. It should be recognized that such efforts are likely to be costly in terms of the time, energy, and resources required to make them work. In addition, there is no guarantee that the cooperation of social agents within such settings can be obtained. If such cooperation cannot be achieved, the prospects for a successful reprogramming effort are dim.

REFERENCES

Baer, D., Wolf, M. M., & Risley, T. Some current dimensions of applied behavior analysis. *Journal of Applied Behavior Analysis*, 1968, *1*, 91–97.

Bailey, J. S., Wolf, M. M., & Phillips, E. L. Home based reinforcement and the modification of predelinquents' classroom behavior. *Journal of Applied Behavior Analysis*, 1970, *3*, 223–233.

Birnbrauer, J. S., Wolf, M. M., Kidder, J. D., & Tague, C. E. Classroom behavior of retarded pupils with token reinforcement. *Journal of Experimental Child Psychology*, 1965, *2*, 219–235.

Buckley, N K. & Walker, H. M. *Modifying classroom behavior: A manual of procedures for classroom teachers*. Champaign: Research Press Co., 1970.

Cooper, M. L., Thomson, C. L., & Baer, D. M. The experimental modification of teacher attending behavior. *Journal of Applied Behavior Analysis*, 1970, *3*, 153–157.

Cossairt, A., Hall, R. V., & Hopkins, B. L. The effects of experimenter's instructions, feedback, and praise on teacher's praise and student attending behavior. *Journal of Applied Behavior Analysis*, 1973, *6*, 89–100.

Greenwood, C. R., Hops, H., Delquadri, J., & Guild, J. Group contingencies for group consequences in classroom management: A further analysis. *Journal of Applied Behavior Analysis*, 1974, 7, 413–425.

Hanley, E. M. Review of research involving applied behavior analysis in the classroom. *Review of Educational Research*, 1970, *40*, 597–625.

Herman, S. H. & Tramontana, J. Instructions and group versus individual reinforcement in modifying disruptive group behavior. *Journal of Applied Behavior Analysis*, 1971, *4*, 113–120.

Kazdin, A. E. Role of instructions and reinforcement in behavior changes in token reinforcement programs. *Journal of Educational Research*, 1973, *64*, 63–71.

Kazdin, A. E., & Bootzin, R. R. The token economy: An evaluative review. *Journal of Applied Behavior Analysis*, 1972, *5*, 343–372.

Krasner, L. & Ullman, L. *Research in Behavior Modification*. New York: Holt, Rinehart & Winston, 1965.

Lipe, D. & Jung, S. M. Manipulating incentives to enhance school learning. *Review of Educational Research*, 1971, *41*, 249–280.

Mischel, W. *Personality and assessment.* New York: John Wiley, 1968.

O'Leary, K. D., Becker, W. C., Evans, M. B., & Saudargas, R. A. A token reinforcement program in a public school: A replication and systematic analysis. *Journal of Applied Behavior Analysis,* 1969, *2,* 3–13.

O'Leary, K. D. & Drabman, R. Token reinforcement programs in the classroom: A review. *Psychological Bulletin,* 1971, *75,* 379–398.

O'Leary, S. C. & O'Leary, K. D. Behavior modification in the school. In H. Leitenberg (Ed.), *Handbook of Behavior Modification.* Englewood Cliffs, N.J.: Prentice-Hall, Inc., 1976.

Parsonson, B. S., Baer, A. M., & Baer, D. M. The application of generalized correct social contingencies: An evaluation of a training program. *Journal of Applied Behavior Analysis,* 1974, 7(3), 427–437.

Patterson, G. R., McNeal, S., Hawkins, N., & Phelps, R. Reprogramming the social environment. *Journal of Child Psychology and Psychiatry,* 1967, *8,* 181–195.

Thomas, D. R., Becker, W. C., & Armstrong, M. Production and elimination of disruptive classroom behavior by systematically varying teacher's behavior. *Journal of Applied Behavior Analysis,* 1968, *1,* 35–45.

Ullman, L. & Krasner, L. *Case studies in behavior modification.* New York: Holt, Rinehart & Winston, 1965.

Wahler, R. G. Setting generality: Some specific and general effects of child behavior therapy. *Journal of Applied Behavior Analysis,* 1969, *2,* 239–246.

Walker, H. M. & Buckley, N. K. Programming generalization and maintenance of treatment effects across time and across settings. *Journal of Applied Behavior Analysis,* 1972, *5,* 209–224.

Walker, H. M. & Buckley, N. K. Teacher attention to appropriate and inappropriate classroom behavior: An individual case study. *Focus on Exceptional Children,* 1973, *5*(3), 5–11.

Walker, H. M. & Buckley, N. K. *Token reinforcement techniques: Classroom applications for the hard to teach child.* Eugene, Ore.: E-B Press, 1974.

Walker, H. M., Hops, H., & Fiegenbaum, E. Deviant classroom behavior as a function of combinations of social and token reinforcement and cost contingency. *Behavior Therapy,* 1976, 7, 76–88.

Walker, H. M., Hops, H., Greenwood, C. R., Todd, N., & Garrett, B. Experiments with response cost in playground and classroom settings. Eugene, Ore.: CORBEH Report #35, Center at Oregon for Research in the Behavioral Education of the Handicapped, University of Oregon, 1977.

Walker, H. M., Hops, H., & Johnson, S. M. Generalization and maintenance of classroom treatment effects. *Behavior Therapy,* 1975, *6,* 188–200.

Walker, H. M., Mattson, R. H., & Buckley, N. K. The functional analysis of behavior within an experimental classroom setting. In W. C. Becker (Ed.), *An empirical basis for change in education.* Chicago: Science Research Associates, 1971, pp. 236–263.

White, M. A. Natural rates of teacher approval and disapproval in the classroom. *Journal of Applied Behavior Analysis,* 1975, *8*(4), 367–372.

Author Index

Subject Index